WET EXIT

A BOLD STORY OF SUICIDE AND SELF-RESCUE ON AUSTRALIA'S LONGEST RIVER

ROD WELLINGTON
WET EXIT

A BOLD STORY OF SUICIDE AND SELF-RESCUE ON AUSTRALIA'S LONGEST RIVER

CROW BOOKS

Cover design by Rod Wellington, with assistance from Tony Cullota.
Interior design by Dean Klinkenberg.
Illustrated map by Jeremy Bruneel.
Greyscale maps by Abstract Marketing Inc.
Cover photograph by Angela Speller Photography.
Author photograph by Rod Wellington.
Poetry by Rod Wellington.

Published by Crow Books.

ISBN: 978-0-9940829-6-1

To anyone who is struggling or has struggled with mental health issues

wet ex·it /wet egzət,ˈeksət/ *n.* **1** When a kayaker capsizes and has to get out of the kayak while still underwater; a self-rescue technique that is one of the first skills taught to novice paddlers. **2** Suicide by drowning.

Fallibility is a motherfucker. So is humility. They're ego killers. They suck.

I never thought myself invincible, but I surely never thought myself incapable either. I spent decades doing awesome self-propelled adventures. I never believed I couldn't. I dreamed. I planned. I executed. I excelled. And then fallibility came along and fucked everything up. Not only did it shred my ego, but it also shredded my suicide plan. Not cool, fallibility. Not cool at all...*motherfucker*.

Living with mental illness fucking sucks. Wanting to kill myself fucking sucks. Suffering through depression fucking sucks. Feeling awkward in social settings fucking sucks. Fearing my way through patterns of paranoia in the workplace fucking sucks. Doubting myself fucking sucks. Being judged by others fucking sucks.

People have told me I'm obsessive and compulsive and depressive and repetitive. They've told me I'm manic and anxious and reckless and blind. They've told me I'm lazy and crazy and twisted and cruel. I've been called an asshole, a thief, a prick, and a cunt—all in one day! People have told me I overthink things.

People have told me medication will help my *condition*. They've told me it works for them, that their brain responds positively to pills produced by heartless pharmaceutical companies with greedy agendas. "Medication smoothed out my brainwaves," they've told me. I bet it did!

Fuck medication. Never used it. Never will. I don't want my brainwaves *smoothed* out. I don't want my reality neutered. I don't want LifeLite™. I want to experience *real* emotional pain, the kind that helps me grow. Sure, it sucks when you're trapped in it, but I think it's better to endure the anguish than to numb it with prescription meds.

i

There was a time in my life when I self-medicated. I used alcohol and recreational drugs to cope with an onslaught of stress that never seemed to recede. I worked shitty jobs, brought home shitty paycheques, and pissed the shittiness away *all* weekend long. And then, one day, I stopped…and everything got *very real*. That was in 1998, 20 years ago. Someone recently asked me, "Is your life better now than it was when you drank?" "No," I replied. "Nothing beats ignorance. It's the most blissful high you can have."

Fallibility is a wake-up call. It's reality *concentrated*. It can't be trademarked because it can't be mass-produced. It can't be mass-produced because it would kill the *fuck* out of everyone. That's why it only rears its ugly head occasionally.

Remember Charlie Sheen? Me neither. Remember when he did that interview on *20/20* and he said he had *tiger blood* in his veins? Me neither. Remember when he was *#winning*? *#MeNeither*. Remember when he did that stand-up comedy tour? Me neither. Remember when Charlie Sheen was *cool*? Me neither.

Remember TV? Me neither. Remember Ronald Reagan? Me neither. Remember mutually assured destruction? Me neither. Remember conspiracy theorists? Me neither. Remember Noam Chomsky? Me neither. Remember UPC codes? Me neither. Remember breast implants? Me neither. Remember colon cancer? Me neither. Remember Facebook without the annoying advertisements? Me neither. Remember old growth forests? Me neither. Remember the reason you got out of bed this morning? Me neither.

I didn't shave today. I didn't shave yesterday. Or the day before that. I've spent the past seven days parked in front of a computer screen, writing this *fucking* book. I'll be glad when it's finished. I'll be glad when someone hands me a $20 bill and I hand them the paperback version of this damned manuscript. I'll be glad when I can breathe fresh air again. I'll be glad when I can go out west again and climb a *fucking mountain*. It's been too long. I used to climb mountains all the time. And then fallibility came along and fucked everything up.

Remember when *fallibility* was a word you had to look up in the dictionary? Me neither. Remember that time when you *didn't* compare yourself to others? Me neither. Remember that time when you laughed all day because life was funny and wonderful? Me neither. Remember that day when you had no suicidal thoughts whatsoever? Me neither. Remember when that special person gave you hugs when you needed them? Me neither. Remember when your dead mother told you everything was going to be okay? Me neither. Remember that time when you went the whole day without crying? Me neither. Do you remember your dreams from last night? Me neither.

Fallibility is a motherfucker. It shows you that you are *not* what you thought you were. It cuts you down to the size you *are*. It makes you the person you *never* wanted to be. It force-feeds you the truth and watches you eat it. It flattens your fangs and fattens your lip. It knocks the chip off your shoulder and grinds it to dust. It grins while you wince. It laughs while you weep. It stays when you leave, and it's still there when you return. It is judge, jury, and *expeditioner*. It's the *evil* explorer. It's a *motherfucker*.

January 27, 2016 – Near the source of the Murray River, Australia

The warm rain fell like water from a thousand faucets—solid columns of liquid silver streaming down from an unseen source. No two streams touched in the windless afternoon. The rain simply fell silently until it splashed upon foliage, upon rock, upon water, upon wood, upon mud, upon me. The lush forest received the wet kiss and drank it deep, deep into a fertile consciousness stripped clean of labels, deep into a place undeveloped by human conception, deep into a oneness that cradled my loneliness like an unrequited lover cradling hope. Beyond dawn lies light. Beyond dusk lies less light, but light nonetheless.

I sat unmoving at the gnarled base of an immature oak and watched the rain run glistening down its rough bark—tiny rivulets cascading over a vertical landscape, each depression a wooden valley filled with a forest of moss and clinging mites. Upon the plateaued precipices clung spiders and beetles and ants of all sizes. They eyed me safely from a distance, a wary distance given to those who entered their home unannounced. They spied me a thousand times over as a million of me stared back. It was a numbers game, a game I'd never win.

I was not their Noah.
Nor was this their ark.
Nor were they the pairs that spread
their seeds into the dark.
No mission lay at hand for them.
No plan they had for me.
And yet this flood that now besets us
will somehow set us free.

Leave it to dry Australia to deluge me with surprises. This was my
third visit to the continent, and this was definitely the wettest of
the three. The rain began just hours after leaving Sydney and stayed
with me for 10 of the first 12 days. Each downpour dampened the
mood of the trip. Each soggy weather forecast seemed like a giant
middle finger thrust in my direction. Australia always had an or-
nery knack of doling out challenges. I'd overcome all the challenges
that came before, but this time things were different.

Even the mighty stumble.
Even the mighty fall.
Even the mighty, each hard of hearing,
must heed resignation's great call.

Before me lies a deep depression, an ancient scar upon an ancient
landscape. It is V-shaped, its steep sides lined with thick forest and
thicker mystery. At its bottom runs an infant river, jovial and unbridled. This river, named Murray, descends from meadows and
mountains and alpine sublime. Its font lies in a place treaded by
few, carpeted green with grasses and regally rimmed with white-
barked gum trees. A short metal pipe, driven into the earth to mark
the river's source, is the only evidence that a human has been here,
evidence that someone else has sought this sacred treasure. Beside
the pipe, cool, clear water emerges from the landscape, beginning a
1578-mile descent to the sea. This stream will cascade over waterfalls and squeeze between rock walls. It will pool and pass its time
until it resumes its journey. Its flow will increase as the rain lingers
on, drenching the steep valley slopes with turbid runoff.

This river lies where life begins,
the life beneath the funnel.
But to reach this life and prosper wise,
one must traverse a darkened tunnel.

In these hills roam brumbies, wild horses who know not the meaning of fences or saddles or iron shoes. These elusive beasts feast on

verdant flats and quench their thirst with river water. They spend years running and grazing and breeding on the same familiar acreage. Aside from sickness and an occasionally fatal snake bite, their existence is seemingly stress-free. Time, it appears, is their only predator.

Their coats and colours vary.
Their bodies, angular and lean.
Their paths are etched into the earth,
but they are rarely seen.

In order to walk through this hilly land of brumbies, one must think like a horse. Here, there are no trails forged by humans. Here, the forest, and all of its riotous vegetation, forms a dense maze through which creatures of simple thought pass. Here, a human must quiet his frenetic mind and follow leads left by animals who chose efficient passage, their course based not on travelling the shortest distance between points, but instead a path whose obstacles are cleverly acknowledged and avoided. Fallen trees are skirted rather than straddled, as are boulders and rocky outcroppings. One must traverse the contour lines rather than climb the slopes. One comes to realize that horses, like rivers, find their way with little effort and little fear. In short, they walk the path of common sense.

I came to this place in January 2016 to finish one chapter before beginning another. A previous river journey remained incomplete and I sought to close the circle.

In December 2009, I began a four-month, summit to source to sea expedition of the Murray River in southern Australia. The goal was to climb the continent's highest mountain (Mount Kosciuszko, elevation: 7300 feet), hike 30 miles from the mountain's base to the font of the Murray, and then kayak the river to its mouth at the Southern Ocean. I would do the entire journey completely self-powered, using only legs, arms, and stubborn determination to reach my goal. Others had paddled a large majority of the river's length, beginning their descents from points further downstream, but no one, as I found later, had started from the river's true source, let alone the country's highest peak. I was setting the bar high. *Very high.*

Mount Kosciuszko, named after General Tadeusz Kosciuszko (a Polish national hero), is located in Kosciuszko National Park in southern New South Wales. The mountain is also home to one of Australia's few ski resorts. I overnighted at a friendly hostel in Thredbo, the small village at Kosciuszko's base, and began my trek to the summit the next day.

The six-and-a-half-mile hike to the peak took about four hours to complete. A well-marked dirt trail climbed through dense forest on the lower slopes, then followed a rusty, gridded, metal boardwalk as it crossed the treeless tundra of the upper slopes. Even in the heat of the warm December day, large patches of dust-covered snow were visible in shadowed depressions near the gently rounded peak. A flat-topped rock cairn/monument marked the summit. I eagerly climbed atop it, grinned madly, and spread my arms wide as a tourist snapped photos with my camera. The grey outlines of distant mountain ranges fanned out in all directions, their peaks all below me. I truly felt on top of the world.

A three-day trek through forests south of Kosciuszko brought me to the source of the Murray. The summer heat and weight of a full backpack made the hike a proper challenge. In many areas, creeks and streams were either dry or too far off the trail to comfortably hike to. The carrying of extra water (and extra weight) became a burden and a necessity.

Two-and-a-half miles downstream from the source, I set up camp on Cowombat Flat, an open alpine meadow. The hooved tromping of brumbies resonated through the landscape as they quickly galloped across the flat and disappeared in the dense maze of gum trees and shadows. I counted 12 of the beasts, split evenly in two groups, each majestically muscled and deliciously undomesticated. They were rebels after my own heart.

The bubbling flow of the Murray—here, no wider than a sidewalk—bisected the flat in an east-to-west direction, while the hiking trail—an old 4x4 track—crossed the river and the flat from north to south. Here, and for the next 1174 miles, the Murray forms the border between New South Wales and the southern state of Victoria.

Marked by a small pile of rocks, a rough foot path spurred off the main trail and led through the forest in the direction of the Murray's source. 100 yards in, the trail vanished. By consulting with my topographic map and GPS, I was able to navigate another quarter-mile through the gums. I emerged in a grassy glade. Beyond the glade, the river and the soggy earth surrounding it had been well-trodden by brumbies. It was obvious they often came here to drink. Here, the infant Murray was little more than an ambling brook. It darted above and below ground, emerging next to the trunks of lofty eucalyptus trees and disappearing under medicine ball-sized clumps of soil and grass called *tussocks*. I pushed through dense stands of underbrush, working my way upstream until the river vanished completely underground. Here, where the first signs of flow emanated, was the source of the Murray. Curiously, and somewhat disappointingly, the metal pipe that supposedly marks the river's source was nowhere to be seen. *Had I somehow stumbled past it? Was it buried beneath the underbrush? Had it been removed?* I lacked the means to answer those internal questions. All I could do was assume I was either at, or close to, the source. According to my GPS, I was within spitting range of the font. *Perhaps this area is similar to the beginnings of other rivers I've encountered,* I thought to myself. *Perhaps ground water flows from numerous caverns and underground streams, welling up in several spots before it coalesces into a defined channel.* If that was true, and I guessed it was, then the spot upon which I stood was a definitely a source—*my* source. That, for me, was good enough. Taking that thought as my cue, I stooped and filled a yellow-capped urine sample vial with clear spring water. The goal: pour the spring water into the ocean at the expedition's conclusion. Whatever would happen between the source and the ocean was anyone's guess. The only thing I knew for sure was this: it was all downhill from here.

I trekked alongside the tiny Murray for its first two-and-half miles. The river meandered across the forest floor, weaving its way south until it entered the treeless terrain of Cowombat Flat. It was here that I left the river and hiked south along Cowombat Flat Track into Victoria.

The river downstream of Cowombat Flat was, to me, unknown. Judging by the topo maps, it had carved out a steep sloped valley lined with cliffs and rocky outcroppings. There was a good chance the river would be narrower than an alley and choked with debris. Trying to descend it in any kind of watercraft would be a waste of time. Therefore, I would have to detour around the next nine miles of river.

My plan was to continue south on Cowombat Flat Track into Victoria until it intersected with Limestone–Black Mountain Road. I'd then follow that road until it intersected with Limestone Creek Track (another 4x4 road) which descended to the river. At the terminus of Limestone Creek Track was Poplars Camping Area, a primitive, riverside campground. I planned to launch my 12-foot inflatable boat from this point.

The river downstream of Poplars flows through a very remote valley. The river here is only accessible by 4x4 track in three spots. Getting in and out of this area is very difficult. To complicate things, the Murray is clogged with numerous logjams and dotted with sections of whitewater. In an emergency, evacuation by helicopter is the only option. Further downstream, the river flows through the famous Murray Gates, an 18-mile stretch of commercially rafted whitewater.

The distance and difficulty of descending this upper section of the Murray presented not only a challenge logistically, but also physically and mentally. Did I have enough experience to successfully paddle this section? The easy answer was no. Was I concerned for my safety? Definitely. Was I still gonna give it a go? Absolutely. I'd travelled too far to turn back now.

The detour (on foot) would cover a distance of 23 miles, more than double the distance by river. Unfortunately, this meant there would be a section of river that I wouldn't see or experience. This fact didn't sit too well with me. When I set out to do a source to sea descent of a river under my own power, I want to experience every inch of that river. If it cannot be paddled, then I want to walk beside it and keep it in my sight. This detour would take me well away from the Murray before reconnecting with it at Poplars Camping Area. I might go on to descend the rest of the river, all the way to the sea, but this unseen nine-mile stretch would always remain a mystery to me. Admittedly, there was sadness connected to that fact. I was grieving a loss. Perhaps it was a loss of pride. By choosing not to walk beside the river for those nine miles, I was essentially admitting defeat. I was resigning. I was quitting. I was failing. I struggled with that sense of failure for weeks during the planning process. In terms of safety, the detour made sense. Missing out on experiencing nine miles of untamed river, however, did not make sense. Somehow, I would have to overcome the guilt and sadness associated with the decision to detour. Somehow, I had to stop it from haunting me.

My decision to detour nine miles of the upper Murray was further influenced by an Australian gent named Trevor Davis. Trevor was the manager of Tom Groggin Station, a 2000-acre cattle ranch located at river mile 50 on the Murray (on the Victoria side, river left). Tom Groggin is the first parcel of privately owned land on the river. Everything upstream of the ranch lies within either Kosciuszko National Park on the New South Wales side of the river or Alpine National Park on the Victoria side. The ranch is almost completely surrounded by park land. This may sound idyllic, and in some sense, it is, but, as Trevor explained to me, it comes with a very serious and dangerous drawback.

In 2003 and 2006 (three years before my visit), wildfires ravaged parkland on both sides of the state border. Massive swaths of land were decimated. Tom Groggin Station managed to escape damage, but the experience was hugely terrifying for Trevor and his family, who chose to stay and protect the ranch while the forest around them burned. Trevor posited that the government's inability to properly manage a huge amount of new undergrowth that had sprung up following previous fires resulted in an abundance of fuel for future fires. Had this undergrowth been maintained, said Trevor, the wildfires of '03 and '06 would've been far less devastating. To hear Trevor speak about the fires and their impact on his family is to hear a man passionate about his dogged commitment to forest conservation and the safety of others.

I met Trevor Davis completely by chance. He and his teenage daughter were spraying weeds in a campground 100 miles south of Tom Groggin Station in the small town of Omeo, Victoria. A few days prior, I had rented a 16-foot sea kayak from a paddling shop in Melbourne, strapped it to the top of a rental car, and embarked on a mission to find a place to store the boat while I descended the first 90 miles of the upper Murray in a 12-foot inflatable canoe. (The sea kayak would be used to descend the flatwater portion of the river, essentially the remaining 1488 miles.)

I arrived at the campground in Omeo and struck up a conversation with the owner, telling him I was hoping to store the kayak at a farm somewhere along the upper river.

"Well, mate, it's your lucky day," said the owner. "The manager of Tom Groggin just happens to be here today. He's camped at site 18. I bet if you ask him nicely, he'll be able to help ya out."

And help he did, *after* he tried to talk me out the notion of descending the upper part of the Murray.

"Have you been on that part of the rivva before, mate?" asked Trevor, his question loaded with concern.

"No," I answered. "Have you?"

"Mate," he replied with a smart-ass smile, "I grew up on that rivva!"

A clean-shaven, light-skinned, red-haired, thinly-built, cowboy hat-wearing bloke in his mid-40s, Trevor went on to explain that he'd spent his whole life in the hills surrounding the upper Murray. Born and raised in the rural village of Biggara, he'd always been around cattle and horses—he'd always been a cowboy. When he secured the position of manager of Tom Groggin Station, he'd found his dream job. Throughout his life, he'd never lived more than 20 miles from the Murray. He'd ridden horses along its rocky banks and herded free-range cattle in remote verdant flats. The river was in his blood, his voice, his words. He understood it when it spoke to him. He respected it immensely. One might say he even feared it. It was from this fear that his concerns for my safety stemmed. His first impression of me was one of doubt. He saw me unfit for the challenge ahead and spent several minutes quizzing me about my outdoorsy credibility. When finished, his skepticism was still evident.

"The rivva up there is no joke, mate," said Trevor. "You really need to know what you're doin'. It's no place for amateurs, no place to screw up. There's heaps of Class III rapids, miles of whitewater, and the forest is thicker than the night. *And* it's bloody remote! No roads in. No roads out. Are you *absolutely* sure you want to do this?"

"I plan to do it with or without your help," I replied, bluntly. "Of course, I'd prefer to have you involved in some regard. It sounds like you know the upper river better than anyone."

"Alright, mate," said Trevor, smiling wryly. "I guess that settles it then. You're comin' home with us."

The three-hour drive to Tom Groggin Station was heavily punctuated with harrowing wildfire stories and government criticism, as well as a few tales about intrepid river travellers who'd tried their hand at descending the upper Murray.

"There were these two Kiwi blokes who got their raft hung up on a huge logjam somewhere below Poplars Camping Area," said Trevor. "They set off their emergency beacon and had to be airlifted out. When the helicopter landed next to my house, I questioned them about the ordeal. All the one bloke said was, 'We had no idea…' I've always wondered if he meant, 'We had no idea it was going to be that hard' or 'We had no idea what we were doing.' It was probably a combination of both.

"And then there was this 70-year-old bushie (a mountain man) who decided to join two young blokes from Sydney for their raft-ing trip. But instead of just joining them in *their* raft, the old bug-ger took his *own* raft and hefted the bloody thing over every logjam and fallen tree from where Kings Plain Track ends at the rivva all the bloody way to Tom Groggin. Apparently, the trip nearly *killed* him! He told me it was the hardest bloody thing he'd ever done. And he's the toughest bushie I ever met! He said he'd nevva, *evva* facking do it again!"

At first, I thought Trevor's animated stories were aimed at deter-ring me from doing the river journey. However, over the course of our drive to Tom Groggin Station, I began to feel that perhaps he was secretly rooting for the underdog—namely *me*. His sto-ries aroused in me an even greater desire to see the upper river firsthand. There'd only been a handful of people who had success-fully descended those first few miles of the Murray. The ones who'd made it as far as Tom Groggin Station had taken leave of the river at that point. None of them had continued onward to the sea, an-other 1528 miles downstream. During my trip planning, I never came across an account of anyone doing a true source to sea pad-dling descent of the Murray. Now, I was finding out why. Others had balked at the challenge of the upper river, perhaps intimidated by its rapids and remote location. With Trevor's invaluable help, I aimed to discover what many had missed. I would then take that knowledge and share it with the sea.

Tom Groggin Station was, in many ways, an idyllic retreat. Built upon an expansive meadow and dotted with barns and outbuild-ings, the ranch was home to a sizable herd of prized Angus cattle. Forested hills ringed the ranch's northern boundary and rocky peaks were visible to the west. To the south, the Murray formed the boundary between Tom Groggin Station and Kosciuszko Na-tional Park. Near the eastern end of the property sat a one-level farmhouse where Trevor and his family resided. Rustic on the outside, but modern within, the air-conditioned house provided a welcomed respite from the mounting heat of the late spring day.

Soon, this place would scorch in the summer's dry heat, tempered only slightly by the property's prominent elevation and the unique mountain ecosystem of southern New South Wales.

"C'mon, mate," said Trevor. "I'll show you the guest accommodations. You'll have it all to yourself."

A short stroll brought us to a spacious, two-bedroom log cabin. Antique farm tools and horseshoes hung from the rough wooden exterior. Loose boards creaked under our weight as we walked atop the planked porch.

"There's a cool story that goes along with this place," said Trevor as he opened the cabin's front door. "Ever heard of Banjo Patterson?"

"Sounds familiar," I replied as we stepped inside.

"Patterson was a well-known Australian poet who specialized in bush stories," said Trevor. "His most famous poem was *The Man from Snowy River*. I know you've heard of that one, right?"

"Absolutely," I said, nodding my head. "It's a classic."

"Well, the man who inspired that poem was named Jack Riley. Legend has it Riley stayed in this cabin when he came through this area. Tonight, you'll be sharing space with the spirit of Jack Riley. Whaddya think of that, mate?"

"I think that's pretty cool!" I said, excitedly.

Trevor reached in the back pocket of his jeans and pulled out his wallet. He extracted a colourful paper bill and handed it to me.

"There's Riley and Patterson right there, mate," he said, pointing to the bill. "On the back of a $10 note, no less. We put our heroes on our money, mate—not some bloody *monarch*! No bloody Pommies in *Aw-strail-ya*, mate!"

I chuckled as I examined the paper bill. My chance encounter with Trevor Davis was producing some incredible experiences already. I was happy. I was in the right place and on the right path.

"Let's say you and me go look at some topo maps and find you the best route to the rivva," said Trevor.

"Sounds good, *mate*," I said, reaching out my hand in thanks. "I'm glad I met ya."

"It's only been *one day*, mate," said Trevor with a wry smile. "Don't rush in with your appreciation too soon. It took me a *year* to get a 'glad I met ya' outta my wife."

I chuckled again and returned his smile.

"Don't tell her I said that, though," he said, grinning as we exited the cabin.

Back at the farmhouse, we pored over a topographic map of the 50-mile stretch of river upstream of Tom Groggin Station.

"Okay, here's my plan," I said, pointing a pencil at the map. "I'm going to circumnavigate the headwaters on foot. I figure it's about 107 miles altogether. The plan is to go to Thredbo, climb Kosciuszko, hike 30 miles of trails to the Murray's source, cross the river into Victoria, continue on Cowombat Flat Track to Limestone–Black Mountain Road, then to Limestone Creek Track, then McCarthys Track, then follow Davies Plain Track to Tom Groggin Track, and take that back here to the station. Then, at some point, walk Alpine Way back to Thredbo. And then, somehow get back to Poplars Camping Area at river mile 11.5, launch my inflatable boat, and descend the whitewater down to the Bringenbrong Bridge."

"Whew," said Trevor, shaking his head. "You *are* an ambitious one, aren't ya?"

"I want to see it all," I replied. "I want to soak it all in."

"Oh yeah, mate," said Trevor. "You certainly *will* soak it all in! But I got an idea that might simplify things a little."

Trevor shifted the map slightly and traced his index finger along the Murray's snaking course.

"The rivva's fairly low right now. You might be alright floating a boat down through the Gates from here, but upstream of here is going to be completely different. I've got a morning free on Thursday. We can take a drive down Kings Plain Track and McCarthys Track and see what the rivva levels are like in that upper part. I can drop you and your backpack at Poplars Camping Area and you can walk back to Tom Groggin. And while we're at it, I'll show where to access an old track that's been closed for the last two decades. You'll see more wildlife on that track, and no trucks. How's that sound?"

"Perfect!" I said, smiling.

"In the meantime, my son'll run you into Corryong and you can top up your food supplies. Feel free to use the station as a home base. You can portion out your food and leave some here. That way, you don't have to carry as much. After you hike back to Groggin, rest up for a day if you want, and then we'll drive you over to Thredbo. Climb Kosciuszko. Do your walkabout. Make your way back to Poplars. I'll keep track of your location with your SPOT. When I see you're getting close to Poplars, I'll drive down there with your inflatable boat and a food resupply. That way, we're not hiding gear in the bush for some drunken yabbos to find."

"That sounds like a good plan," I said. "And there's one more thing I need to sort out. I had a phone conversation with a guy who lives beside the Murray near the Bringenbrong Bridge. He gave me permission to leave my sea kayak in his barn. His name's Tom Lednar. Do you know him?"

"Of course I do, mate!" said Trevor, smiling wide. "Tommy's an old mate of mine. We grew up together!"

I laughed and shook my head at the absurd serendipity. Things were falling into place quite nicely and I couldn't be happier.

The drive to Kings Plain Track and McCarthys Track was a bumpy one. The dirt tracks were rough and rutted and we had to proceed slowly at times, especially on the short, steep climbs. Trevor explained that he had a contract with the government to maintain these roads with a grader. He was making mental notes of the locations of bad spots as we went.

After a jarring descent, we reached the river's edge at the end of Kings Plain Track. A small opening in the trees on the opposite bank signalled that vehicles occasionally ford the river and continue into the bush on the New South Wales side. The river level was low here, less than 18 inches in the deepest spots visible from the bank.

"You might be doing more walking than paddling, mate," said Trevor as we stood on the grassy bank. "And by the time you get back here after your walkabout, the rivva's bound to be lower than it is now."

Another 30 minutes of driving—including a steep, rough descent on McCarthys Track—brought us back to the river at Poplars Camping Area. Here, three miles upstream from the Kings Plain access, the river looked even lower. I leaned out over the flow to get a look upstream and down. The view for about 25 yards in either direction showed what I expected: plenty of exposed rocks in the riverbed and no real navigable channel. Trevor was right. I would be doing more walking than paddling.

"What do you think my chances are of hiking beside the river from Cowombat Flat downstream to here?" I asked. "It's about 14 miles shorter than walking the 4x4 tracks all the way around."

"Just upstream of here, maybe a mile or so, Limestone Creek empties into the rivva," said Trevor. "It's a big creek and its outflow probably doubles the rivva's volume. Most of what we're seein' here is outflow from Limestone. So, *upstream* of Limestone there's gonna be way less water, certainly not enough to float a boat. Plus, the rivva carves its way through a steep valley up there, so walking is gonna be *very* difficult. There'll likely be tons of natural debris in the rivva itself, so walking in the rivvabed may not always be possible. You might be forced up the steep banks into the thick undergrowth—lots of blackberry. It would be a brutal slog, mate. I wouldn't want to do it. My advice: stick to the 4x4 tracks. You don't want to burn yourself out before you even get on the rivva."

I respected Trevor's input. He probably knew more about this area than anyone I was likely to meet. I hated to let go of the idea of not seeing that nine-mile stretch of river, but it seemed to be the safest and most efficient way of approaching this part of the expedition. Still, compromise does not sit well with me. I'm an all-or-nothing person. I like to find the extreme points of things and slowly analyze all that lies between those points. Doing anything less than that is compromising, and compromising is not acceptable.

I didn't say it aloud, but I resolved right then and there to return after the expedition to hike this missing stretch of river. I would have to return to Tom Lednar's place to retrieve my inflatable boat anyway, so a 100-mile drive over to the source area wouldn't be much of a stretch. Walking that nine-mile section of river would close the circle, so to speak. It would give me the completion I craved. For now, however, I'd stick to the detour plan and bypass the area on foot via the dirt tracks. I would still be covering the distance under my own power and that's what mattered most to me.

The three-day, 30-mile walk from Poplars Camping Area to Tom Groggin Station gave me a good chance to examine the mountainous terrain. When the dense, jungle-like forest of gum trees parted and revealed a viewpoint, a wide, V-shaped valley thousands of feet deep showed its face. It was simultaneously beautiful and menacing. In a week's time, I'd be somewhere down in those green depths, hauling my inflatable boat over rocky shallows, slowly making my way downstream. And I would be doing it alone. That was the scary part. There would be no givers of advice, no local lenders of knowledge. There would only be me. I would have to follow my gut. I would have to own every decision. I would have to find a way out of the unseen jungle.

A resupply drive to Corryong went as planned. As did the shuttle to Thredbo. I climbed the country's highest peak, and then hiked 30 miles into the bush to find the source of the continent's longest river. The 23-mile detour walk took me down rough dirt tracks and graded gravel roads. The route was scenic, but my body was sweaty. The summer heat had arrived with a vengeance and I was more than relieved when, after two-and-a-half days of trekking from the Murray's source, I reached Poplars Camping Area.

Just as Trevor had predicted, the river level was lower than when he'd dropped me at Poplars 12 days prior. Walking from bank to bank without wetting my knees was an easy task. Unless the river pooled or narrowed considerably, I would be dragging the inflatable boat over and around the many exposed rocks and boulders that littered the river. The math was simple in this section of the upper Murray: the wider the stream, the lower the level. And, with an absence of rain in the forecast, the level was bound to drop even further.

Below are journal entries from the first six days of river navigation on the upper Murray (Poplars Camping Area, river mile 11.5 to the Leather Barrel Creek confluence, river mile 40). These excerpts are well-detailed and give a comprehensive look at my descent of this remote stretch of the river. Days 1 to 8 of the expedition were spent summiting Mount Kosciuszko, hiking to the Murray's source, and trekking the dirt track detour to Poplars Camping Area as part of an on-foot circumnavigation of the Murray headwaters. Days 8-13 were spent descending the Murray from Poplars Camping Area to Tom Groggin Station. I arrived at Tom Groggin Station (river mile 50) on January 11, 2010. (The 30-mile, on-foot section from Poplars Camping Area to Tom Groggin Station was completed December 26–28, 2009. The 17-mile, on-foot section from Tom Groggin Station to Thredbo via Alpine Way was completed on January 13, 2010.)

Day 8 (January 6, 2010)

Big thanks to Lynda Davis (Trevor's wife) and her friend Kim (son Adam and daughter Brooke) for delivering food, gear, and the SOAR S12 inflatable canoe to Poplars Camping Area. Poplars Camping Area is located 11.5 miles downriver from the source of the Murray and is the highest point on the river accessible by 4x4 vehicles. After thoroughly reviewing topographic maps of the area, and having taken a firsthand look at the river at both the Kings Plain Track and Poplars access points, Trevor Davis and I determined that Poplars would be the best place for me to launch the boat. We also determined it would be unwise and unsafe to attempt a traverse of the nine-mile section of the Murray from river mile 2.5 (where it intersects with Cowombat Flat Track on Cowombat Flat) to river mile 11.5 (at Poplars Camping Area). If time permits, I will attempt this nine-mile riverbed walk at the end of the expedition.

Using SOAR's magical EZ Pump, I inflated and launched the S12 mid-afternoon. I was very excited to finally get on the river. The boat was heavy with gear and ten days of food. I was able to paddle the first 100 yards, but then had to enter the river and pull the boat over the shallow rapids. Thus became the tedious routine of exiting and entering the boat every time I ran aground, which happened about every 30 seconds. Low water was the norm and I encountered several logjams over the next two hours, requiring me to portage the gear, food, and boat separately over the debris—a very time-consuming ordeal indeed. During those first two hours, I managed a distance of one-and-a-half miles. At this pace, I was looking at 7–10 days of backbreaking progress to cover the 38.5 miles of river from Poplars to Tom Groggin Station. At 4:00pm, I located a rare flat spot along the riverbank not overgrown with blackberry or scrub and set up the tent. As a small cloud of honeybees developed a profound interest in the yellow nylon rope attached to the boat and a rust-coloured spider with a leg span the width of my palm emerged from the underside of the riverbank (after I almost stepped on it!), I retired to the relative safety of my tent wondering what other potentially poisonous and cringe-worthy creatures were lurking along the banks and hiding in the crevices of logjams. Tomorrow would be another opportunity to find out.

Day 8 progress: 1.5 miles

Day 9 (January 7, 2010)

First full day on the river. Eight hours of pulling, pushing, lifting, walking, and paddling—not necessarily in that order, but paddling would definitely be last on the list. Low water meant that plenty of rocks were exposed, requiring me to be in and out of the boat hundreds of times during the day. Plenty of walking in 6–8 inches of water, pulling the boat behind me. When the water was too low, I had to walk backwards in the stream, wrenching the boat forward inch by inch over the rocks. Progress was tedious and tiresome. There was no time to daydream. I was forced into the present moment, forced to focus intently on the position of my feet on the slippery rocks. Each foot, clad in neoprene boots, instinctively felt for purchase. Each footfall had to be measured and accurate. Unrushed safety was the name of the game. An injury in this remote area—miles from help of any kind—could mean death. Aside from the camping area at Kings Plain Track, three miles downstream from Poplars, there was no access to the river whatsoever. No roads in or out. No trails. Walking out through the thick forest was a near impossibility. Three years prior, two seasoned whitewater paddlers from New Zealand had underestimated the section of river below Kings Plain and had to be airlifted from the river by helicopter. Their exasperation was expressed in this meagre response to their rescuers: "We had no idea…"

For me, Kings Plain represented the last exit on a river of no return. After that, I was truly on my own. The refuge of Tom Groggin Station was a lengthy 35.5 miles downstream, a world away at the sloth-like pace I was producing. But the seriousness of the situation never weighed heavy on me. Instead, an air of contentment and purpose enveloped me and gently guided me downstream. I had ventured here to see the river as a whole, complete from source to sea. I had come to see firsthand its progression, its maturity. Like the ego-bruised Kiwis who had come before me, I knew little of what to expect. I knew only that the work would be hard and that I was completely committed to the task at hand. Such as it is when you head-up a zero emissions expedition. Such as it is when you choose a challenging and unorthodox career like mine. This is my work. So be it.

Many years ago, my good friend Scott McFarlane penned a catchy little tune entitled "Little by Little." As I stood knee deep in the warm current with an impatient blue boat bumping the backs of my thighs, surrounded by lush foliage and virgin old-growth trees that had never felt the sting of a chainsaw, a random chorus of lyrics from Scott's song streamed forth from my lips.

Little by little we're getting smarter,
little by little we're moving on,
little by little we're taking patience by the hand,
little by little we come to understand this song,
take it little by little, you can't go wrong.

I smiled and slowly waded downstream. The expedition now had an official theme song.

Did I mention logjams? Eight times during the day I had to remove the gear from the boat and haul everything over piles of debris. Some of the fallen trees blocking passage were huge: 8–10 feet in diameter and more than 100 feet long. During one such portage, I came face to face with a big, rust-coloured spider on the underside of a monster tree. A spike of adrenaline shot through my body and I did my best to remain calm as I crept past it, my nosetip mere inches away from the fuzzy beast. I wondered how many more went unseen by my wary eyes.

I also encountered several smaller fallen trees. Most times, it was possible to either move the trees aside or go under or over the trees without removing the gear from the boat. Thick scrub and blackberry prevented me from portaging along the banks.

Near the Kings Plain river access, I came across a group of teenagers wading in the shallow water.

"How far to Poplars Camping Area?" they asked.

"Are you planning to walk there?" I asked back.

"Yes," they replied.

"Well, I started at Poplars yesterday," I explained. "It's about three miles upstream and it has taken me a total of five hours to come this far."

"Oh!" they said, sounding surprised. "Maybe we'll just stick around here."

Smart choice, I thought to myself.

As I passed a small huddle of parked 4x4s at the camping area, I turned back to see the teens happily splashing each other among the boulders. Kings Plain was my last chance to exit from the river. If I had any doubts as to how tough things would be downstream, this was the place to bail. The teens' laughter came to me on a gentle breeze. Their innocence and naiveté was not lost on me. Nor was their summertime celebration of freedom and recreational abandonment; playful afternoons devoid of stress and toil. A pang of sadness washed over me as I realized I did not share the contentment found in their passive pursuits. I had chosen a different path, a path whose rewards I hoped would reveal themselves in good time, rewards I hoped would balance out the sadness, the stress, the sinking feeling of being alone. Little did I know, these would be the last humans I would see for several days. Tugging the boat behind me, I turned and plodded downstream.

Eight hours of toil brought me four miles to a large logjam at the north end of a narrow island. In the center of the island was a raised, flat area free of debris—a perfect place to set up camp. As I lay back on my inflatable mattress and listened to the nightly frog serenade, I could feel my overused muscles complaining loudly. Progress had come at a price. Sleep and time would quiet the complaints and I rested in the assurance that it was indeed progress that I was making. I was achieving my goal, little by little.

Day 9 progress: 4 miles

Day 10 (January 8, 2010)

Began the day by hefting the boat and gear down a
semi-dry channel that bisected the island I was camped
on. I filmed the portage for posterity. An hour later, I
repeated the same procedure in yet another semi-dry
channel that bisected yet another island with yet another logjam on its northern end. I filmed this portage
as well. This time, though, I decided to challenge myself further and not remove the gear from the boat. This
particular channel had one added feature that the last
one sorely lacked—its surface was composed of sedi-
mentary rock that had been eroded by the river's current, producing a series of deep, V-shaped troughs. It
resembled the bevelled surface of a giant record album
covered with slime. As one can easily imagine, walking
backwards on the surface of a giant record album covered with slime while pulling a 12-foot inflatable boat
heavily laden with gear was indeed an intrepid task.
My favourite part was sliding backwards into a deep
pool at the end of the channel and desperately clinging
to the boat as I drifted downstream. It's always nice to
have that stuff on film.

Luckily, other than during those first two follies, I
was spared having to portage the boat and gear on this
day. Most obstacles in the stream—fallen tree limbs and
the like—were easily sidestepped. I was not, however,
spared the tedium of pulling the boat over rocks and
shallow rapids. For the third consecutive day, I continued the tiresome trend of exiting and entering the boat
hundreds of times. Ironically, my canoe paddle was the
driest piece of equipment I possessed.

As the cool water from the surrounding creeks entered the fray, the river began to swell. The banks slowly
closed in as I descended into a deeper valley. The slopes
became much steeper, each side a crush of lush foliage

and giant, white-barked gum trees. At one point a pair of brumbies (wild horses) stared out through a veil of green ferns, their eyes locked to mine as I drifted past. Brilliantly coloured gang gangs (parrots) swooped and called to their partners as birds of cleverer camouflage darted in the trees and chirped out sunny songs of playful joy.

All was not joyful below my knees, however. Thanks to my frequent watery forays, the sunscreen lotion on my lower legs quickly washed away, leaving them to bake in the sun when I was seated in the boat. Equally annoying was the fact that the zippers on my kayak boots had become jammed with sand and refused to zip up. The oversized zipper sliders chafed away at the tender skin on the inner sides of my feet. Raw sores formed and I winced every time I stood in the rocky riverbed and wrenched the boat downstream. And because an exotic river trip wouldn't be complete without a good infection, the skin between the toes on both feet developed a nasty red rash—inflamed and itchy, painful and peeling.

Save for the sound of one jet plane, an abandoned sandal bobbing among some boulders, an empty Coke can, and a wayward canoe paddle wedged in a weedy bank (which joined my gear arsenal for a few days), I saw and heard no other signs of human activity. It was as if humans had never existed. The landscape here thrived in ways immeasurable. The trees had seen neither axe nor chainsaw. No roads had been built. No trails blazed. The land had been, by virtue of its shear remoteness, virtually untouched by human hands. "How many places have I seen in my lifetime as pristine as this?" I wondered aloud. The answer, sadly, was "very few." "Very few" was also the number of people who had been privileged enough to set eyes upon this virginal Eden. I knew I was one of only a handful of people worldwide to have seen it. For this fact alone I was thankful. This privilege, it seemed, was the reward for my toil.

As the warm afternoon wore on, my dry canoe paddle was finally called to action. I steered the boat through numerous boulder gardens, over two-foot drops, and down bumpy staircase rapids. The Murray was picking up steam. The cold-water creeks were pouring their caches into the river, churning up the challenge and forcing me to intensify my focus on the numerous obstacles in my path.

By 4:30pm, I was busily scanning the banks for a decent spot to set up camp. It took me another two hours to find one. Rounding an S-curve, I spied an exposed strip of sandy bank at the base of a cliff that was 200 feet high and nearly vertical. Gum trees and ferns clutched precariously to the rock face. Looking back upriver, I could see a distant ridgetop looming over the leafy crowns of the gum trees. Somewhere up there on Davies Plain Track, 4x4s were grinding their way up the dirt road, long out of sight of the river below.

Tired and sore, I cooked up a meal of instant rice and canned beans and washed it down with mouthfuls of filtered river water. Sleep came quick as darkness fell over the forest, the cool evening air a sober reminder that I was still 2460 feet above sea level.

Ah yes, the sea—the ultimate destination of this expedition. Dreamy mists hung heavy over the mountains while a half-moon winked its yellow eye between white, wispy clouds. I took leave of my camp and drifted, free from fallen trees and logjams, free from foul-smelling, fungus-ridden feet and toe jam. I drifted onward to a distant ocean, an ocean that lay an unfathomable, 1554 miles downstream. Then, in the space of an exhalation, I was there, standing tall at the river's mouth, straining to hear a faint but familiar voice over the roar of the pounding surf. The voice was that of my good friend, Scott McFarlane. As moonlight fell upon my grinning face, I recognized his words. "Little by little," he whispered. "Little by little."

Day 10 progress: 7 miles

Day 11 (January 9, 2010)

Daylight filtered through the forest canopy as I woke to yet another day on the river. The current quietly gurgled over the shallow rapids in front of my tent as the ever-present bird sounds tickled my waking ears. I made my morning meal of instant oats, mixing in two generous tablespoons of brown sugar, a teaspoon of spirulina (blue-green algae), and a healthy handful of raisins and peanuts. Then began the twice-daily routine of filtering river water, certainly the most tedious of camp chores. Then came the pack-up of gear followed by the strap-down of gear in the boat. Finally, at 9:00am, I was ready to once again launch the SOAR S12 and hit the river.

It didn't take long to find the first obstacle of the day: a smallish tree that had recently fallen across the river, completely blocking passage. Fallen trees of this size were annoying, time-consuming hiccups that set me cursing aloud. They were too big to move and too long to go around. Going over was the only option, and "over" meant that *everything* had to come out of the boat.

Take a moment right now and slip your feet into my neoprene boots. You are standing knee-deep in the warm, rushing current. The sun is burning the back of your neck and the raw, pink skin on your tender feet tingles irritably. Directly in front of you is an obstruction that prevents you from progressing downstream. You've seen and dealt with many such obstacles on the river so far and secretly hope you won't have to deal with many more. Secretly, you know this will not be the case. At your side is a 12-foot inflatable boat full of gear. You've actually brought along too much gear and too much food and it's all *very heavy*. In one of your bear-resistant canisters is a large nest of wires, cables, and connectors that have served no purpose over the last three days, other than strengthening your muscles from lugging it around. A soggy, unused wetsuit weighs down one bag while a whitewater helmet is tucked far inside another bag, right next to that two-person tent with the broken zipper. Rounding out the bulk of gear are two roll-top drybags that house the expensive cameras and a larger drybag that contains the camping gear.

You unhook the bungee cords that hold the gear securely in the boat. Near the uprooted base of a fallen tree is a small patch of grass on which to pile the gear. You struggle with the empty boat, which alone weighs a hefty 70 pounds, forcing its rounded bow up onto the log. You back away to take a photograph. With a guttural grunt and a few choice expletives, the boat finds its way to the downstream side of the log. You shoulder the heavy packs and precariously straddle the fallen tree, then haphazardly toss the gear bags back into the boat and strap the kit down. Smiling, you raise your arms in triumph and exclaim excitedly, "Easy!"

Just around the bend, out of sight, is another obstacle. It's bigger than the one you just dealt with. You'll see it in about 90 seconds. You will curse and shoot your eyes skyward. Then you will go through the whole routine again. And again. And again. And between the obstacles, you will repeatedly jump from your boat and pull its reluctant bulk over the rocky shallows, zig-zagging down the riverbed in a valiant attempt to find the path of least resistance. And you will try to do all this with a smile on your face, believing that if you are happy, at least outwardly, the toil of such tedium will be far less encumbering. Yes, the trick is to dupe yourself into a state of contentment, all the while being fully aware that to treat such a trick thusly is to enter into a dangerously deceitful game with yourself. It takes a great deal of practice to fool yourself. Lucky for you, your present river adventure has offered up plenty of opportunity for *foolure* (failure) and you've become fairly adept at self-trickery. Congratulations.

~ ~ ~

It is the routine of river travel, or any kind of travel for that matter, that grinds you down mentally. Mealtimes and bedtimes. Biting insects and stinging insecurities. The aforementioned *happiness hoax*. The paddle strokes. The hours alone. Hours of drifting thought. Free in the mind. Trapped in the mind. Mindful awareness. Mind full of fear. The duel with duality. The unpredictable predictability. Sun—too much of it. Water—never enough of it. The rote. The route. The routine. Repetition. Routine—is it boring? Hardly. Is it essential? Essentially, yes. Repetition. Do you understand? Repetition. Have you learned your lesson today? No? Repetition. Repetition. Repetition.

But wait. Why I am trashing *routine*? Isn't routine the glue that holds an endeavour together? Isn't routine the structure, the constant, the reliable, the tried, tested, and true? Isn't routine, then, the blueprint for success? Q: What is the basic definition of success? A: The completion of a routine. Routine, therefore, is a *discipline*. People generally seem to dislike routine and repetition. Routines and repetition appear constrictive, habitual. Take, as an example, the routine schedule of the common working person in the Western world— the routine of a 9–5 workday. It is the very adhesion to this routine that has helped make democracy a *success* (sarcasm inferred). Routine is not something that has been imposed on people. People follow the rules of routine that they alone have created. The act of *breaking free* from routine is simply the first action of a new routine.

How ironic is it then, that the very thing that structures our goals—routine—is the thing we come to loathe throughout our endeavours for success? And the funniest part is, *we create our routines.* Our actions are incredibly self-defeating! We may even blame others for the *misfortune* of routine that seems to have been mysteriously imposed upon us by others. That is a seriously ridiculous fabrication which nicely illustrates our inability to claim personal responsibility for something we personally created. Are you bored with routine? If so, have a look at what you are resisting. Routine is a blueprint for progress, a blueprint for growth. Are you resisting growth? *Resisting* is a mental activity. Routine, in and of itself, is not a state of mind, it is a state of being. Routine, like growth, requires little thought; it only requires quiet commitment.

Even though we've established that the adherence to routine is a mental activity rooted in discipline, we cannot overlook the physical aspect of adhering to routine. When this physical aspect is applied to the success of long distance, self-propelled expeditions, adherence to routine plays a vital, yet less important, role when compared to the mental aspect.

If you've properly prepared for a rigorous journey by training your body to withstand the repetitiously punishing demands it will undoubtedly encounter, the physicality of such a trip is of little issue. Much like a grandfather clock whose pendulum is set in motion, the body will perform tediously routine activity seemingly effortlessly until it breaks, or until the mind tells it to quit. Long, arduous, physically demanding expeditions fail because the minds of the participants fail. If you have not succeeded, it's because you believed you would not succeed. Fear is the mind killer and doubt is fear's accomplice. Focus on these two obstacles (fear and doubt) and you will become a log in the jam. Eliminate these two obstacles and your river will flow unhampered.

The body will adhere to its routine, whatever that routine may be. Lungs will breathe routinely. The heart will beat routinely. Present the body a blueprint and

watch it perform. Routine is the structure, the constant, the reliable, the tried, tested, and true. Routine
is the very thing to fall back on when the mind says,
"No, I can't" or "No, I won't" or a myriad of other self-
negating thoughts. Routine knows otherwise. Routine
is progress—pendulum progress—slow and calculated,
precisely proven through experience. When doubt and
fear fail, routine succeeds.

~ ~ ~

A highlight on this day was coming across a Sambar
deer standing motionless in the middle of the stream.
From my silent vantage point in the drifting boat (the
river here was deep enough to actually float the boat),
I was able to see that this particular species of Australian deer resembled the mule deer or elk found in
North America. It was a large beast—four feet high at
the shoulder, solid medium brown in colour with no
visible antlers. There was no time to take a photo or
grab the camcorder. I was lucky enough to lock eyes
with it for 20 seconds before it turned away and calmly
galloped down the riverbed, its hooves splashing the
water and loudly clunking the rocks underfoot. Seconds later, it made a quick turn into the forest and
disappeared.

The increase in flow meant I was doing more
paddling than in days previous. There were many
straight sections where the river widened and subsequently got very shallow. In one section, the river
formed a deep pool between smooth cliffs. It eventually closed in around me and funnelled the flow
through a four-foot-wide natural sluice. Several
stands of old growth trees lined the banks and I
saw one of the biggest gum trees I've ever seen in
Australia. White and yellow cockatoos began to appear in the foliage, a sure sign that I was dropping
in elevation.

For the second day in a row, I saw no humans. And while the humans were thankfully in short supply, the logjams were not. All told, I did six portages on the day, as well as deal with numerous fallen trees and branches littering the stream. At one dogleg bend in the river, a mass of logs and branches was embedded on the south end of an island, creating a huge obstruction. Luckily, a narrow channel had formed through the debris. In order to reach the channel, I had to remove most of the gear from the boat, balance it on branches, and then heave the boat over a large log. The water here appeared to be about eight feet deep, so I had to be careful not to drop any gear. Once back in the boat, I had to break off several branches to clear a route. I then poled the boat through the flotsam and onto the safety of the island. After a short rest, I plodded downstream.

Finding a place to set up camp proved overly difficult. I searched for two hours before I came across a bare spot along the bank. It appeared to be the terminus of a game trail, a place where animals commonly came to drink from the river. In order to erect the tent, I had to yank out several handfuls of an invasive spiky grass that seemed to be everywhere I didn't want it to be. The needle-sharp tip of this knee-high nasty plant can easily penetrate skin or poke out an eye. I came to label this green inconvenience *lethal grass* because if ever you stumbled and fell into a patch of this stuff, you'd surely be impaled on it.

Adding to the morose camp setting was an abnormally wretched-looking black mud spread wide along the riverbank. The river water here was crudely opaque and nose-curlingly offensive. After wading through this filth, the fungal rash on my feet flared up fivefold. It then occurred to me that, because this site saw regular use by animals, maybe I had been thoughtlessly wading through a funk of fecal matter. As I crawled into my tent for the last time that day, smearing the black muck across the nylon floor, the ever-present expletives found their way through my clenched teeth. I quickly awarded the site the dubious honour of being the second worst place I've ever camped, topped only by the infamous Squalor Gallows campsite on the upper Mississippi River. (That story appears in my first book, *Part-Time Superheroes, Full-Time Friends*.)

At least I could take comfort in the fact that I'd come seven miles further downstream and was now within two days of Tom Groggin Station if I kept at the current pace. I was now on the third of six topographic maps of this area of the upper Murray. Progress was being made and routine was being adhered to. With any luck, the morrow would see an abatement of time-consuming logjams and an influx of flow. If the maps were to be believed, and there was no reason they shouldn't be, the influx was coming soon in the forms of Cascade Creek and Leather Barrel Creek. I hoped for less portaging and more paddling. After all, that's what I was there to do.

Day 11 progress: 7 miles

Day 12 (January 10, 2010)

I launched the boat at 9:00am, relieved to be away from the black filth and lethal grass. Unfortunately, much of the muck from the campsite was tracked into the boat, coating the seat and floor of the S12. It didn't take long for it to wash off, however. Plunging over a two-foot drop in the first rapid of the day, water came pouring in over the sides of the boat, filling it to the brim and flushing out the filth through the 16 self-bailing holes in the boat's floor. Soaked from the waist down, I smiled and paddled onward to the next rapid.

I decided to set a distance goal for the day, something I hadn't yet done on the river. Leather Barrel Creek is a major tributary that enters the Murray at approximately river mile 40. It is also the largest creek to enter the Murray up to that point. With the creek being nine miles downstream from last night's camp, I decided to push for that important confluence as my day's goal.

By mid-morning, the temperature had already hit 86°, very warm for this high up in the mountains. I was thankful for the shady relief the valley's steep slopes provided from the sun's early onslaught. By noon, though, the sun had found its apex and was quickly searing any exposed skin in its path. My already well-roasted lower legs were rapidly changing from pink to red and singing unhappily in pain. Their only relief came from my repeated forays into the drink to pull the boat over rocky shallows.

Cascade Creek entered the party at river mile 37.5. It added to the river's volume, along with several anonymous feeder creeks. In the placid pools that formed between successions of roaring rapids, a welcomed serenity unfolded. Only the smooth sound of my paddle pushing water and the shrill, yet serenading chorus from crowds of invisible cicadas punctuated the heated, humid air. Curious dragonflies darted to and fro, momentarily landing on the boat to tilt their multi-eyed heads in my direction, then launching themselves in playful pursuit of their brethren.

Less welcome were the ever-present black flies. Although not biters, they were nevertheless frustratingly annoying—far more so on land than on water. Snack breaks and bladder relief took place mostly on, or in, the river. (And yes, I did take time to silently apologize to those people living downstream.) Even less welcome, but also far less frequently encountered, were the March flies. Unlike the larger and somewhat lazier horsefly, these nasty little pricks wasted no time taking samples of my sunburnt flesh. The March fly's routine was simple yet effective: land, eat, and leave—quickly. I'd like to boast that I managed to squish dozens of them with my gloved hands, but I'd be lying to you.

As I descended in elevation, their numbers seemed to increase. The hotter the day became, the quicker and more maddeningly evasive the flies became, and the more *unhinged* I became!

Luckily, my wish for an abatement of river obstructions came true, for the most part. I still encountered many fallen trees and the occasional logjam, but did not have to remove the gear from the boat all day. A new challenge came in the form of boulder gardens. From high above, I must've appeared like a slow rat in a large maze as I guided the boat on foot through the remains of these ancient rockslides. Many times, the boat had to be pulled up and over the huge, smooth boulders due to the S12's wide girth and inability to squeeze between them. When the workout got too strenuous, I could always find relief by splashing water on myself.

Rapids increased in size and intensity. Two-foot drops were frequent. Several Class II rollercoasters materialized to test my limited whitewater skills. Many times, where the water was still low and the exposed rocks plenty, I had to exit the boat mid-rapid and urge it over the drops. Standing in a rushing surge of churning, waist-high water, attempting to pull a heavy, flooded boat over large rocks was not what I expected when I began planning this trip. Back then, I imagined myself riding atop the river, not being half-immersed in it.

~ ~ ~

In December 2008, when I first started laying the plans for this expedition, I realized that if I was going to tackle the Murray River from source to sea I was going to have to descend 68 miles of potentially dangerous whitewater in the river's upper reaches. Frankly, that idea scared the crap out of me.

My experience with whitewater prior to the Murray was confined to co-piloting a canoe through a handful of Class I–II rapids on the upper Mississippi River in the summer of 2001. The closest I'd come to running anything that could be considered a "challenge" was a frothy Class II beast near the city of St. Cloud, Minnesota. Here, the youthful Mississippi winds its way quickly around a sharp bend, then tumbles over a shelf of half-hidden rocks. Although we were well aware of the St. Cloud rapid on our map, myself and long-time fellow adventurer and best mate, Scott McFarlane, chose not to scout the rapid. Our eagerness and ignorance got the better of us that morning, landing us in a precarious situation as we were swept around the bend and into the turbulent fray. Thanks to Scott's precision paddling strokes and his shouted words of encouragement from the stern, we managed to white-knuckle our way through the mayhem. It's hard to forget the disorienting mix of exhilaration and fear we felt upon being spit out of that noisy ruckus of rocks and river. We smilingly rejoiced in our triumph, but wholeheartedly agreed it was definitely something we didn't want to go through again. Lucky for us, it was the last navigable rapid on the upper Mississippi.

For many years, the Murray River downstream of Tom Groggin Station had been frequently descended by whitewater rafting companies keen on giving their customers a barrel of thrills on what is known as Australia's longest set of continuous rapids. Here, the river plunges through the constricted confines of the famous Murray Gates, winding its way 18 miles through 30 Class I–IV rapids until it finally slows its pace to become the calm flatwater river as seen near the settlement of Biggara.

After almost 10 years of drought, the Murray was significantly mellow in early 2010. Low snowfall meant that the Australian spring runoff was confined to a few weeks in September and October. Because of this, many rafting companies closed shop and moved on to other pursuits. A few thrill-seeking rafters and kayakers made the yearly spring run through the Murray Gates down to Biggara, but just like the annual rainfall amounts, their numbers were dwindling.

My choice to descend the upper Murray during the month of January (a low water month) had been dictated by my work schedule. At the time, I was employed as a landscape maintenance person, cutting lawns and planting flowers. Given the seasonal aspect of the work, the dormant Vancouver winter months of December, January, and February were times when I generally did my travelling. Running the Murray in spring made good sense when considering flow volume, but getting to Australia before December was impossible due to my commitment to work.

Even given the probable low water levels of January, I still fully expected the Murray to give me a run for my money. I decided that if I was going to tackle the river's untamed upper reaches, I'd better be ready for whatever the Murray might present—low water or not.

In May 2009, I signed up for a whitewater kayaking course in North Vancouver, Canada. The local creeks and rivers on the North Shore serve as ideal training grounds for novice and pro paddlers alike. Although I had plenty of experience with plastic and inflatable sea kayaks, this was my first time in a whitewater kayak. I have to say, it wasn't very pleasant.

The first lesson took place in the relative safety of an indoor public pool. We practiced wet-exiting from an upside-down boat. That seemed easy enough: pull the handle of the sprayskirt forward and slide out of the cockpit. I found I didn't mind being upside down underwater and gravity seemed to cooperate well when it came time to bail out of the boat. There was no panic, no stress. I left the pool feeling quite confident with my new paddling skills. *This might be pretty easy after all,* I pondered to myself, smiling.

Then we got on the river.

North Vancouver's Capilano River in May is ice cold. Even as I stood in the sunny parking lot beside the river, silently cursing and sweating under layers of nylon and neoprene, I could feel the chill of the Capilano. Unlike the warm pool, if I fell out of the boat in this water not only would be it be scrotum-shrivellingly cold, but I would also be unable to touch bottom—a fact that frightened me far more than possessing a set of temporarily shrunken genitals.

One of the first drills we were instructed to do was to rock the boat side to side, using our paddle as a brace. Much to my liking, we practiced this balancing manoeuvre in shallow water close to the riverbank. Of course, I pushed the envelope a little too far and fell past the point of no return, tipping over on my left side with my head fully submerged underwater. My immediate reaction was to flick my body in the opposite direction in order to right myself. After three attempts I panicked, thrashing the water with my paddle in a desperate attempt to right the boat. Luckily, the instructor was close by and calmly coached me through the ordeal. Despite his gentle reassurances, I remained emotionally shaken by the experience. I mentally grappled with that frightening feeling of helplessness, trapped and disabled in a boat below the surface of a freezing river, unable to properly exit the boat in the shallow water. I played the scene over and over in my head that day, all the while wondering what the Murray River would have in store for me. *If it's anything like this, I'm gonna hate it immensely,* I thought. Still, I stuck it out and pressed on with the lesson, my stubborn persistence on full display.

We practiced our "T" rescues, just as we had in the pool. This manoeuvre is done in pairs. One kayaker capsizes their boat while the other paddler comes to their rescue by butting the bow of their boat into the cockpit area of the capsized boat, essentially forming a "T." The object here is for the capsized kayaker to reach up and grab the bow of the rescuer's boat and use it as a stabilizer while they right their own boat. Let me tell you that hanging upside down in a cold, swift moving river while you voluntarily wait for someone to come to your "rescue" is not a very pleasant experience. After the debilitating brain freeze kicks in, the whole experience goes downhill real fast. After the fifth "T" rescue, I called it a day.

The following weekend, we returned to the pool. If I was going to tackle the treacherous whitewater of the upper Murray, I would need to be able to perform perhaps the most important of whitewater self-rescues: the Eskimo roll. Over and over I went, at least 15 times. Only once did I manage to perform the roll properly. The afternoon was a fiasco. For an instructor who prided himself in saying that all his students would leave the class knowing how to roll, I was the exception. He was visibly annoyed and sent me to the opposite end of the pool to practice my hip flicks. I felt like a failure. My confidence sunk like a lead lifejacket. I left the pool with a bruised paddling ego—dejected, downtrodden, and downright angry. My time of dealing with impatient, non-empathic instructors was over. I would have to take training into my own hands.

Flowing east out of the Cascade Mountains and into the dry western edge of British Columbia's Okanagan region, the Similkameen River seemed like a good place to regain some paddling confidence on my own terms. Warm, shallow, and swift enough to present a decent challenge, the river provided me with four days of hands-on whitewater experience. I'm proud to say that I only capsized once, going sideways over a sizable drop near Bromley Rock Provincial Park. The dunk shook me up, but I quickly regained my composure, drained the boat of water, and continued downstream, logging in a total of 60 miles over four days. I considered the trip a success, but remained wary of the tippiness of the plastic whitewater kayak. The Murray certainly promised to be more treacherous than the tame Similkameen. This fact alone prompted me to examine the possibility of using a different type of boat.

Back in 2005, Australian paddler Rowen Privett descended the Murray River from Tom Groggin Station to the Southern Ocean. I contacted Rowen in December 2008 after viewing his website, Murray Quest 2005. Rowen, who works as an outdoor education instructor and is knowledgeable in both whitewater and sea kayaking, provided a ton of logistical support and encouragement in the early planning stages of my expedition. He and I agreed that the use of an inflatable boat would increase the safety factor I was seeking, as well as being, in Rowen's words, "user-friendly." Brand names like Innova, Incept, and Aire were bandied around, but I already knew the boat I wanted for the Murray expedition: the SOAR S12. (Big thanks to Rowen, Josh, and their friend Matt Neale for sharing their knowledge and experience.)

I contacted the California-based company SOAR (Somewhere on a River), makers of inflatable boats best suited for moving water. CEO Larry Laba was gracious enough to offer the use of a 12-foot inflatable canoe for the upper portion of the Murray expedition. At 40 inches in width, the SOAR S12 promised to be not only a stable vessel, but also roomy enough to store all the gear and food required to sustain a solo adventurer in the remote upper reaches of the Murray. Seeing that the dimensions of the boat resembled a canoe more than a kayak, Larry suggested that I use a 60" canoe paddle rather than a traditional kayak paddle to propel the S12. It had been many years since I held a canoe paddle in my hands, but I welcomed the renewed challenge of using a single blade. With the arrival of the S12 came the paddling peace of mind I'd been seeking. Here was a robust, inflatable boat that I could trust to get the job done safely. (Thanks to Larry and the staff at SOAR for their support and encouragement.)

Finally, all the pieces of the whitewater puzzle were assembled: training, logistics, gear, and even a little dose of sponsorship. My self-confidence was high, equalled only by my determination. I felt ready to take my whitewater experience to the next level. It was time to meet the Murray.

~ ~ ~

By late afternoon, the mercury had soared well into the mid-90s, accelerating not only the prolific growth of the surrounding foliage, but also the speed and numbers of the damned March flies. Unlike the previous three days, finding proper campsites was a veritable non-issue. Sandy beaches began to appear at regular intervals and each successive one was an invitation to set up my tent and seek refuge from the flies. The problem was, most of these beaches were fully exposed to the scorching sun and the thought of baking in a nylon sauna for hours until sundown was not very inviting. "If I set up the tent in this heat," I said aloud, "it'll be *roast until ghost*." Plus, I still had to reach my goal for the day: Leather Barrel Creek.

The aforementioned creek lay only a half-mile downstream when I rounded a sharp bend and bumped the boat over a short drop and into a deep pool, right next to a beautiful beach. It was too tempting to refuse. I nudged the nose of the boat up on the sandy bank and sighed. I had failed to meet the day's goal, but at least the beach was sandy and fecal-free, a deep contrast to the previous night's muddy filth-fest. "Paradise!" I exclaimed, as a wide grin spread across my face. "Peace at last!"

And then the flies moved in.

I frantically scurried around on the hot sand, erecting the tent in record time and diving into its comforting sanctum. After happily exacting revenge on a few of the miscreants who'd foolishly followed me into my plastic domain, I laid down on my inflatable mattress for a soothing, well-deserved rest.

In less than three minutes, the temperature in the tent became unbearable. I flung open the zippered door, fought off the barrage of flies, and dove headlong into the cooling waters of the Murray. I surfaced to find a swarm of buzzing beasts ready to feed on my saturated scalp. I thrashed the air with my arms, sending the vermin into a fury, and then dove into the cool, clear depths of the pool.

Smiling with relief, I made a mad dash over the scalding sand and ducked back inside the tent. Owing only to convenience, and not common sense, I fired up the stove and cooked up a quick curry feast, which, in the stifling heat, doubled my body temperature and prompted another mad rush to the river for relief.

As the sun eventually found its way behind the dense nest of green foliage, a pair of deer emerged on the opposite side of the river and silently descended to the bank for a drink.

Inside the humid tent, I consulted my topographic maps. At my current pace, Tom Groggin Station would easily be reached by the following night. I was looking forward to a day off. The thought of a taking a refreshing shower and downing a cold drink put a smile on my face. My maps also confirmed what I suspected: plenty of rapids in the coming day. That thought didn't bother me as much as the challenge that lay beyond Tom Groggin—the Murray Gates. The thought of passing through the Gates provoked no smiles on my face, only the blank, chilly stare of fear one expresses in times of uncertainty. Though the Gates were still a lengthy 18 miles downstream, I could hear their restless roar. It came to me quietly at first, like the sound of croaking frogs upon the evening breeze. Then it intensified as the last remnants of daylight faded on the forest floor. As the deer finished their drink and slipped silently into the shadows, I shuddered in my sleeping bag, frozen in fear on the warmest night of this young year.

Day 12 progress: 8 miles

Day 13 (January 11, 2010)

The sixth day on the river was punctuated with a dra-
matic capsize while careening over a four-foot-high
drop several miles upstream of Tom Groggin Station.
I miscalculated the approach and went over the drop
sideways, completely flipping the boat. The ordeal
happened quickly. I remember thinking it strange that
there was water behind the lenses of my sunglasses.
That's when I realized I was underwater. I popped to
the surface to find the boat overturned and my paddle
circulating in a nearby eddy. A yellow nylon rope—one
end of it tied to the boat and the other end attached to
my camera bag—was taut, its length stretched into the
unseen depths of the pool below the rapid. I panicked,
thinking the bag and its contents were lost to the river.
As I hurriedly reeled in the rope, I felt weight on its
end and was immensely relieved when the bag broke
the surface. Thankfully, the cameras were dry. A quick
inventory of gear showed nothing had been lost. I was
grateful that I'd wisely secured everything to the boat.

Less than a mile downstream, I cautiously approached another similar-sized drop. I'd successfully
navigated the same drop during a short trial run a few
weeks prior and remembered that a large rock lay at
the bottom of this drop. The rock had been almost
completely submerged last time. This time, however,
because water levels had dropped considerably, the
rock was substantially exposed, creating an unavoidable obstacle as the boat careened over the drop and
landed square on top of it. The force of the water tumbling over the drop pinned the boat in place, filling it
in seconds. I grabbed hold of the bow line, scrambled
overboard, and swam to a nearby boulder to assess the
situation. Laden with water, the boat proved too heavy
to heave off the rock, so I swam back to the boat, got

in, and removed all the gear. After some serious effort, and a lot of grunting and cursing, the boat floated free of the river's grip.

I arrived at Tom Groggin Station in late-afternoon and passed under the first two bridges on the Murray— a car bridge and a narrow, elevated suspension bridge for foot traffic. Despite the bothersome onslaught of March flies, I was undoubtedly relieved to see the familiar setting of the ranch and to know that the first and hopefully *hardest* part of the upper river was behind me. I expected the 38.5-mile descent to take 10 days, but I'd finished it in six. Not bad for a novice whitewater paddler. I hoped to carry that well-earned confidence forward to the next 24 miles of intimidating rapids. Some of the toughest whitewater in Australia lay before me, and the thought of descending it alone scared me shitless. I could bolster all the self-confidence I wanted. I could worry about it until I nervously shook in my neoprene boots. I could avoid it and complain about it and silently wish it away, but one thing remained true: at some point, the fear would need to be faced.

Day 13 progress: 10 miles

After a day of rest and reorganizing, I strapped on my hiking boots and walked 17 miles of Alpine Way from Tom Groggin Station to the village of Thredbo at the foot of Mount Kosciuszko, thereby completing my 107-mile circumnavigation of the Murray headwaters. Free from the intense focus needed to navigate the river's rapids, I daydreamed as I ascended the winding highway through the Australian Alps. I thought back to my 5200-mile bicycling journey across Oz in 2003–2004. I'd ridden roads like the present one many times, grinding up formidable, jungle-lined hills and screaming down bitumen switchbacks as the wind and heat evaporated the sweat from my overworked body. That continental crossing often demanded every ounce of determination I could muster. Somehow, I managed to dredge up the required resolve and got the job done. Somehow, I needed to do it again—this time, on the country's longest river.

Before I resumed my descent of the Murray, I joined Trevor and his family to break bread with his seasonal neighbours who lived part-time in their summer home on the ranch's west side. I learned that the upper Murray (the river upstream of the Swampy Plain River confluence) was originally known as the Indi River (pronounced inn-dye). Some maps still use that name. I also had the privilege of meeting the old bushie who rafted from Kings Plain access to Tom Groggin Station a few years prior. He made his living crafting leather goods (his belts were top-notch) and lived in an off-the-grid cabin in the woods near the town of Khancoban, 30 miles north of Tom Groggin Station. We compared notes and shared harrowing stories of our descents. "Nevva again," he remarked when Trevor asked if he planned to have another go at it. "Nevva again."

Besides tolerating the incessant scourge of March flies and nervously speeding down frothy rapids squeezed between towering canyon walls, the descent through the narrow gorge of the Murray Gates went better than planned. This 24-mile section took two days to paddle. Water levels were low and dropping daily in the January heat, which meant that the boat had to be walked through numerous boulder gardens. Still, the series of 30 rapids (all of them colourfully named) doled out abundant challenges that helped hone my meagre whitewater paddling skills. And just to ensure that my ego remained in check, I inadvertently went through the most treacherous rapid backwards, wide-eyed with fear and manically clutching the boat's safety line for dear life. Sheesh.

Eventually, the steep valley walls receded as the quieted Murray entered pasture land near the village of Biggara. Herds of cattle slowly splashed their way across the river in its shallowest bits. Fences, bridges, and barns communicated the presence of humans, unwelcomed after weeks of floating and trekking through an Edenic upper river.

Sixteen miles on, I passed through the Swampy Plain River

confluence and traded the 12-foot inflatable boat for the 16-foot plastic sea kayak stored in Tom Lednar's garage. Thus marked the end of the 90-mile-long upper Murray, and the beginning of the 1488-mile flatwater pursuit to the sea.

It's hard to paraphrase the next 10 weeks in a pair of paragraphs, but it's suffice to say that heat, drought, and perseverance had a lot to do with it. Ignorant owners of motorized boats reigned supreme in sections of the river deemed *recreational*. Their belligerent comments stung hard with gender-specific put-downs about my dreadlocked appearance, as if a beer in one hand and a fishing pole in the other somehow permitted them by law to be bold and boorish. I'm sure their American redneck cousins would be proud, and any retort suggesting such would've undoubtedly been met with more derision. More often than not, I bottled the anger and simply paddled on.

Meanwhile, my fucked up financial situation was providing stress of a different kind. Long before I climbed Mount Kosciuszko and kicked off the expedition, I had to nearly drain one bank account to pay for a rental car and a rental kayak. I had money in two other accounts in two other banks, but no way to transfer funds between banks. The situation was complicated by the fact that several automatic withdrawal payments came out of the drained account every month. The longer the account sat idle, the longer those payments went unpaid. I didn't have a mobile phone during this expedition, so I had no way to contact the banks directly. Online banking and email were not options because 99% of the time I had no Internet access. Towns were few and far between on the Murray, and the few pay phones I did manage to find were often inoperable. When I found one that worked, I was stymied by the time difference between Canada and Australia. The Canadian banks were often closed during Australian daylight hours. In the rare cases where the time difference made contacting the banks a possibility, I was inconveniently nowhere near a town. It was a conundrum of epic proportions. Not only did a long list of important payments go unpaid for three months, but my employer also took my lack of communication as proof that I had no intention to return to work following the expedition. When my employer's patience expired, he hired someone to replace me. Thanks to all the drama, as well as the time wasted in dealing with the drama, I had to twice reschedule my return flight and borrow a sizeable amount of money just to finish the expedition. By the time I reached the river's end, I was jobless, financially crippled, and impossibly stressed out. Ironically, paddling and trekking 1578 miles to the sea was the easy part!

To help alleviate some of the anxiety, I sought comfort in my plan to return to the river's beginning and hike those nine unseen miles I'd passed on three months prior. It had taken me 87 days to paddle (and walk) 1578 miles from the Murray's source, yet the journey to me was still incomplete. One final goal remained: fill the missing gap.

I rented a car in Adelaide, drove to Melbourne to drop off the rental kayak, drove north to Tom Lednar's house to retrieve my inflatable boat, and then drove to the vehicle access point closest to the Murray's source. A six-mile walk brought me to Cowombat Flat. I crossed the river into New South Wales, pitched my tent, and went in search of the elusive metal pipe at the Murray's source. An hour of combing the forest floor yielded nothing but muddy boots and a sour frown. Dejected, I returned to my tent.

Cowombat Flat stretches west until its meadows become rocky and woody. There, where the tiny Murray is joined by the larger Pilot Creek, a rough rock wall abruptly directs the flow south into a shallow, steep-sided canyon complete with 12-foot waterfalls. Burdened with a weighty backpack, but keen to proceed, I entered this section cautiously. It was unlike anything I expected to see.

I carefully skirted the plumes and pools of the waterfalls and picked my way along the canyon wall until the flow levelled and doglegged north. Before me stood the most intimidating valley I'd ever laid eyes on. Nothing, and I mean *nothing*, gave any hint that a human had ever been there before. If the section of river downstream of Poplars Camping Area seemed extraordinarily remote when I paddled it in January, this place was even more so. The narrow channel was choked with fallen trees, living trees, ferns, vines, saplings, and woven nests of natural detritus. The only place to trek was in the forest.

For the first mile, I followed game trails (most likely established by brumbies) that snaked along the contour lines about 20 vertical feet above the river on the left descending bank. Numerous spur trails disappeared into the forest to my left and right, some leading down to the river, some ascending the steep slope to the out-of-view ridgetop. I was careful not to follow these side trails, reminding myself that they'd been created by animals whose intentions differed from humans. The animals didn't follow these trails in order to arrive at the first vehicle access on the Murray. They followed these trails to food and water sources and safe havens, places where humans rarely tread. Our goals may have differed, but our paths were still the same.

When the brumby trails petered out, I took off my leather hiking boots, slipped on my neoprene kayaking boots, crossed the knee-deep stream, changed back to the hiking boots, scrambled up the rocky bank, and went in search of more paths. I found none. I pressed on through thick undergrowth, the supple saplings slapping and scratching my face. With the footing unstable and the forest inhospitable, I dropped down to the river's edge, switched boots, and tried walking in the stream. Progress slowed to a crawl as I repeatedly stubbed my toes on unseen, slimy rocks and cursed loudly at my calamitous circumstance. Two times I tumbled, landing in nests of blackberry, badly scratching my exposed arms and legs.

After a quarter-mile of stumbling my way downstream, I was immensely frustrated by the lack of progress. I took leave of the river and made camp on a rare flat spot of open ground. A full day of difficult hiking had netted me little more than two miles. A quick inventory of food showed I had only a two-day supply left. Seven miles of river walking followed by seventeen miles of road walking lay between me and my rental car. If I could cover those seven miles in one day, I stood a good chance of not running out of food. Unfortunately, based on the hiking conditions I'd encountered so far, and coupled with the extremely steep terrain I would inevitably encounter the following day (as illustrated on my topo maps), that prospect seemed highly unlikely.

Early the next morning, I slowly plodded through the dense forest on the left descending bank. I found no trails and no scat—no signs that animals had passed this way recently. I did, however, come across the eroded beginnings of a foreboding rock wall that stretched along the left bank. I dropped my backpack and scrambled to higher ground to survey the terrain. Perhaps 300 yards downstream, a sheer rock wall towered hundreds of feet above the river. I had two options: 1) climb the eroded portion of the wall, emerge atop it, and somehow navigate a descent on its other end, or 2) cross the river and attempt to bypass the wall through the dense forest. I chose the latter.

Rocky outcroppings and waterfalls forced me further up the steep, opposite bank. When footing allowed, I turned to see whitewater pouring over sizeable drops in the canyon below. Paddling this section, I thought, would indeed be a formidable, if not impossible, task. Shit, *hiking* it was hard enough!

Up into the thick underbrush I pushed. This proliferation of scrub, I determined, was the "fuel" of which Trevor Davis had spoken. The growth here was new, less than two years old. If lightning struck this area, the fresh tinder would burn quick and hot. Walking through this stuff was immensely difficult. I used the combined weight of my body and backpack to propel myself forward, leaning into the brush at an impossible angle until it yielded. The further I proceeded, the thicker and more taxing it became. After an hour of arduous toil, I emerged into a small opening that afforded an unobstructed view downstream. Beyond the rock wall was a huge, flat area with few trees. Beyond that was more forest and more steep-sided valley, but no rock obstructions. If I could somehow reach the flat area, the next mile beyond it looked entirely passable. It wouldn't be easy, but it was doable. I checked my watch. It was noon. That was a shock. I expected to see 10 or 11:00am. I hung my head in despair. It had taken me two hours to walk less than a half-mile. The gravity of that indisputable truth hit me hard in the gut. At the present pace, it would take days to complete the next six-and-a-half miles of river and 17 miles of road before I arrived at my rental car. I would run out of food before then. I would grow weak from lack of nutrients, thereby increasing the risk of injury. Even a minor injury here might cost me my life. A decision had to be made. Would I proceed, or would I retreat? I was just over two miles into the river trek. If I turned back, I could take comfort in the fact that I was familiar with the route. I could retrace my steps to Cowombat Flat and then hike the remaining six miles of dirt track back to the car. That certainly seemed like the wisest option. The other option, of course, was to proceed into an overgrown unknown. I thought about rationing my food supply. I thought about foraging for food. I thought about starving to death. Worst of all, I thought about not completing what I came here to do. I thought about how I would perceive myself as a failure, that somehow, after all the adventuring I'd done in my life, I had still managed to miscalculate how much food to bring. I had wanted to keep the backpack's weight to a minimum, so I brought only three days' worth of food. Even with the firsthand knowledge I'd acquired from paddling the upper Murray, I still managed to underestimate the difficulty of this nine-mile trek. I truly believed I could cover that distance in a day. That naiveté was bound to make me a dead man or a failure. How could I have been so stupid?

I removed my backpack and retrieved my video camera. It was time for a confession.

The six-minute clip, spoken like one of those last-words-before-death videos that surface on the Internet from time to time, ended with me looking absolutely devastated. In short, I gave in. I caved. I balked. I backed away from the challenge and retraced my steps. I weighed the options, I weighed my stupidity, and then I retreated. I forced myself to eat the nauseating truth: I had failed. Less than seven miles from my goal, I had given up. I was *gutted*.

Is this how climbers feel when they turn back just shy of summiting Mount Everest? I wondered. *Are they shattered and sickened by their lack of resolve? Do they think themselves quitters? Or do they honour their attempt? Do they take pride in their accomplishment, the near-completion of their goal? Do they find solace in the success of climbing thousands of feet to reach the high point of their journey? Is it really not about the destination, but rather the journey itself? Surely, when it comes to climbing mountains, summiting is always the furthest goal. Surely, the destination defines the journey. Surely, those who fail to reach the destination fail to reach their goal. Surely, others must share the disappointment I feel in this moment of retreat. Surely, this vile pain cannot be mine alone.*

To my surprise, I shed no tears that day. The tears, I discovered, would come later. The loss was massive. The impact bigger still.

For to grieve a thing we once thought ours
is to know we never truly possessed it.

Redemption, it seemed, lay in one final act, one final decision, one final option: to return to this sacred place at a later date and, with proper preparation, complete the incomplete. The question was: *when?* I had climbed Australia's highest peak. I had paddled its longest river and bicycled its enormous breadth. I had seen and done plenty in this beautiful land down under. Was there *really* a need to return? The answer, I later learned, was *yes*.

~ ~ ~

In the summer of 2011, a year and a half after paddling the Murray River, I was pushing a gas-powered lawnmower around a gated community stuffed into a well-wooded (but ultimately down-trodden) corner of a Vancouver, British Columbia suburb.

Cutting grass was an integral part of my landscape maintenance job, a position I'd held, off and on, for the better part of eight years. At no time during my landscaping tenure was I truly happy (in fact, I was miserable every day), but on the day in question (it was sun-filled and warm, as I remember), a generous grin crept across my face as my mind eagerly wrapped itself around a glorious idea that had just popped into my head.

That morning, while shovelling the contents of a typical breakfast into my mouth (cold brown rice, soy beverage, spirulina, and sliced banana), I sat reading an interesting paddling story in Coast & Kayak magazine about a small group of kayakers who had recently floated the beautiful White Cliffs section of the Missouri River in central Montana. The photos alone spoke volumes. White sandstone cliffs, carved long and tall from eons of erosion, towered over the parched Montanan prairie. The sky spread wide with sapphire and puffy white as shades of tan blended into an inhospitable landscape of russet-coloured hills and spiky vegetation. I was mesmerized.

The images and words from the magazine article stayed with me throughout the workday, drifting into daydreams that happily distracted me from the inane drudgery at hand. I dredged up fond memories of past river journeys and thought long about the Murray and Mississippi rivers, two mighty waterways I had travelled the complete length of. Those had been arduous adventures, wrought with rollercoaster emotions and unforeseen challenges. But both journeys had also immersed me deep in a natural world of beauty, wonder, and personal growth, three factors sadly absent from my work-a-day world.

Even though I knew virtually nothing about the Missouri, other than it flowed through the badlands of Montana and emptied into the Mississippi north of St. Louis, I was quickly becoming obsessed with it. I wondered if it was the longest river in North America. Or was yet another "M" river (the McKenzie in northern Canada) the longest? River trivia tumbled into my head as I struggled to name the longest river on each continent. The Nile, the Amazon, the Murray in Australia; those I knew. The other four? No clue. (I could see that some after-work Google research was in order.) But if in fact the Missouri River *was* the longest in North America, and if I was to paddle it from end to end, I would be able to claim I had kayaked the longest river on two continents from source to mouth. *Hmmmm,* I thought. *That would be pretty cool.* And then, without warning, the words of a thick-accented Australian bloke I'd met years prior came flooding back. When he learned I was attempting to paddle the Murray from source to sea, he asked, without hesitation, "So, mate, where do ya go from here? Are you gonna paddle the longest river on each continent?" I laughed and promptly answered with an exaggerated headshake, "Ha! Not a chance!" The idea of doing such a thing was ludicrous. *Honestly,* I said to myself, *who would be foolish enough to undertake something like that?*

For years, I had been trying to come up with the idea of doing a multi-staged, self-propelled expedition, one that would allow me to take my adventuring to the next level—a level at which I could actually earn a living from it, particularly through public speaking, multi-media presentations, and book sales. I was seeking a new career direction, a direction that would better reflect my passions and dreams as they related to self-propelled exploration. Missing was the precious seed that would allow this desired direction to flourish. My British adventurer friend, Dave Cornthwaite, had his Expedition1000 project, and that was proving to be successful for him. Sebastian Terry, an Australian friend of Dave's, had his 100 Things project, an ongoing bucket list that had become more of a lifestyle than a quest. He too was carving out a living.

Maybe I should paddle the longest river on each continent, I said nonchalantly to myself as I directed the rumbling lawnmower along an arrow-straight fence line. *I've already paddled* one. I mulled that thought over for a few short moments and then decided to up the ante. *Why not just paddle the longest river system on each continent from source to sea?*

"Wait!" I shrieked over the roar of the mower. "That's it! That's the key I've been looking for!"

The whole idea came to me in a flash. It was one of those A-HA! moments that grabs you and will not let go, a realization that your consciousness has just lurched forward and planted you firmly in the unwritten unknown. Within a millisecond, I knew there would be no turning back. It took only a millisecond more to convince the doubtful and fearful part of myself that a new direction had indeed been wrought, a defined direction that had eluded me for almost a decade, a direction defined not only by passionate adventure-seeking, but also a desire to establish a career that both reflected my self-propelled passions and my intense longing to be free from two-and-a-half decades of unrewarding work. I knew I had worthy gifts to contribute to the world, gifts not extended through the grip of a rumbling lawnmower or the slivered shaft of a shovel, but gifts that contribute to the betterment of the world, gifts that hopefully inspire others to better themselves, to push past their imagined boundaries, to cultivate the courage to take risks, to seek out happiness, purity, and truth. This *is my career direction,* I said to myself, *to say and do the things that best enhance my life and the lives of those around me at any given moment.* By committing to such a decision, I had discovered a missing piece of my life puzzle and the discovery made me giddy.

And then, more questions arose in my mind.

Has it been done before? Has someone actually taken the initiative to descend the longest river system on each continent?

At the time, I did not know. I'd recently read (albeit briefly) about some bloke undertaking a similar project. Strangely (maybe because he was a friend of Dave Cornthwaite), his name came quickly to me: Mark Kalch. I resolved to find out more about Mark's project when I got home from work.

A quick Google search revealed that Mark Kalch, an intrepid explorer in his own right, also possessed a grand ambition to paddle the longest river system on each continent from source to sea. He called his project, "7 Rivers, 7 Continents." His website stated he'd already paddled the Amazon (in 2008) and was readying himself for a source to sea descent of the Missouri–Mississippi river system beginning on May 1, 2011, which meant his expedition was already well underway.

I admit to feeling both dismayed and relieved at this discovery; dismayed because I had briefly pondered the idea of Mark and me perhaps adventuring together down the Missouri, but relieved that his intended solo descent would stay that way, and mine, whenever its fruition would come, would likely also be a solo endeavour.

Upon delving further into Mark's website, I discovered that I shared with him similar career ambitions, at least as to how they related to pursuing a decade-length, multi-stage expedition. His career as a competitive athlete, explorer, and motivational speaker seemed successful and well-established.

I held back from contacting Mark straight away, chalking up the fear I felt to a lack of proper preparation and a true lapse of spontaneity. I was worried he'd think I was perhaps stealing his idea of descending the great river systems of the world from source to sea. Of course, I had no such intention. I was not seeking out competition or an appropriation of his ideas. Instead, I believe I was seeking mere companionship; a planning partner or avid accomplice, one with whom I could share ideas and information, and one to whom I could offer support and encouragement while he pursued his goal. I decided that contact with Mark would happen when it happened and I went about my own expedition planning and research.

Weeks later, on May 31, Mark revealed via a blog post on his website that his 2011 expedition plans had been halted. He had, in fact, never reached the Missouri River. Nor had he even left his European home. His right shoulder—injured earlier in a whitewater kayaking mishap—now desperately needed surgery, the results of which would postpone the start of his Missouri–Mississippi descent to May 2012.

Maybe there's a possibility of working together after all, I thought as I re-read his post and grimaced at the bloody surgery photo. *Things* do *happen for a reason, be they unfortunate or otherwise.*

And so, as ridiculous as it sounds, I began working up the courage to email Mark and inform him of my expedition plans. I say "ridiculous" because it seems absurd to me that I should be intimidated by such a person as Mark Kalch. (I think he would comply with that thought.) Maybe I was intimidated by his ample list of expedition accomplishments and his obvious career successes. I'm not sure. What I do know is that shyness, low self-esteem, and tricks of the mind are strange things indeed. Fear can grip us tight at times when we need it not to. Surely, we are all better off without such fears. Risks, whether big or small, are always better overturned, exposed, and undertaken.

It took a full month to work up the courage to contact Mark Kalch via email and inform him of my expedition plans. Thankfully, but perhaps not surprisingly, his prompt reply was well-peppered with friendly tones of respect and encouragement. A formidable bridge had been crossed and the view from the opposite bank appeared to be full of grace and good fortune.

Back on the river research front, the task of choosing which of the seven longest river systems I would descend first was occupying my mind. Like most pursuits, the decision was based on the availability of money. I didn't have the funds to finance an overseas expedition, so it was pretty much a shoe-in that I would begin with the closest river system, the Missouri–Mississippi. I set a launch date (June 2012, a year hence) and excitedly began to grasp the enormity of the undertaking.

~ ~ ~

The following is a blog post I wrote in August 2014. I was living in Chatham, Ontario. I was unhappy. I needed challenge of a different kind.

> I've spent the majority of the past year rooted in front of a computer screen. Occasionally, I would venture outside, go on a short adventure or two, and share some words and photos of those little journeys on Facebook. When I wasn't sleeping, walking, or riding a bicycle, I was seated in front of a computer, working on the manuscript for my first book, *Part-Time Superheroes, Full-Time Friends.*

Seasons went by. I noticed them pass, sorrowfully. I longed for summer to arrive, and when it did I spent most of it inside, working. Summer receded. Leaves fell. Snow came. I continued working and longed for summer to arrive, again.

My book project progressed at a painfully slow pace. Graphic design projects crawled along, always at the designer's pace, never at mine. In their defence, however, I complicated the process by adding new ideas to the projects—enlarging them far beyond what our initial conversations and action plans had been. Mock-ups were sent via email. They were reviewed and critiqued. Replies and further instructions were then sent back and the whole process went through another cycle. Over and over. Dozens of times repeated. Frustration loomed. Emotions fumed. Words were heated. Knee-jerk reactions deleted. Anger festered. Knuckles whitened. In abbreviated computer-speak, there was much SMH and little LOL. I took solace in the fact that things were indeed progressing. That line of thinking made the rage somewhat palatable. But every time I stuffed the anger, it would arise elsewhere.

The anger bled into other areas of my life, most noticeably social interactions. I became withdrawn, isolated, scared of judgement. I would walk at night so I wouldn't have to interact with others. The local police took notice of my nightly actions and I was frequently followed and occasionally questioned. Perhaps the innocent findings of one officer were never passed on to the others because none of them seemed to ascertain that I was simply walking to relieve stress. The interactions were never ugly, but I resented their interest in what I deemed a simple activity. If *they* were out for a nightly walk, I would have no interest in *their* activity. I hoped they would return the favour. They rarely did.

Over time, the resentment became very real. Hatred fogged my nightly walks. I focussed hard on positive things and affirmed that my life in Chatham was not as bad as I thought. Truth be told: life *was* bad—and it was getting worse.

My relationship with my father turned sour. (No surprise there. That pattern has been happening since I was a child.) Words were minced and voices raised. Pride on both sides was bruised. Expectations weren't met, which led to inevitable disappointments. Ideas and morals don't always span generations. It happens in most families. Acceptance is the key to moving on. Although, in this case, acceptance didn't enter the frame for either party.

My fragile self-esteem took a nosedive. Depression took firm hold of me. I relented and submerged myself fully into it. I piled on work and junk food—comfort blankets that gave me an illusion of being in control. It was all about *control*.

My health plummeted. The muscles and self-worth I'd amassed from paddling the longest river system on the continent withered. I gained weight. I noticed more pigment spots appearing on my face, arms, and back. Hair grew out of my body where none had grown before. On my head, it was thinning noticeably. I had to shave my face more often. I wondered, *What is happening to me?* Somehow, I had entered yet another physical maturation process and I wasn't pleased with the change. I was overly critical of my body image, always in a negative way. (This has been a lifelong issue.) I began to question my goals and passions. *Is this the right path to take? Should I chuck this idea of adventuring and writing and speaking and get a* real *job?*

I was fast approaching a tipping point. I knew it was coming. I'd stood on that precipice before in a different place, in a different time. Back then, I'd taken the leap, and later, reaped the rewards. But this time, I was too scared. I backed away from the precipice and slinked back to the familiar depression. I was depressing myself, holding myself down, holding myself back from enjoying life.

In the past, I've blamed the city of Chatham for my problems, especially if my problems were occurring while I was there. This time, I began blaming the *people* of Chatham for my problems. The ones who ridiculed me as I walked down the street (presumably for the way I looked—dreadlocks can bring out the ire in the ignorant). It sucks being pointed at and laughed at—*directly* laughed at. It's like daily bullying. That stuff didn't end in elementary school. I'm still being bullied and it sucks. I deflect a lot of it. I bury a lot of it. I fume about it. I hurl insults back occasionally. Sometimes I talk rationally to the ignorant few (both male *and* female) and explain how their actions and words are hurtful. Rarely does it have a positive effect. In the end, I move on. I leave the toxicity behind and seek understanding in other locations.

Familiarity breeds contempt, and I am *highly* contemptuous. I hold grievances against a great many people in my life, too many actually. I know it's unhealthy and a huge weight to bear every day, but I insist on carrying the burden. It won't break me—I won't let it—but it consumes a lot of my time and energy.

I was thinking about that last line when I had my final spat with my father in early July 2014. My dependence on him (financially and emotionally) had bottomed out. My self-esteem had taken too many hits from his poisoned words. I was sick of my lack of responsibility. I was sick of submerging myself in the hole I'd unwillingly (or willingly) dug for myself. The tipping point had finally arrived. I didn't want to leave Chatham with hate in my heart, but that's what it had come to. If I stayed, the situation was bound to get worse. I've experienced *worse* in various forms in the past. It wasn't fun and I had no plans to go to that dark place again.

For months, Vancouver had been calling. Memories of riding my bicycle through city streets on warm nights flooded into my head. (I've become too car-dependent. Simply put: I need to ride.) I need to feel healthy and happy again. I owe that to everyone around me, and to myself. I need to look at my body and be content with how it looks today. I need to smile (and mean it). I need people around me who accept me as I am. (I immersed myself in the Vancouver punk scene many years ago simply for that reason—they accepted me, and vice versa.) But I also need not be scared of those people who are different from me. I don't want to create a safety bubble around myself composed of people just like me. I need diversity. I don't need bullies or hecklers. I need people with patience, understanding, and less fear. They don't need to know the meaning of life, they just need to be honest. And they need to smile. I like people who smile. I like strangers who smile. I like people who aren't afraid to smile. And yes, Chatham has many people who smile. There are many people in Chatham who accept me for who I am. I appreciate that. I need to work on accepting them. That is my work away from the computer.

On many levels, Chatham is a good place to live. But I cannot be there anymore. I need challenge of a different kind. I need new stimulation. I need the non-judgemental nature of nature. I need trees and rocks and lakes and rivers and mountains and oceans. I need mosquito bites and gnat bites and annoying no-see-ums. I need a sunburn. I need to paddle in clear water. I need to camp beside a lake. I need to smell a species of flower I've never smelt before. I need to meet strangers. I need to smile. I need to live.

And that is what I've set out to do. I am driving west across this beautiful country. I am seeing my homeland with new eyes. I must say, it is astoundingly awesome! I am smiling at strangers. I am breathing fresh air. I am warming my face with the sunrise. I am bedding down with the sunset. I am gazing long at great lakes and listening hard to people's stories. I am connecting with others. And I am weeping in joy for doing so. I am shedding the burden of anger, hate, and grievance. I am becoming whole again. I am becoming *me* again.

In the coming weeks, you'll see photos and read stories from this new journey. You'll see transformation. You will no doubt relate to my journey, for you, too, have taken such journeys in your life, and will undoubtedly do so again. In the past, my expeditions and road trips have been more about the destination than the journey. This one is different. This one is all about the journey. I am learning that lesson daily and I am grateful for it.

(Rest assured that I am not giving up my passion of adventuring and sharing insights from those adventures with others through speaking and writing. If anything, this experience is galvanizing those passions. I am now more committed to them than ever. It is my life work and I will press onward regardless of the struggles.)

~ ~ ~

I'm not able to tell you when the suicidal thoughts began, but I do know they were connected to my job. I hated my fucking job.

> *I hated that I stayed so long*
> *and pricked a prong upon the crown*
> *and came to drain the blood within*
> *in hopes that I might somehow win*
> *the approval of others*
> *those miserable blood brothers*
> *who raced through days*
> *of toil and trivial security*
> *propped up and worshipping*
> *a dank, rotted purity*
> *a male pose calamity*
> *a macho propensity*
> *a benign ego density*
> *an opt-out intensity.*

When came the poison, the pills, and the noose,
so came the pain, the pleasure, the truce.
So came the exit, the ending, the freedom.
So passed a life that would no longer need him.

I'll kill not those
who cause me pain,
but leave them with
a death profane.

It's true. Every great purge begins with profanity.

Fuck...

The following is a blog post I wrote in May 2015.

> This is Part 1 of *Lead with Your Heart*, a week-long series about letting go and moving forward. If you like what you read, please consider sharing this post with others. Your actions might save a life, or at least initiate a decision to pursue a new direction. We can all use a little help as we navigate life's unpredictable path. Honesty and openness go a long way in providing anonymous answers to seekers of truth, and we are all seekers of truth.

~ ~ ~

Everyone dreams of quitting a job they hate. But not everyone returns to a job they hate once they quit. Sometimes, it pays to stay away. Unfortunately, I learned that lesson the hard way.

Vancouver, British Columbia, January 2002

"You're looking for a job, right?" asked Andreas.

"Well, I have a job," I answered, "but I need another one."

"Why do you need two jobs?" he asked.

"I don't need two jobs," I said. "I just need to quit the one I have."

"Why do you wanna quit your job?"

"Because I hate it."

"I see," said Andreas. "That's a good reason."

There was a slight pause before Andreas spoke again.

"A percussionist friend of mine works for a landscape maintenance company. He told me they're looking to hire another person. I have the owner's number. You want it?"

"Sure," I replied.

"My friend says they pay a fair wage and the work is seasonal, nine months a year," said Andreas. "My friend goes on U.I. for the winter months. It works out good for him."

I took the number and got the job. The hiring process was simple. No resume. No application form. Just an informal meeting over coffee. By the time our cups were empty, the job was mine.

Four years later, I quit.

During those four years, I was absolutely miserable every day. Sure, the pay was good (I funded two bicycling expeditions with the earnings), but the laborious work was bitterly unrewarding. I resented my boss and everyone I worked with. I felt overused and underappreciated. There was no opportunity for creativity. Mental challenges were limited to one sizeable quandary: whether to quit on any given day or not. Five days a week, I struggled through a quagmire of mindless grunt-work and emotional desperation. "If this is all the future holds for me," I posited, "then I'd rather be dead." And dead I became—lost in a dark sea of suicidal ideation and hopelessness. I drifted rudderless in that sea for four years, and every two weeks, I collected a paycheque. And then, I quit.

Somehow, I made it through without killing myself. Somehow, I summoned the courage to move on. And somehow, things got worse.

Utterly despondent, but sporting a false grin, I stumbled from job to job—ten in one year. I lived alone. Ate my meals alone. Endured my pain alone. Faced the future alone. And then, I discovered kayaking.

I looked into possibly taking a wilderness leadership course at a local college. I remembered that my old friend, Andreas, had taken the same course after quitting his bakery job. I wanted to connect with him and pick his brain. Unfortunately, I'd lost contact with him. But I knew someone who might have his phone number—*my old boss*. Trouble was, my old boss was pretty much the last person in the world I wanted to talk to. I hadn't spoken to him since we parted ways, almost two years prior. Surely, the sound of his voice would trigger feelings of past anger and erase any positive progression I'd made since quitting my landscaping job. Strangely (or perhaps not strangely), my conversation with him didn't produce a desire to slit his throat. Nor did it net any contact info for Andreas.

"All I know," said my old boss during our phone conversation, "is that he moved to Vancouver Island and became a kayaking instructor. I haven't seen him in years."

And that's when I should've politely thanked him for his time and hung up. But I didn't.

"So, what's new with you?" I asked, nervously dragging out the small talk.

"Oh, you know," he said, "same old, same old."

And that should've been the cue to end the conversation. But it wasn't.

"How about you?" he asked. "Are you working?"

"Yes," I answered, hesitantly, almost knowing what was coming next. "I work in a bottling factory in Burnaby."

"Do you like it?" he asked.

"No," I said, grimacing. "Not really."

"I see," he said, suddenly sounding interested. "One of my guys quit at the end of last season and I haven't hired anyone yet. Might you be interested in coming back to work here?"

And that was when I *definitely* should've hung up the phone. But I didn't.

"Maybe…" I said, *very* hesitantly this time.

"How much were you making per hour when you worked here?" he asked.

I told him.

He offered to increase the amount and stated a number.

"Is that a figure you might be interested in?" he asked.

He was a shrewd fucker, that's for sure. His offer was 40% more than what I was currently making at the bottling factory.

"Whaddya say?" he prodded. "Are ya interested?"

Suddenly, my hesitancy was gone, replaced entirely with images of dollar signs.

"Sounds good," I said. "When do I start?"

"March 1st," said my old/*new* boss. I could almost see him smiling in his greedy, manipulative way, the way he did when he overcharged customers or guilt-lessly fucked over his employees. "See you *then*."

And just like that, I was back to raking leaves and cutting grass five days a week; back to what was familiar, back to what was routine, back to the same mistake.

My second tour of duty wasn't as intense as the first. I smartly distanced myself from the petty personal politics that always hinder employee relations. I used the increased income to pay off debts and undertake a four-month kayaking expedition in Australia in 2009–2010. I dropped down to part-time hours when stress levels became difficult to manage, and muscled through the wet autumn grind to re-pad my wallet for the off-season downtime.

But even with the job's generous scheduling flexibility, I could not keep depression at bay. Suicidal thoughts crept in again, slowly edging out smiles and social interaction. Paranoia and silent resentment ruled the roost. Isolation became the favoured escapism. Stagnation became the norm. Instinctively, I knew something had to give.

At the end of four years, I quit—for the second time. This time, however, I had a plan that would take me light years away from landscaping. Routine had kept me rooted, but the thirst for adventure would set me free.

I put my belongings in a storage locker and set off on a quest to paddle the longest river system on each continent from source to sea. It would be an ongoing project, likely taking 15–20 years to complete. I called it the Magnificent Seven Expedition—its name a nod to the number of rivers and continents I'd visit in order to complete the challenge. The name was also an homage to The Clash, an English rock band. The lyrics to their song, *The Magnificent Seven*, contained both a poetically rousing call to arms, and, in my case, an apt encouragement: "Wave bye-bye to the boss, it's our profit, it's his loss."

And profit I did.

I went on to become the first North American (and second person ever) to kayak the Missouri–Mississippi river system from source to sea, a total distance of 3800 miles. Along the way, I made dozens of new friends, many of whom helped make the adventure a grand success.

Following the river trip, I based myself in my hometown of Chatham, Ontario and laid the groundwork for a book manuscript chronicling the kayaking expedition. At the same time, I put the finishing touches on my first book, *Part-Time Superheroes, Full-Time Friends*. The creativity was flowing fast and unhindered. My landscape maintenance job, and all the negativity it entailed, seemed distant and irrelevant now. I had created an exciting, new career—one filled with passion and purpose. I was moving forward. I was leading with my heart.

And then, in August 2014, something shifted in my mind. Past resentments resurfaced. A stubborn inability to forgive others dominated my inner thoughts and outward actions. Focus waned. Self-confidence plummeted. My old acquaintances, *Paranoia* and *Isolation*, returned. They set up shop and refused to leave, no matter my efforts to evict them. The same old despondency took hold. The suicidal thoughts came back with a vengeance. The cruel, calloused hand of *Fear* gripped me hard and shook me senseless. My only recourse was to escape.

I sent an email to my old boss in Vancouver and requested his help.

"I'm moving back to Vancouver at summer's end and I need to make sure I have work lined up before heading west. Do you need an extra hand this autumn?"

His reply was swift.

"Yes. I'll have work for you," he wrote. "Call me when you get here."

And just like that, I was back to raking leaves and cutting grass five days a week; back to what was familiar, back to what was routine, back to the same mistake.

By the afternoon of the first day, with a gas-powered hedge trimmer belching fumes in my face, the suicidal ideation returned. It flooded over me, smothering me. I had 11 weeks to go before the end of the season. *This is gonna suck,* I said to myself. *Every awful step of it is gonna suck.* And it did.

For 40 hours a week, I laboured through the drawn-out autumn routine of cutting grass and raking leaves while the cold rain poured down. And for 60 hours of those same weeks, I systematically worked my way through a storage locker crammed with useless articles from an irrelevant past and set upon the task of purging them from my life.

I created five piles of stuff: one to sell, one to donate to charity, one to leave on the sidewalks of Commercial Drive (my old neighbourhood in East Vancouver), one to be boxed and shipped to Ontario, and one destined for an alley of my choosing. Nothing went in the trash. It was all somehow recycled.

I earned $575.00 by selling the worthy bits on Craigslist, but everything else was given away. When I was finished, I'd eliminated 85% of my worldly possessions and had greatly lessened the weight on my shoulders. And then came the final and most meaningful purge: my landscape maintenance job.

True to my word, I stuck out the full 11 weeks. Almost surprisingly, the experience was worse than I'd imagined it would be. The familiar, low-level horror of suicidal ideation was ever-present. With its re-emergence, I realized for the first time that, prior to this job, I'd never entertained the thought of killing myself. How is it I was spared those desperate thoughts for the first 35 years of my life? Had self-pity somehow replaced my life's purpose when I made the decision to pick up a rake and clean up someone's yard? Had I drifted so far from my life's passion that death seemed a more fitting, self-imposed sentencing than following my heart's intent? How could I regain traction and move onward unhindered, free from the weighty blanket of worry, second guesses, and mindless, unrewarding toil? The answer was profoundly simple: just fuckin' do it. Now. *Right* now.

I felt the ugly gears of negativity grind to a halt.

MOVE! I shouted to myself, forcefully jarring myself from a self-imposed stupor. *Choose action! Enact change! Sure, risk and fear are ever-present. But so are optimism and opportunity! The choice to move forward needs to be made NOW! The road to simplicity begins right now! Heed the unheeded! Purge the unneeded! Build the biggest bonfire and don't wait around to watch it burn! MOVE! FORWARD! NOW!*

I cordially shook hands with my boss on the final day of work. We wished each other success, and then parted ways. I packed my tools, work clothes, rain gear, boots, and a heap of bitterness into a large duffle bag. I drove to a grungy alley in an industrial section of East Vancouver and placed the bag beside a dumpster. I removed the lens cap on my camera, pressed the shutter button with a determined index finger, and walked away.

It was a scene I had fantasized about many times while toiling away in someone's yard in some lonely corner of a gated community in some nondescript suburb of Vancouver. I held fast to that fantasy, knowing one day I'd act it out, knowing one day I'd possess the courage to follow through, to move on, to lead with my heart.

"I care not who finds the bag," I said aloud as I turned the ignition of my Ford Focus and set the car in motion. "I care not what becomes of its contents. I care only that the contents and their negative meanings possess me no longer. I am no longer chained to that identity. I am free to become me—the me who walks boldly into the future brimming with brilliant ideas and creative intent. I choose change. I choose growth. I choose life. I choose *me*."

~ ~ ~

For as long as I can remember, I have struggled with self-doubt. Every day I cringe in fear at the thought of being judged by others. That fear is wholly debilitating. It breeds anxiety, paranoia, anger, sadness, self-hate and, finally, inevitably, depression. It ebbs and flows, but it never dissipates. It is cyclical. It always returns, like an unwanted and unwelcomed adversary that holds a mirror in one giant hand and reaches out with the other, tightly gripping my head and holding me still against my struggle, forcing me to view the pain etched upon my face from years of frowning.

This fear is simple, invisible, encompassing. It is unwavering, unforgiving, unmatched. This same fear is also an illusion, a toxic product of *my* mind alone. No one implanted it in my head. It was introduced to me through the process of pure observation, the familial osmosis of youth.

My father is a Navy veteran—disciplined, hardened, stubborn, and stoic. He is also an admirably responsible man—utterly devoted to his family, his marriage, and his work. He is also completely devoid of empathy. I suppose he is like many men who find it difficult to express their emotions, mostly because doing so is seen by society as a weakness. He once told me that he only cried twice in his life—when his mother died, and when his wife, my mother, threatened to divorce him. I've rarely seen him sad or angry, but I *have* seen him fearful many times. I've seen him spiteful and verbally abusive. His hurtful words mask a fear unacknowledged.

If men, strong men like my father, could get past their fear of being judged by others for simply being *honest*, they could be leaders, not slaves to their unfounded fears. By allowing themselves to be vulnerable, their courage would shine. There is so much to gain by taking an honest risk, and every man is completely capable of doing so.

I'm positive my father has a vision in his mind of what he would like me to be, but he's never shared it with me. Nor have I asked him to share it, perhaps because I'm afraid it will contradict everything that my life currently is, which in turn, would most likely lead to a showdown of wills with him—something neither of us are comfortable engaging in, mostly because we don't want to hurt each other. We would rather be silent and safe in our respective comfort zones. I don't ask and he doesn't tell.

Over the years, I have created a vision in my mind of what I think *his* vision of me looks like. My vision consists of cobbled together remnants of verbal slights directed my way from childhood onward, with the negative abuses far outweighing the positive praises. I've allowed his insults to manifest and fester. I've allowed them to influence, foster, and feed the crippling self-doubts that stream through my mind daily. I secretly hate myself for doing so. I also realize it is completely unfair to blame my father for my own undoing. I torment myself with my own imagined fears. This is not only unfair to myself, it is unfair to everyone around me.

Still, there is an undying need to prove myself to my father—to gain his acceptance, praise, and recognition. That need is not as prevalent as it once was, but it still gnaws at me annoyingly like a persistent phantom hound—always felt, but never seen.

I'm not able to tell you when my father began hearing voices in his head, but I do know the voices are somehow connected to me. I may not hear them, but I hear all about them.

> *Each voice is conceived, concocted, created from truth—*
> *distorted, demanding, mean, cold, uncouth.*
> *They exploit and direct and mock and reproach.*
> *They critique and accuse and further encroach*
> *on the last shreds of sanity that surely remain*
> *entrenched in a mind flooded full with disdain.*
>
> *Gone are the days of judgement and reason,*
> *replaced by a case of progressive brain treason.*
> *Call it dementia or Alzheimer's Disease—*
> *a future laced deadly with no guarantees*
> *of escaping a world of paranoia and fear,*
> *confused and corrupted by every word that you hear.*

He'd been on this earth for 82 years when the voices started. At least that's when he began to tell me about the people who visit him daily. They lurk out of sight—just beyond the living room window frame, just beyond the backyard shed. They scurry away before he flings open the curtains. They're quick. They know he's coming. They never tell him their names, but they always call him Bob. They yell his name incessantly from the neighbouring yards. All through the night and all through the day they mock him. "They want my money," he says. "All of it!" They tell him that he hired them to watch over his property like security guards, and now they've come to collect their fee. "But I never hired them!" he tells me repeatedly. "I don't owe them a cent!" Earning, saving, and retaining money has always been important to my father.

And then there's the little girl who sings only to him. "She's about eight-years-old and has a beautiful voice," he says. "When the men take a break from yelling their demands, she starts singing." She knows only two songs—*Amazing Grace* and an untitled piece apparently penned by her. She sings only in the daytime.

My father began to share his auditory hallucinations with me in early 2015. At that time, I was putting the finishing touches on my first book. I was busy as fuck and never had time to fully develop an interest in what he was mentally enduring. At the time, his delusionary behaviour was leaking into my life on a daily basis. He was convinced that the men whose voices he heard were extorting money from me. He also felt they were trying to get to *his* money by going through me. He believed his retirement savings—which, upon his death, will go to his children—were at great risk of being pilfered by these imaginary conspirators. He was suspicious of my behaviour, but never risked an accusation. He was angry, confused, scared. His behaviour was erratic, confrontational, bizarre. The voices taunted him and he aggressively retorted, yelling at them at all hours of the day and night, playing into a dangerous mind game that he alone created.

This would be a good time to mention that I travel a lot. It's not uncommon for me to spend four or five months on the road promoting my books. I organize my own book tours and visit with paddling friends all over the United States. When I'm not on the road, I usually stay with my father at his house in Chatham, Ontario. Ten years ago, he sold the family home in town and downsized to a two-bedroom trailer in a retirement mobile home park on the outskirts of Chatham. The one-level trailer, my father believed, would allow for better mobility for his ailing wife—my mother—who suffered from a degenerative muscle disorder. In the later stages of her life, until she died in 2010 at the age of 73, my father was her primary caregiver. When I stay at my father's house, I sleep and work in the pink-walled bedroom my mother occupied. Gone are the wheelchair and elevated hospital bed. Gone are her clothes and most of her keepsakes. Gone is her silent despair at having to endure a progressive and incurable illness. Gone is the shelfful of prescription medications that she overdosed on intentionally. Gone is the debilitating depression that haunted her through other suicide attempts years prior, resulting in a brief but horrible hospitalization. Gone are the self-directed negative effects that unfortunately stem from society's stigmatization of mental illness—shame, blame, embarrassment, confusion, hopelessness. She lived in secret pain and sour desperation. She endured a life she didn't want, a life she didn't ask for. Bitterness, regret, anger, and fear muddied her final years. Perhaps no one knows that better than my father. Perhaps he took all that into account when he moved the shelf of pills to an upper cupboard, out of my mother's reach, thus removing her only exit plan, her only escape from herself.

Suicidal ideation and depression have a prominent history in my immediate and extended families. I am the youngest of three children, the only male. My sister closest in age to me has attempted suicide several times. My oldest sister planned her own death, but abandoned the idea once the plan was enacted. My nephew attempted suicide during his teenage years. Several friends of mine have committed suicide. A former girlfriend attempted suicide many times during our relationship. Her step-father committed suicide. The first funeral I ever attended was for a teenage friend who had taken her own life.

It seems as though suicide and suicidal ideation have always been lurking in the shadows, ready to pounce when least expected. Reflecting on it now, I guess it was only a matter of time until my burdens became too weighty, until the unending stress overwhelmed me, until I enacted a suicide plan of my own—a foolproof plan no one could overturn.

Living in a trailer with an ailing parent is very difficult. As much as I dislike using this label, my father is a *shut-in*. At 83, his hearing and eyesight have faded. He relinquished his driver's licence and sold his vehicle. Pains in his back, hips, and legs restrict his mobility. He's never had close friends and makes no effort to surround himself with others. He spends hours playing solitaire on his computer. He prefers solitude, but enjoys himself when people visit his home. Facebook provides a social outlet. Sometimes he'll share with me an old story from his Navy days. Most times I'll listen, even though I've heard each story a dozen times.

Living in a seniors' trailer park is uninspiring. I do not involve myself in *their* community. I'm merely a guest, and I'm embarrassed to live there. When people ask where I live, I purposefully fail to mention that I reside in a trailer park. I'm afraid they'll look down on me and associate me with the supposedly downtrodden slice of society that typically inhabits a trailer park. I'm embarrassed that I don't have my own place. I'm embarrassed that I live in my father's home. Years ago, I owned enough possessions to furnish a one-bedroom apartment. I worked hard at a job I hated in order to purchase those things. They weren't treasures, but each one had a function. And now, those things are gone. They disappeared through a series of intentional purges. They had no purpose in this new life of transience. In some ways, I mourn the loss. Also gone is privacy. Living with an ailing parent offers little in the way of privacy. Thin walls divide me from my father. Private conversations involving others are impossible. I never invite people over. If I meet with people locally, which is a rarity, we meet at a café or restaurant. I crave solitude. I crave my own space. I am grateful that my father has opened his home to me, but, due to the lack of privacy, living in my car sometimes seems a better option.

I occasionally ask my father for money with no intention of repaying it. I'm not sure why I feel entitled to his money. He never says no, but I know he regrets giving it to me. I know my asking for money contributes to the voices and scenarios he creates in his mind. I contribute to his illness and I feel guilty for doing so. It pains me to admit it, but I'm using him and I can't stop. Sadly, this pattern has played out for decades. I choose to remain dependent on him in order to maintain my lifestyle. By doing so, I remain trapped in my dependence.

Finances and suicide are closely linked in my head. The less money I have, the less secure I feel. The less secure I feel, the more hopeless I feel. The more hopeless I feel, the less purpose I have in life. With little purpose to life, death seems like the next logical step. At that point, the main question I often ask is, "What's the point in living?" Lack of money often contributes to a feeling of being trapped—trapped by my own decisions, trapped by my lack of motivation, trapped by my fears. Lack of money = despair. I use my father's money to leverage myself out of despair, at least temporarily. When the money dries up, I'm back asking for more.

For two years now, book sales have been my only means of earned income. Sales are meagre and not self-sustaining. I try my best to alleviate the need to approach my father for money. I refuse to get a *job*. I'd rather invest that time in growing my business. I started my publishing company (Crow Books) as a way to gain independence. So far, it's only partially succeeded. I feel if I was to transition to a job in order to generate income, it would be a regression. It would become a dependence of another kind. And because my experience with jobs has been nightmarishly bad at the best of times, that scenario would only lead to more suicidal ideation. I seriously hate this conundrum I've created and I have no idea how to solve it. The only recourse is to continue to write. Hopefully, the writing will reveal a path that's clear.

In the summer of 2015, I spent three months in the U.S. promoting my first book. My time on the road was filled with adventure and good memories. As the road trip wound down and the glum prospect of returning to my father's house in Chatham became an unavoidable reality, my festive mood tanked big-time and suicidal ideation began to creep into my thoughts. I resented myself for the decision to return to Chatham. *Surely there must be other options,* I desperately thought. I was not looking forward to the inevitable arguments with my conservative father. He has never supported my life decisions. They have always been too radical for him to accept. He bottles his displeasure and unleashes it in times of anger. Verbal confrontations erupted from time to time, with both of us silently fearful of a physical clash. Sooner or later, I reckoned, someone was going to get hurt and I didn't plan on it being me. I resented my father's presence in my life. He was supposed to die years ago. He'd become a burden to me. In fact, he'd been a burden my whole life. I never liked him and it's unlikely that I ever will. If he died, I wouldn't miss him. His permanent absence would be a welcomed relief, just as it had been with my mother.

In September 2015, I connected with my adventurer friend, Dave Cornthwaite, in Memphis, Tennessee. He and Richard Day, a close friend and native Memphian, listened attentively as I shared my suicide-related fears with them. Each offered practical and empathic advice. Both suggested that I relocate, that I not return to Chatham, especially not to my father's home.

The following month, while en route to Ontario via Minnesota, I received a Facebook message from Dave. His message came as a surprise. It offered hope at a time when hope was most needed. It also offered something more tangible than hope. It offered *recognition.*

> Hey buddy. Hope Minnesota is treating you well. Reckon you'll be on the water next year? I'm helping Aquapac put together a shortlist for their outdoor champion 2016. Free gear plus £1000—interested?

Basically, the message asked if I was interested in a sponsorship deal with Aquapac, a British manufacturer of waterproof cases and bags. The company's annual "Outdoor Champion" acts as a brand ambassador of sorts, loosely promoting Aquapac and its products via the adventurer's outdoor pursuits during the course of a calendar year. Dave held the title in 2011, the year he stand-up paddleboarded the length of the Mississippi River. Other water-based adventurous folk (Roz Savage, Sarah Outen, Emily Penn), all friends of Dave's, held the title at different times. To be considered for a title previously held by a handful of inspiring adventurers helped me feel good about myself. After years of struggling to score sponsorship deals, it seemed I was finally being recognized by the paddling/adventuring community for my accomplishments. I sent a quick email reply to Dave to let him know I was interested.

> Thanks for thinking of me for the Aquapac list. Am I interested? You betcha. Now that the first book is complete, I'll be spending a lot more time on the water in 2016. Planning three expeditions, starting in March: Buffalo River source to sea (Buffalo to White to MS to Gulf)—approx. four weeks. It's a National River, similar to a National Park. It's incredibly beautiful. Then paddle the MS from source to sea for less than $2016, then kick off a summit to source to sea journey of the Darling–Murray starting October (climb Mount Kosciuszko, bicycle from Kosciuszko to the source near Brisbane, then paddle to the ocean.) Oh, yeah…and release another book. Sign me up! Ready. Fire. Aim.

Those were lofty paddling plans for a guy who had no money and no chance of earning a substantial income from book sales. It was early October. The prospective start of that Buffalo River expedition was still five months away. I was camped on an island in the middle of the Mississippi River in lower Minnesota. I was roughing it, squatting on public land because personal funds were almost non-existent. I had no idea how I was going to finance *one* expedition in 2016, let alone *three*. Sheesh. I wondered if I had bitten off more than I could chew. *Maybe I shouldn't have blurted all those plans to Dave. Dammit!* I shouted to myself, feeling the foul familiarity of self-doubt gnawing at me. I knew the slope of self-despair was a steep and slippery one. Once initiated, the descent would be swift and ugly. Prompt positive action was needed if I was going to leave this island of isolation with a sound mind intact. I quickly ditched the detrimental self-pity and tapped into a vein of golden intention. *Fuck it!* I exclaimed. *I'm pushing on with this plan! All I need is some trust, some truth, and some faith. I got this!*

I arrived in Chatham in mid-October, still buoyant from a summer filled with crazy experiences. My well-earned joy, however, was short-lived. By the end of the first week, life was static again. The initial air of acceptance that wafted between my father and me evaporated. It was replaced with a dark cloud of resentment. I distanced myself from him in hopes of reducing my anger. One less trigger = far less stress. Sadly, it wasn't the only trigger.

An outstanding debt to a local dentist also needed to be dealt with. Regrettably, I sold my kayak and paddling accessories to pay off the bill. Weeks later, the tooth responsible for the transaction abscessed and needed to be extracted, costing me more money and sending me further into debt. Several other teeth were sending similar signals and the resultant stress and worry was making life in Chatham miserable. Depression, it seemed, wasn't right around the corner—it was already here.

And so began the construction of a grand, faultless scheme—a secret plan to take my own life. I would tell no one and keep the despair hidden best I could. The element of surprise spurred me on and I dwelled long on how friends and family would marvel at my ability to plan such an elaborate ending. In death, the recognition I craved would finally arrive. Unfortunately, I wouldn't be able to bask in its glow. I began to wish that suicide came with a second chance—an opportunity to die, but also a chance to live again. Of course, it doesn't work that way. Still, suicide gave me something to live for. It gave me purpose, something to focus my energy on. My mission was succinct, but not uncomplicated. The goal was to live long enough to die correctly.

Death by suicide is never simple. It is an effective product of earnest decision-making. Even if the act is spontaneous, it still comes loaded with intention. My intention was to go out on top, to do something so elaborately difficult that people were sure to sit up and take heed as I lured them toward my demise. My death would come as an abrupt retirement notice, like when a sports icon retires upon winning his or her final championship. Its intention would be to stun and surprise the masses. It would also be my middle finger salute to all those who had badgered, bullied, and doubted me along my path. It would also be directed at society's inability to accept those who exist on the fringes of its garden of righteousness—the derelicts, the misfits, the punks, the poets, and the paupers. I have been one and all of those. I, *we*, have been marginalized, scrutinized, criticized, and penalized. To anyone, alive or dead, who played even a small part in those processes, I raise a rigid digit and say, "Fuck you!" The act of suicide, therefore, became my parting shot, a way of saying, "I no longer want to participate in your sick game. I'm taking my ball and going home."

As the suicidal ideation progressed, my exit strategy became more elaborate. I isolated myself. I took inventory of my possessions and decided to recoup what money I could from the sale of camping gear. Doing so would eliminate the need to depend on my father for money. I was determined to support myself during this time of transition. Planning my death became a way of regaining my power. I viewed my reliance on my father as a weakness. I berated myself for having depended on him in the past. I viewed it as an embarrassment and I was careful not to share the dependence with others for fear they might see me as a manipulative cheat who was unable to pull his own weight. I hated that others might be too quick to judge without knowing the whole story—the familial history of suicidal ideation and depression, the unwillingness to play by society's rules, the steadfast perfectionism, the lack of true intimacy as a result of self-imposed isolation, the overwhelming craving for intimacy and companionship, my twisted all-or-nothing thinking that led me to believe that all future jobs would annoy me as much as the jobs of the past. Only *I* knew the complete story, and only *I* could share it. Only *I* could set the record straight. People were sure to judge me for having exploited money from my aging father, but at least I could defend myself through the words in my story. Even in death, those words and their inherent truth would set me free. The niggling need to defend myself from naysayers and caustic critics drove me to write this book. I needed to know, prior to death or perhaps after death, that the truth was accessible to those who seek it. There exists a need to defend myself before suspicion even enters the picture, to perhaps be ready for it before it occurs, as if the question of it occurring is more a matter of *when* than *if*. From this toxic need rises paranoia, the crippling culprit that keeps all this stuff unspoken. Silence is the great planner, the creeping corrosion that consumes all.

And so began the final purge. Superfluous possessions were quickly divested courtesy of Craigslist. Camping tents, paddling apparel, waterproof drybags, camera equipment. I packaged up my cigar box guitars (handmade by my friend Patrick Mallette in Blair, Nebraska) and shipped them to my good friend Richard Day in Memphis. So went a camera tripod and head to my friend John Henry, also of Memphis and one of the main characters in my second book, *River Angels*. In fact, all three of those men were river angels. They had all helped me at some point during my river journeys and I felt a need to give them something back. It was a way of saying thanks, as well as saying goodbye.

Money from the sale of possessions was spent on groceries, credit card payments, and relevant camping gear I planned to use en route to my death. I received confirmation from Aquapac that I'd been chosen as their 2016 "Outdoor Champion." Unbeknownst to them, the news helped solidify my suicide plan. The $1500.00USD sponsorship money would go towards purchasing a plane ticket to a far-off country. In an effort to best utilize the windfall, I aimed to leave Canada after the money was deposited in my bank account at year's end. This way, I wouldn't squander it on credit card payments or numerous other distractful indulgences. The money's arrival was perfectly timed. I promised myself it would be used wisely. Doing so ensured that my plan would see its end.

The Magnificent Seven Expedition, my quest to paddle the longest river system on each continent from source to sea, was about to enter its second stage. Stage One played out on the Missouri–

Mississippi river system over the course of 256 days in 2012–2013. I logged 3800 hard-won miles during that trip. I discovered en route to the Gulf that no one had paddled the complete waterway in one go. As it turned out, Australian adventurer Mark Kalch, whose 7 Rivers, 7 Continents project mirrors my own (or perhaps mine mirrors his), began his journey down the Missouri–Mississippi one week before me. He went on to get the first descent. I got the second. He got the gold medal. I got the silver. His efforts got him nominated for the inaugural Spirit of Adventure Award, given out yearly by Canoe & Kayak Magazine, the largest paddling magazine in North America. My efforts on the Missouri–Mississippi netted me no ink in the magazine—no award nomination, no honourable mention. Nothing. As much as I disliked the idea of there being silent competition between Mark and me, I had to admit that resentment and jealousy had crept into the equation. In some ways, my thunder had been stolen and I was none too happy.

Life has an odd way of doling out circumstances. Years ago, I had no idea I'd come to the point where death—and the quick journey to it—would appeal more to me than happiness and life sublime. I had no idea that what I perceived as a finely crafted plot to end my life was actually the product of a spiralling depression, a fragile state of mental illness that tricked me into believing I was on the right path and that death presented me with the freedom I craved. Of course, *I* tricked me. *I* created the illness. *I* created the depression. *I* created the plot. *I* created the ending. I would use what I loved to kill the thing I didn't love: *me*. I would travel to Australia and climb its highest mountain, just as I'd done in 2009. I would then pedal a bicycle from the base of that mountain to the source of the continent's longest river system and paddle that waterway to the ocean. Summit to source to sea. It would be elaborate, difficult, harrowing. It would test me like no other adventure I'd undertaken. I would grow strong and aware. I would regain power over myself, freeing myself from the shackles of parental dependence. After reaching the river's mouth and basking in the glory of success, I would leave the sandy beach and venture into the ocean. There, in the unseen depths of bluish green, in the tranquil troughs between the whitecapping waves, I would find my final solace. The ocean would be my pillow, and suicide would be my sleep.

In 2009, Dave Cornthwaite embarked on a source to sea kayaking descent of the Murray River in Australia. His journey finished in November, a few weeks before my Murray descent began. The boat he used for that trip was a yellow, 16-foot Wilderness Systems sea kayak named Nyala. Its name was inspired by the young lion cub in the film, *The Lion King*. When Dave learned I was planning a summit to source to sea descent of the Darling–Murray river system (Australia's longest waterway) in early 2016, he offered me use of his boat which, conveniently enough, was stored at the home of Peter Dodds, a friend of Dave's who had taken a keen interest in his 2009 descent. Peter and his family twice joined Dave on the river, including the final 350-mile stretch to the sea. The Dodds reside in a lovely rural home near Canberra which, conveniently enough, is a two-hour drive from Mount Kosciuszko, the place where I planned to begin my 2016 expedition. I accepted Dave's boat offer and was glad that it eliminated the need to either secure a sponsored kayak, rent one, or buy one. With those logistical quandaries out of the way, a darker, secret use of Dave's boat began to brew in my head. Not only did I plan to use his kayak to descend the river system, but I also intended to paddle it through the Murray's mouth and far out to sea. When the shore appeared as only a faint, dark line upon the horizon, I would remove my life jacket, place it in the cockpit, and exit the boat. As long as no one interfered, death by drowning would be my departure from this world. At some point later, my body and the boat would be found. A suicide note, eloquently penned during the river descent, would be discovered in a sealed drybag. The hows and whys would all be answered. The climax of my final chapter would unfold, leaving only words and wise whispers in its wake.

Crown me king of a wandering tide
that surges upon the morrow
like wind upon prairie wheat,
chafing not the grains of goodness
but stalking seeds of willful intent—
the meat of which
remains tender in memory
and ripe in vision strong.

I now take you back to November 2015, two months before I embarked for Australia. Credit card payments have become unruly beasts, their amounts far exceeding my meagre means. Money from the sales of frivolous camping gear has been squandered on the insurmountable debt. I view my financial dilemma as wholly unmanageable and begin to brainstorm a solution. Filing of bankruptcy before my departure to Australia, I decide, will eliminate the troublesome monthly payments while on expedition. Bankruptcy, although drastic in its irrevocability, seems like the only course of action worth pursuing. I view this option as a responsible one, a measure of maturity defined in settling my own matters rather than leaving them in the quivering hands of my grieving family. The law of the land has granted me a monetary exit, a second chance, the duration of which need not be lengthy nor detailed. There will be no annual budgets or cost evaluations to uphold. I need only a gently arcing bridge to carry me quickly to a future current. Curiosity and determination will drive the machine from that point on.

In the autumn of 2015, I was asked to be a literary guest at the River Arts Festival in Dunnville, Ontario. The two-week festival, presented in numerous performance spaces and galleries around town, focuses on local and regional writers, artists, and musicians. Not only would I be paid for the gig, but a free vegan meal at The Minga (a local restaurant) was also offered. My arm didn't need to be twisted to produce a solid "Yes" to that proposition.

For a town with a population of 6000 to have a vegan restaurant as cool as The Minga is testimony to Dunnville's concentration of progressively-minded individuals. The not-for-profit restaurant houses a generous performance space perfectly sized for acoustic musical acts and hands-on art workshops. Paintings by local artists hang on a long wall stretching half the restaurant's length while a row of public-use computers lines another wall. An open concept kitchen is neatly tucked behind a wraparound front counter and the friendly staff dish out an amazing selection of raw and cooked vegan offerings.

Meeting me at The Minga was Jody Orr, one of several organizers of the River Arts Festival. We seated ourselves at a long, wooden dining table and, over tea and appetizers, discussed Jody's 11-year involvement with the festival. Pulling from two decades of experience as an organizational and community development consultant, Jody's intricate and specialized knowledge had certainly contributed well to the festival's ongoing success.

During our pre-dinner conversation, Jody's attention turned to the arrival of another festival organizer. Her comment made it obvious that I'd been the subject of an earlier conversation.

"I told you he had longer dreads than you, Kitty," said Jody, smiling.

I turned to see a petite dreadlocked woman removing her winter coat and scarf as she strolled confidently toward our table. Her raw natural beauty and white bright smile lit the room afire. She was stunning. I felt my heart beat faster. The ensuing warmth felt foreign, but fantastically arousing. Here was a woman like none I'd seen before. Here was a woman I could write poetry about. Here was an opportunity to foster a personal connection with a beautiful female and I refused to let it slip by.

Kitty Pawlak sat in the empty chair to my left and dug a shiny fork into a bowl of tossed greens and shredded beets. Her shoulder-length dreadlocks, colourfully decorated with blue thread, green beads, and silver trinkets swayed as she talked enthusiastically about her upcoming trip to Central America. A recent spate of chilly Ontario weather had her longing for warmer climes. Her love of food and travel dominated our conversation and special attention was given to her prized puppy, Mawa, a mongrel she'd been introduced to while vacationing the previous year in Mexico. Her compassion for dogs (and animals in general) wouldn't allow her to go home without Mawa and the subsequent snuggles with her new puppy became a favourite leisure activity. "She's my little space heater in the wintertime," said Kitty, smiling.

Throughout our meal, I discovered Kitty Pawlak was a River Arts Festival co-organizer, a part-time cook and server at The Minga, a musician, an actress, and a talented artist. She also created kickass handmade shoulder bags from scraps of gifted fabric and repurposed accessories. She also tended a large garden at home and possessed encyclopedic knowledge about food production and environmentally sound farming practices. She could turn any meal into a vegan masterpiece. In short, she was amazing and I was amazingly enamoured.

That night, Kitty joined the audience at Dunnville's public library as I discussed the writing process and publication of my first book, *Part-Time Superheroes, Full-Time Friends*. My new dreadlocked friend sat cross-legged on a folding chair in the second row and posed poignant questions about adventuring and book writing. The spotlight was mine and I used it to flirt and tease the crowd, with a sizable amount of attention directed toward Kitty. When the event wound down and signed copies of *Superheroes* went home with their new owners, I stood face to face with Kitty and asked what the coming night held for her. She said she had to return to The Minga to clean up. I offered to help with her work chores, but she kindly refused, saying that she and her co-worker, Frances Jane, could handle it by themselves. I smiled and gently relinquished my pursuit. We bid each other good night and I watched longingly as she exited the library.

I sat for an hour in my car in the library parking lot that night, meticulously replaying the evening's events in my mind. I'd spent almost three hours in the presence of a woman who matched nearly every attribute I look for in a potential partner. During the course of the previous three hours, I'd progressed from being stubbornly interested in her to being mildly obsessed. I knew the inherent danger in assigning such spontaneous importance to a stranger, especially a female stranger, especially an impossibly cute female stranger with dreadlocks that worked at a vegan restaurant and liked to embark on crazy adventures in foreign countries. Aligning myself with that kind of female obsession was downright risky. I was either setting myself up for a painful free-fall or an unbridled romance of rockstar proportions. I was betting on the latter and shirking off the former. It was clear to me now—I was hooked.

For the next two weeks, I piloted an overloaded obsession train as it manically sped through darkened valleys and over joyful peaks. Emotions scattered themselves across my mental landscape like pollen in a windstorm. Fear, sadness, anger, guilt, and overwhelming happiness were constant companions. Self-doubt ran rampant. Self-confidence lunged in and out like a prize fighter, steadfastly jabbing onward to a unanimous victory. Reality wavered. Fantasy faltered. Life seemed scarily amazing and amazingly scary. If there was one useful takeaway from this nerve-wracking ordeal, it was this: hope—the all-important beacon that drives a determined optimism forward through life's daily struggles—had become my persistent partner. I felt *alive*. Suicide seemed conquerable. The whirlwind of emotional energy brought on by Kitty's presence in my life gave rise to a greater purpose for living. *Might she be the one who saves me from* me? I wondered. *Might it be love that provides the much-needed salvation?* The answer to both questions, I hoped, would be an emphatic "Yes."

As I carried that hopeful positivity forward, one nagging question remained unanswered: was Kitty in a relationship? *Dammit!* I thought. *That would've been a good question to ask during our dinner at The Minga.* My overworked mind somersaulted with what-ifs. How would I handle the news if she *was* in a relationship? What would happen if the door labelled *HOPE* suddenly slammed shut? And…what might happen if she was *single*? *That* was a thought worth hanging on to. I concluded that the best course of action was to seek an answer face to face.

A quick glance at the River Arts Festival online calendar showed that LMT Connection (a funk band from Toronto) was scheduled for the festival's finale. I summoned the courage to send Kitty a Facebook friend request and attached a short message informing her that I would see her at the concert.

"Cool!" she replied. "LMT will be off the hook! See ya there!"

In the meantime, I had a meeting with my father and explained my Australian paddling plans. I told him that the Aquapac sponsorship had been finalized and that they would present me with $1500.00USD at the beginning of 2016. I was free to use it however I pleased. The money, I reckoned, would go toward the purchase of a plane ticket. I explained that the paddling expedition would last for approximately six months and that my trip budget called for about a thousand dollars per month in expenses. Those funds, I hoped, would be supplied by my father.

Asking my father for money was always a nerve-wracking endeavour, even though he'd often told me he would never say "No" to such a request. The fact that I always seem to wait until the last minute to ask causes unneeded stress. I usually harbour a hope that he'll offer before my asking, but that rarely happens. Instead, I struggle through waves of guilt and embarrassment before asking, with those emotions stemming from my financial dependence on him and my perceived lack of self-sufficiency. Self-anger infiltrates the mix when the guilt reaches its tipping point. I blame myself for my lack of self-discipline and dependence on others. I feel inadequate in those stressful moments, a failure to those who know me. I could say the burden is mine alone, but I know these requests of financial assistance adversely affect my father as well. Perhaps the most obvious example of this is his persistent lack of confidence in my abilities. I believe he sees me as an ongoing child dependent, one who refuses to join the status quo and assume the responsibilities of an "adult." If this is true, he sees me as less than I am. And while I am more than what he may give me credit for, I slight myself as well, eroding my self-confidence with thoughts of inequity and incompetence. A secondary and equally damaging aspect (to him more than me) is how these monetary requests filter into his psyche and churn up newly imagined scenarios that play into his deteriorating mental condition. Whether it is dementia or Alzheimer's that robs him of joy in nearly every present moment, any dealings with money seem to fuel the actions of the sinister characters who inhabit his addled mind. I believe my financial dependence on him has contributed to his stress and paranoia. He has woven me into those characters who choose to "steal" away his retirement savings. My asking for assistance has led to me becoming the unconscious adversary. I have become the enemy. I have become the disease.

Thankfully, my father offered to fund the entire expedition as well as pre-trip expenses like bicycle repairs and gear purchases. He also saw the rationale of me filing for bankruptcy rather than supplying me with money for endless credit card and line of credit payments. By paying for the bankruptcy proceedings, he was essentially saving himself money in the long run. Fortunately, my father had never experienced the negative societal stigma associated with bankruptcy. He'd kept his financial head above water throughout his working years and was now able to comfortably live out his retirement on savings and pensions. Thankfully, he withheld judgement of me on the day we discussed my financial matters. He chose not to berate or belittle me for my questionable financial dealings. Instead, he saw himself financially able to free his son of burdens and to support his son's paddling adventure. He was also, quite unknowingly, contributing to his son's suicide.

The second drive to Dunnville, Ontario in November 2015 was filled with nervous energy. I had a loose list of questions I wanted to ask Kitty Pawlak, most of them pertaining to her relationship status. How and when those questions were asked would depend on the setting and the mood of the given situation. I needed to be flexible, not domineering. The last thing I wanted was to alienate her with a sense of control. I wanted her to be comfortable in my presence. I wanted her to trust me. I wanted her to know I liked her. I wanted to leave Dunnville knowing I had asserted myself honestly and thoroughly. I wanted to leave knowing all my questions had been answered satisfactorily. I wanted to know where I stood with Kitty and what relationship possibilities existed. Putting myself in a position to ask those questions would place me well outside my comfort zone, and being *that* far outside my comfort zone might make me a nervous wreck. I couldn't fuck this up. I needed to be real. I needed to make a positive impression. I needed to make myself vulnerable. I needed to take a sincere risk. I needed to grow beyond the present me, to be a better me, a more adventurous me. I needed to know I was capable of loving someone, and that someone might love me back. I needed reassurance. I needed a hug.

The hug arrived soon after I stepped through the front doors of the Royal Canadian Legion building in downtown Dunnville. Kitty's smile and warm embrace were welcomed ice-breakers. "It's nice to see you!" she exclaimed. "I'm happy you're here!" Her cardinal red leggings and dark blue tank top clung to her body like a second skin. She was dressed for dancing and looked every bit as sexy as the first time I saw her.

While the band set up their instruments, Kitty and I chatted about her upcoming trip to Central America. The lure of warm weather and sandy beaches was strong. She longed to immerse herself in thick jungles and pristine saltwater. A disdain for the bland flatness of southern Ontario had rooted in her and she yearned for locales exotic and new.

Our conversation turned to alcohol consumption when she offered to buy me a drink from the bar. I explained briefly why I quit drinking in 1998—a drunken fist fight with a police officer was a profound turning point—and how I'd remained sober for 17 years. "It started as a weekend challenge—just to see if I could go a couple days without drinking." I said. "One weekend led to one week which led to a month which led to a year. It's been an ongoing experiment, an ongoing challenge. So far, I've successfully passed the test."

She revealed that she'd also struggled with alcohol dependency and a gambling addiction. Weight gain and depression were the unwelcomed side effects. "I usually limit myself to one or two drinks now," she said. "Most times, I don't drink at all. I'm also much more active now. Dancing is my drug of choice."

And dance she did as LMT Connection cranked out its fiery brand of stripped-down funk. I resisted the urge to join her on the dancefloor for fear of being judged by others. A darkened table just outside the glow of the stage lights became my roost that night. I tapped my foot and nodded my head to the pulsating rhythm, well aware that the object of my affection drew stares from men and women alike as she lost herself in the music and danced freely with eyes closed and arms undulating. I sat transfixed, secretly wishing I had the courage to join her as she sweated out years of useless fears and toxicity. I longed to impress her, to embrace her, to leave the concert with her on my arm.

Unfortunately, due to the music, dancing, and lack of adequate courage on my part, I'd neglected to ask Kitty about her relationship status. Throughout the night, we'd bonded on subjects like travelling to exotic countries and the inherent vices of self-medication, but I still had a mental list of questions I needed answered. Thankfully, my opportunity to do just that arose when we were invited to join a small group of Kitty's friends at the home of Dick Passmore after the concert.

Conversation flowed freely around a large wooden dining room table at the Passmore house as I delicately engaged Kitty in conversation. I learned she was in a relationship with a guy named Adam. They'd been together for the better part of four years and shared a house in a rural town about 15 miles northeast of Dunnville. He would be joining her on her upcoming trip to Central America.

My heart sunk a little when the news was revealed, but I also sensed an air of bitterness when Kitty spoke about her partner. It seemed as though there was tension between her and Adam.

As the questions continued to flow, I realized no one at the table had asked about Adam. In fact, his name hadn't been mentioned all night. I thought that to be exceptionally strange.

"Where is Adam tonight?" I asked.

"At home," she replied, flatly. "Probably asleep on the couch with the TV on."

"Does he join you at social gatherings like the one tonight?" I asked.

"Not usually."

She faced me with a blank look, a look that barely hid her desperate yearning for intimacy. I returned her solemn stare and immediately sensed that her relationship with Adam had reached an impasse. It was on its last legs. They both knew the end was near. The trip to Central America seemed like a last-ditch effort to salvage their relationship. Part of me hoped their plan might fail, but part of me felt it might not. I placed a silent bet on the former and posed my next question, one designed to cut to the heart of the matter and expose the true pain.

"Are your needs being met?" I asked.

"No…" she replied, casting her gaze downward. Her short answer spoke volumes. My question had reached its target.

She lifted her eyes to meet mine. They were unloved eyes, tearfully filled with sadness and disquieting pain. My heart sank a second time as I fought off the urge to offer a comforting hug.

> *And as my courage waned,*
> *and as my urge refrained,*
> *I watched her eyes return*
> *to the lie that often burned*
> *a desperate brand upon her soul,*
> *betraying self and self-control.*

For the remainder of our time around the Passmore's table, Kitty Pawlak spoke loudly and jokingly in a makeshift Spanglish accent, an obvious departure from our deeply personal discussion. She had erected her wall. She'd seen her truth reflected in my eyes and had turned away when it became too painful to bear. She would impart no more sad emotions on this night. I took her avoidance in stride. Everyone reaches a saturation point sooner or later. She had shared until she bled truths, and for that I felt grateful. She had given me more than I had asked for. My questions had all been answered, but I still had one secret to share.

We wished our afterhours companions goodnight, took leave of the Passmore's warm home, and walked out into a blustery November evening. We shuffled down the sidewalk shoulder to shoulder, sharing our favourite highlights from the night's proceedings. I was happy to finally be alone with her. A rare, silent moment enveloped us as swirling snow sped snakelike through a vacant intersection. The swaying stoplight switched green and I seized the opportunity to share my secret.

"This isn't easy for me to say, Kitty, but...*I like you.*"

The corners of her mouth dimpled and a half-smile formed for a brief second before fading back to neutrality.

"Oh, Rod..." she said with a lamented pause, "I'm in a committed relationship."

I nodded knowingly. Her heart belonged to someone else and I, the adventurous author who'd driven far to divulge those three precious words, now had to set free the fantasy of *Rod and Kitty* and wish well this new friend as she embarked on a journey that was sure to shape the coming year. But just as each night becomes the morrow, so does hope reside in the belly of impossibility.

Faith may lie hidden,
but it always stands ready
when despair decides to exit.
Faith will face
the frantic race
and become our rival's nexus.

"Adam wants children," she said with a voice both staid and solid, "but I don't."

That sounded like a serious deal breaker to me. After all, it's hard to find fair parallels when opposition to procreation permeates a partnership.

She explained how her living arrangement with Adam had devolved into a matter of convenience. They shared a house, *his* house, but the sheen of their *together-dream* had faded. A crossroads had revealed itself and both of them were staring down the inevitable.

"Your relationship is essentially over," I said. "You *are* aware of that, aren't you?"

She nodded. Her sad eyes knew the truth.

"I don't know if our time in Central America will repair the damage we've done," she said. "I don't know if we'll love or hate each other at the end of our six weeks together. What I *do* know is that I can't *not* go."

I nodded. My sad eyes knew the truth. The only path forward was paved with uncertainty. There were no concrete answers. There was only the lingering sadness of loneliness and the frosty air of reality.

Our walk concluded and we embraced a final time.

"Good luck with your new book," she said.

"Good luck with Central America," I replied.

She turned and silently walked toward her parked car. Before she reached it, I shouted, "Hey, just so you know, I'm not interested in having children."

Pivoting mid-stride, she looked back in my direction. A wide smile spread across her face. Without a word, she got in her car and drove away. It would be weeks until I heard from Kitty Pawlak again.

Expectations and disappointments rule my world. They're two of the cruelest reality checks I can think of. Time and again, I lead myself down a rosy path full of hope and opportunity only to have my dreams crushed by an undeniable truth that stared me in the face from the get-go. I view these sources of misery like an evil pair of tag-team wrestlers who somehow manage to repeatedly lure me into a ring and then proceed to pummel my sorry ass while a sadistic crowd cheers them on. They work together to achieve one purpose: humiliation. One dangles a carrot while the other lurks all ninja-like just out of sight with a sledgehammer, ready to deliver the deciding blow. They are cunning and relentless and I hate them profusely. I view them as malicious enemies, yet their words and actions are scripted entirely by me. That doesn't mean I'm always aware of my role in their wicked game. I'm a forgetful fuck-knot when it comes to stuff like that. I can know and not know at the same time. I can become obsessed with expectations and subsequently forget that the inevitable disappointments aren't far behind. I seem to be aware and inept at the same time. How is that even possible?!

Expectations were high the day I purchased a plane ticket to Australia in January 2016. The Aquapac sponsorship money arrived in my bank account, accompanied by a generous monetary gift from my father. Together, the amounts added up to less than a comfortable sum to fund a six-month paddling expedition. Minus the expensive plane ticket, accommodations, and car rentals, the meagre remainder meant that a budget had to be established to make the money last. I don't usually work with a budget when I plan and execute an expedition. I'm not extravagant with my spending, but I make sure all bases are covered and all needs are met. In order to pull off this paddling trip without sacrificing too many luxuries, I would need to drastically trim expenses where possible. The first cut would come in the form of the cheapest plane ticket I could find. I did some research online and made of a list of ticket prices that fit into my budget. Then I went to a local travel agency and booked a flight for cheaper than any I found online.

Now, I don't know what your life is like, but when I get something offered to me for free, it usually comes with a catch, and that catch usually leads to some form of disappointment. It's like when you search out a shorter route to your destination only to find it actually took longer to get there by taking the shortcut. It would've been easier and faster to take the long way, but you didn't. And it's not like it's the first time it's happened to you. Fact is, it's probably the *hundredth* time it's happened to you, but you went against what you know and did it anyway. Why the *fuck* do we do that?! I'll tell you why. Because we *forget*. We forget that we create these fucked up expectations in our heads that are fostered by our *do-no-wrong* egos, and we expect our scenarios to play out *exactly* as our egos designed them. And do they? Well, sometimes they do. Most times, however, they don't. And what happens when they don't? We become disappointed. And resentful. And angry. And sad. And it's sad that we end up sad. And who's to blame for our sadness? *Us*, of course. You. Me. Us. No one else. Just *us*. And I don't know about you, but when I discover that *I'm* to blame for my own shit, I feel shittier than I did when I was simply disappointed, and a *whole lot* shittier than I did when I was in the joyous throes of my ego-driven expectation. I've got two words to say to my ego: "SUCK IT!"

When the travel agent explained the flight times and lengths of the layovers, I should've taken that as the first opportunity to change my mind. A three-legged flight lasting nearly 48 hours seemed entirely doable when I pondered it over for about four seconds while seated in the agent's office. *I don't mind sleeping in both the Chicago and San Fran airports,* I thought. *Plus, when I'm not sleeping, it'll give me a chance to catch up on some reading.* Had I been able to remember that I actually detest spending more than ten minutes in a crowded airport, I would've opted for a more expensive ticket. I would've gladly paid an extra $200 for flights that actually *connected* on the same calendar day. But, of course, I didn't. I bought the cheapest ticket the agent could find. I opted for the convenient shortcut and paid the price with my mental health. Dumb. D-U-M-B. I knew better, but still went ahead and created a headache for myself. I certainly didn't need another headache. I had enough of those already. And I certainly didn't need more stress. I had plenty of that already. And yet, thanks to ego and blind stupidity, I created more of everything, more of what I didn't need.

The stress of dealing with the bankruptcy proceedings, the income tax paperwork connected to the bankruptcy proceedings, and the fact that I couldn't publicize the upcoming expedition and its preparations *because* of the bankruptcy weighed heavy on me prior to my departure. If you've claimed bankruptcy because you haven't the money to pay your monthly bills, and then you magically acquire enough money to fund an overseas expedition but decline to claim that money as income, then you've probably created a potentially detrimental scenario for yourself. It's best to keep things quiet and not splash your international paddling plans all over social media. (Admittedly, confessing it in book form isn't the smartest thing to do either.)

And then there was the situation with Kitty. The fact that I had been on an emotional rollercoaster prior to our second meeting (at the concert in Dunnville) weighed heavy on me. Couple that fact with the discovery that she was in a relationship and was out of the country—and out of reach—for six weeks, and the mental burden becomes even more weighty.

And then there were the dealings with pre-expedition logistics. That stuff had been extremely stressful and time-consuming. The selling of gear, the purchase of gear, the bicycle repairs, the online research, the commissioned illustration of my route in Australia, the nerve-wracking process of acquiring funds from my father. It all added up to more weight, more burden.

And then there was the suicide plan and all the inherent depressive emotions associated with that. Everything I was doing in Canada, I was doing for the final time. The visits with family. Driving my car. Eating my favorite foods. Sleeping in a warm bed. All the things familiar were about to be cast away. I was excited and sad. I craved the purge, but I also knew I'd miss the things I'd become accustomed to. In six months' time, they wouldn't matter anymore. In six months' time, *I* wouldn't matter anymore.

On January 18, 2016, I showed up at the airport in London, Ontario with two massive duffle bags, a fully packed bicycle box, and a head full of optimism. Lugging that much gear through crowded airports was sure to be difficult, so I made double sure when I booked the flight that the luggage would be checked through all the way to Sydney. Somehow, the travel agent got it wrong. I was charged $200.00USD for the bike box and was told I would need to claim all my luggage, including the bike box, when I landed in Chicago. This meant I would need to somehow move all my gear through O'Hare Airport and check it all in again for the flight to San Francisco. And then, do it all again in San Fran. Ugh. The thought of pushing two carts full of gear through an airport didn't sit well with me. It would be next to impossible to push both carts at the same time, so I would likely need to leapfrog them and leave each of them unattended for periods of time. That idea didn't sit well with me at all. *Plus*, the luggage could not be checked-in upon arrival in Chicago because the flight to San Fran was scheduled to leave the following day. This meant I would need to keep all the gear with me all night in the airport and hope that no one stole anything if I fell asleep. Ugh. I hadn't even boarded the first flight and already the expedition was becoming complicated. As my optimism waned and my anger increased, another potential trigger was introduced.

In order to temporarily house a bicycle, kayak paddles, and a bunch of paddling gear, I had procured the largest bike box I could find. Fully packed, it weighed 75 pounds, just under the 80-pound limit. I hadn't given much thought to the box's dimensions because they were well within the airline's accepted restrictions. Unfortunately, what I didn't count on was whether or not the box would fit through the luggage x-ray machine at the London airport.

"And what if it doesn't fit?" I asked the x-ray machine attendant.

"You'll either have to repack it," she replied, "or send it freight."

"Great…" I said, frowning. "I don't even wanna think about how much it'll be to ship this box to Sydney."

I hefted the box onto the wide row of metal rollers and pushed it toward the machine's narrow opening.

"Looks like you've got about a quarter-inch of clearance," said the attendant as she slowly guided the box into the machine. "Consider yourself lucky."

"I'll consider myself lucky when I land in Sydney with my sanity still intact," I said. "Until then, I'll take this as a sign that things are getting better."

I should've known better than to voice that assumption.

With the duffle bags checked in as luggage, I proceeded to the security line-up and spent the next 15 minutes unpacking my daypack and having the security staff pick through my hair with gloved hands. Couple that with two trips through a revolving x-ray machine and a humourless interrogation about the bike chain bracelets on my left wrist (which I've been wearing since 1997, the year I bicycled across Canada), and I was left feeling frustratingly humiliated. Thankfully, I managed to keep my cool and proceeded to the seating area at Gate 12 to dissolve into the comfort zone distraction of my phone. What I found there quickly changed my mood from anger to excitement.

My eyes widened and my heart accelerated when I saw that Kitty Pawlak had left a Facebook message while I was dealing with my luggage. It was our first correspondence since our late-night talk in Dunnville in November.

"Yay!" I squeaked, gleefully. "I guess she likes me!"

I nervously clicked on the message and read its contents.

> Are you interested in a little adventure? Lacie and I are going for one now. Thought if you were interested, we can meet up halfway or something.

"Fuck..."

I mouthed the word more than spoke it. It hung heavy on my lips like early morning fog hovering above a cold lake—it wasn't going anywhere anytime soon. It lingered and festered and fouled my mood. It was the unwelcome silent voice of disappointment and bad timing. It was an ugly reminder that my priorities lay elsewhere, entrenched in self-loathing and motivated by depression.

An opportunity had arisen, pitched by a beautiful woman over whom I'd obsessed for months. I longed to be with her, to embrace her, to express my want for her. I pined for her smile, her words, her kiss. Sadly, I'd made my defining choice. I'd chosen death over life and love. I'd balked when beauty came calling. I'd lazed when action was needed. I'd lost before acquiring. The embrace I craved was now veiled in vapour. The image of beauty was dissipating. Sadly, I knew I'd never see her again.

> 'Tis cruel the life
> that robs chance
> from our passing grasp.
> 'Tis crueller still
> to watch it pass
> with hands never once extended.

As expected, my arrival in Chicago was hampered with baggage bullshit. I struggled through O'Hare, pushing two carts loaded high with luggage, cursing under my breath each time I encountered a doorway too narrow for the bike box to slip through. After a lengthy discussion with a staff supervisor at the American Airlines baggage check, I was able to check-in my bike box. Thankfully, I wouldn't have to deal with it again until I arrived in Sydney. My duffle bags, however, could not be checked-in. I was left with the unfortunate chore of toting them around the airport until my flight departed the following morning. The idea of spending the night in one of North America's busiest airports didn't sit well with me at all. Surely, I wouldn't get much sleep. The constant worry that someone might steal my luggage if I fell asleep weighed heavy on me. I bided my time by making hotel and car rental reservations over my phone. Doing so provided me with a sliver of assurance that things would go smoothly once I landed in Australia. Getting there, it seemed, was the tough part. For more than an hour, I toyed with the thought of cancelling the trip and returning to Ontario. It wasn't too late. I could probably get a refund on the unused portion of the plane ticket as well as the travel insurance policy. I could use the rest of the money for other things. It could cover the costs of producing another book. A manuscript I'd been working on was 70% finished. It would be nice to complete it and sell it to those who wanted it. *But what about me?* I wondered. *What happens when the inevitable downturn of depression kicks in again? What happens when the craving for a permanent exit from this dismal reality permeates my waking hours? Will I burden myself with guilt because I hadn't followed through with my elaborate suicide scheme? Will I feel like a failure because I never finished the river expedition?* The answer to the last two questions was "Yes." Not following through meant failure. Not killing myself meant failure. Not flying to Australia meant failure. *Spending the night in this god-forsaken dungeon of an airport means failure!* I shouted in my head. *The abhorrent stress of this day* reeks *of failure!* And so, in the name of self-preservation (the kind of preservation one performs before their final curtain call), I booked a room in a nearby hotel and slid my pitiful ass into a bathtub full of steaming relief.

A frigid blast of winter wind greeted my unprotected face the next morning as I hauled my bags out to the waiting shuttle bus. Fifteen minutes later, I was standing shoeless with a thousand other souls, each of us awaiting our obligatory turn in the revolving x-ray machine. Then came the obligatory purchase of overpriced airport food followed by the obligatory four-hour wait for the connecting flight to San Francisco which, of course, was delayed due to the shitty weather.

The 12 hours I spent haplessly wandering around the San Fran airport in search of solitude were punctuated with several strolls outside the building, soaking up some much-needed sun and appreciating the balmy 60-degree temps, both precursors of what I hoped to find in spades in Australia.

Solitude, however, was nearly impossible to find at the San Fran airport. I spent a total of two hours holed-up in a bathroom stall, the only acceptable refuge devoid of sideways glances and suspicious stares. My time in line at a Subway restaurant was punctu-

ated with barely veiled whispers of derision coming from those in
que behind me. The comments were obviously directed my way.
The accompanying laughter bordered on disrespectful mockery.
The words "dreads" and "freak" and "hippie" made their way to
my overattentive ears, causing my fists to tighten in anger. I wished
to lash out with knife in hand and watch the crimson run freely
from their gaping jugulars. Instead, I stayed silent and allowed the
ridicule to permeate me in sickly ways. Anger rose until sweat wet-
ted my t-shirt's underarms. Paranoia bent my mind so hard that
positive thoughts and helpful affirmations never reached fruition.
Healing intent got trampled by crippling fear. My self-esteem, it
seemed, was already on holiday. My self-confidence, it appeared,
had already claimed its bags and boarded a red-eye to nowhere in
particular. *It's not too late to return to Ontario,* I told myself as I fidg-
eted uncomfortably alone at a dining table set for a party of four.
*This detestable hell can end with one quick trip to a ticket counter.
One transaction. One flight back. It's that easy. So, what's it gonna be?
Are you gonna stay stuck in this protracted paranoia and festering fear
of judgement, or are you gonna enact a table-turning tactful retreat?*

My face must've been a painfully indignant sight to my fellow passengers when I finally boarded the night flight to Sydney.
Staving off the inevitable seemed inevitable. I was on a mission to
destroy myself. Anything else was irrelevant. There would be no
turning back.

The first order of business at the Sydney airport was to secure the
rental car I'd booked online two days prior. A quick scan of the
rental car kiosks revealed the usual corporate logos (Hertz, Budget,
Avis, etc.), but not the company I'd chosen to do business with.
When a more thorough search up and down the busy corridor
produced no results, I approached the Hertz counter and queried
a male staff member.

"They're located off-site, mate," he said. "You call them and
they'll deliver your car here."

"Well, shit," I said, shaking my head in disappointment. "I'm pretty sure that little fact wasn't mentioned on their website."

"I'm not surprised, mate," replied the Hertz rep. "It's amazing what some of these companies *don't* tell you."

I nodded in agreement.

"You don't happen to have their number, do you?" I asked.

"Sorry, mate, can't help you with that," he replied. "Try searching it online. There are free Internet kiosks just around the corner, next to the storage lockers. They're yellow and white. You can't miss them. Feel free to come back here if things don't work out with your rental vehicle."

A Google search produced the desired phone number, as well as a long list of customer reviews about the rental company. None of the reviews were favourable. Each one was a horror story spelled out in such gory detail that my own sordid affairs seemed trivial in comparison.

"Why the *fuck* didn't I read these before I booked the car?!" I angrily wondered aloud as I scrolled through dozens of disparaging reviews. Shaking my head in disappointment, I closed the web browser and marched back to the Hertz counter.

"Sorry to hear it didn't work out, mate," said the Hertz rep. "It's probably for the best, though. Hang tight here a minute and we'll get you sorted with a nice SUV that'll suit your needs just fine."

Rental papers were signed. A security deposit was charged to my credit card. I was handed the keys as the rep showed me on a photocopied map where the car was parked.

"It's the red Toyota in E7," said the rep, pointing his pen to the parking stall on the map. "It's a great little SUV. I've driven it a couple times myself. If you have any problems with the vehicle, don't hesitate to call the number highlighted on your contract. One of our operators will be able to assist you. Have a great trip!"

I thanked him and corralled my luggage carts together for the final push to freedom.

"Oh, one more thing," I said to the Hertz rep as I turned to leave. "Do you think the other company will charge me for the car I never picked up?"

The rep paused briefly as he pondered my question.

"It's hard to say, mate," he replied. "Every rental car company handles their charges and refunds differently. If I was you, I'd give them a call straight away to see where you stand."

"Will do," I said. "And hey, thanks for your help."

There's nothing quite like stepping through airport doors into glorious Australian sunshine and soaring summer temps. Winter, at least the Canadian version of it, instantly becomes a distant memory. For as long as I live, I'll never forget the welcomed blast of heat and humidity I've encountered each of the three times I've exited an Australian airport. I dream of that moment for months prior to it happening. I *long* for it. I view it as the first physical confirmation that I've finally arrived, that I've finally ditched the chilly trappings of puffy parkas and woolly hats and crossed over into a balmy environment that positively and prominently resonates with every fucking cell in my body. I don't detest the cold, but I certainly dislike it. If I never see another snowflake in my life, it definitely won't be a loss.

Up to this point in my 50-hour, airport-to-airport-to-airport-to-airport adventure, I'd rarely smiled. There was, without a doubt, never really much to get happy about. The choice to remain miserable had been a constant one and every annoying hurdle I'd encountered only exacerbated my already foul mood. But when I stepped out into that steamy Sydney afternoon, a wide grin spread across my face as I leaned my head back and soaked up the delicious sunshine. It was the first highlight of the trip. I hoped for more such highlights, and hoped their arrival would come sooner rather than later. I've since learned that the success of wishful thinking, as well as the arrival of its supposed inherent rewards, depends equally on three things: intention, commitment, and open-mindedness— three things I'd forgotten to pack before leaving Canada.

With all my gear securely stowed in the SUV, I took my place in the driver's seat (right-hand drive—something I don't think I'll ever get used to) and vainly tried to familiarize myself with the location of all the necessary controls, trying my best to remember

how I successfully operated rental vehicles without maiming anyone during my last visit to Australia. Finally satisfied with my systems check, and ready to assume the unwelcome heap of risks and
responsibilities of driving on the left side of the road, I cautiously
guided The Red Beast through the maze-like parking garage, exited the airport property, merged into a claustrophobic tunnel with
hundreds of other vehicles, and came to a grinding halt. I was stuck
in rush hour. On a Friday. In the middle of summer. In the most
populous city on the continent. My timing was oh-so perfect. My
planning, impeccable as ever. I sighed, rolled my eyes, and slowly
grumbled, "Just get me to the fucking beach..."

Traffic thinned as I sped south on a multi-lane motorway to the
oceanside city of Warrambool, Victoria. I stopped there for a swim
in 2004 when I bicycled across Australia. Warrambool's city beach,
I determined, would make a lovely "first stop" this time around.
I always found it psychologically helpful to start an overseas trip
with a dip in the ocean. It gave me something to look forward
to during the planning stages of the expedition. (The thought of
swimming in warm surf can be very motivational on a cold, winter
day in Canada.) It also provided a baptismal of sorts, a ceremonial
cleanse before the real work began.

Saltwater seduction,
weightless and worry-free,
savouring life in those scant liquid moments,
the long-sought, sweet apogee.

Eyes drawn shut. Ears beneath the surface. Body belly up, drifting
slow atop the gentle ocean swells. Serenity stilling life's clock. Joy,
a silent friend.

When the floating concluded and my feet touched the sandy
ocean floor once more, I turned and slowly walked toward the
shore. It was then that I realized I hadn't looked west in almost
an hour. Things in the sky were not how they had been. Not even
close. Gone were the long streaks of white, wispy clouds. Gone

was the radiant Australian sun, its fierce, relentless rays now swallowed by a horizon-wide trough of menacing cloudbank advancing swiftly from the northwest.

"Oh crap," I thought as I quickened my steps toward the beach. "That doesn't look good at all."

And then it began. There was no slow build-up, no incremental increase in intensity. There was only a blinding lightning flash and an instant deluge, as if the ocean had suddenly come ashore with vicious intent to reclaim the earth.

Out of breath from a spritely sprint to the car, I landed wet in the driver's seat and piloted The Red Beast south toward the resort town of Shellharbour. I clung to the hope that the storm was simply localized and that a simple relocation would end the inundation. I was wrong. Dead wrong.

The triple-lane highway heading south narrowed to one lane as a river of rainfall cascaded across the pavement. The wet windshield distorted the red glow of taillights as the wipers worked manically to clear the view. Cars crawled through the flood like ants through molasses. Gridlock in both directions pushed patience levels past their limits. Horns blared. Aggressive actions replaced common sense. Automotive anarchy lurked just beyond the next intersection.

I lost track of how many hours it took to reach Shellharbour. It was three times the norm, I'm sure. During that time, the force of rain and frustration never diminished. If anything, it amplified.

Torrents of water poured down the sloped streets of Shellharbour as I circled the city block that housed the hotel I planned to seek refuge in. Not surprisingly, empty parking spaces were nonexistent within a 1000 feet of the hotel. Every stitch of clothing on my body was soaked by the time I reached the hotel lobby.

The room, which I'd booked online, was overpriced and underwhelming. I'd requested one with a bathtub, thinking a soak would be therapeutically necessary by this stage of the journey. Hell, I'd even purchased Epsom salts specifically for the occasion!

Sadly, the bathtub was nothing more than a short, narrow

trough. I would've had a better soak in the bottom of a shower stall. Worse still was the fact that the room's tiled interior was partially flooded with rainwater. (And the room was on the second floor, no less!) A rising puddle had amassed on the elevated walkway, entering the room under the door.

"In all my years working here, I've never seen this happen!" said the shocked hotel manager as he withdrew his keys from the door. "I'd offer you another room, but this is the last one."

What's a wet, tired guy to do? Go look for another room in another hotel on a Friday evening in peak tourist season? Not likely. I paid. I stayed. I laid my weary head down and made the best of a shitty situation.

It's worth noting here that this was in fact the *second* hotel room I'd reserved for the same weekend in the same town. (Both rooms were booked online during my tenure at O'Hare Airport in Chicago.) This hotel room situation resembled that of the rental car scenario back at the Sydney airport where I had read the reviews of the rental car company *after* booking the car. There wasn't much logic applied to that act of ineptness and no more was applied to this one. Customer reviews were savage at best for the first hotel I booked at, prompting me to rebook at another hotel. Room prices were fairly equal between the two places, but reviews for my second choice were far more favourable. In hindsight, I bet the people who wrote those reviews never did so after weathering a monsoon. I bet they never tried to take a bath in room #17 either. As I mentioned earlier, booking two rooms at two different hotels was a dumb thing to do. It seemed like a logical decision at the time, but it would come back to bite me in the ass later.

I stayed two nights and three days in Shellharbour. It rained the whole bloody time. It rained when I swam in the rough surf. It rained when I wandered the downtown area in search of an affordable meal. (Never found one.) It rained as I packed and repacked the mountain of paddling and cycling gear I'd brought with me. It rained when I stood beneath a towering gum tree and listened to the intimate chatter of unseen parrots. It rained when I took photos of the ocean. It rained when I later looked at those photos of the rain raining on the ocean. It rained when I cursed the rain, and it rained when I didn't curse the rain. And, finally, it rained when I departed Shellharbour, piloting The Red Beast west to the home of Peter Dodds near the capital city of Canberra.

Peter Dodds has his eye on the good life. Being an optometrist helps with that. For the past 35 years, this polite, soft-spoken eye doctor and businessman has been carefully testing and correcting the eyesight for thousands of patients. During that time, Peter made an important decision to incorporate onsite lens manufacturing into his business. The decision bolstered sales significantly, making Canberra Vision Care among the top eyeglasses providers in Greater Canberra. His wife, Gemma, and daughter, Carli (the youngest of three children), are both employed at Canberra Vision Care.

It was raining, of course, when I arrived at the Dodds' spacious, rural residence. Nestled at the quiet end of a picturesque cul-de-sac, lushly ringed with low, rounded hills topped tall with forests of gum trees, the house—modern in style, yet aesthetically traditional—seemed to blend efficiently into the landscape. Small flocks of white cockatoos and pink gallahs screeched their way from tree to tree, unfettered by the endless drizzle. Equally unfettered was Peter Dodds, who smiled and shook my hand as he opened the front door and invited me into his home. Before hashing out the details of my upcoming expedition, the Dodds and I talked warmly about our mutual friendship with British adventurer, Dave Cornthwaite.

Peter and Gemma met Dave during his 2009 kayaking descent of the Murray River. Always keen for an adventure, they joined him on two occasions, both times in their motorboat. Their second outing provided Dave with safe accompaniment when he crossed Lake Alexandrina in South Australia, about 20 miles upstream of the Murray's mouth. At journey's end, they acquired Dave's kayak.

"We've paddled his boat a couple times since," said Peter, "but mostly it's been sitting on a kayak rack in our garage for the past six years. It still looks as good as the day Dave finished the Murray. It still has the sponsor stickers and his website address on it. In fact, we had it out on the water a few weeks ago, in anticipation of your visit."

Taking his phone from his pocket, he spoke as he scrolled through photos from the recent kayaking outing.

"Dave emailed me about a year ago, saying that I was to help you in any way I could," continued Peter. "Of course, I plan to honour my friend's request. As you know, Dave has offered you the use of his kayak for as long as needed. If there's anything we can help you with, please don't hesitate to ask. Firstly though, let's get you a good home-cooked meal."

Over dinner, we discussed the complicated transportation logistics for my upcoming expedition.

"Here's how things are shaping up for the next six weeks," I said, pointing to a map of southeastern Australia. "The plan is to drive my rental car up this dirt track to a small parking area about six miles from the source of the Murray River. I'll hike in via Cowombat Flat Track, search out the source, and then continue hiking downstream approximately 11.5 miles to Poplars Camping Area. From there, I'll walk these tracks and roads back to the car. It's about 17 miles from Poplars to the car. Hopefully this rain will bugger off and things will dry up. If not, it'll be a muddy slog the whole way."

"I'm curious, Rod…" said Peter. "Why are you going to the Murray source? Haven't you been there already?"

"Well, yes and no," I answered. "I went to the source area back in January 2010 before descending the river, but I never actually located the metal pipe that supposedly marks the beginning of the river. When the river journey ended, I drove back to the source area and searched for the pipe again. I never found it. So, I need to go have another look. I'm determined to find it this time. Also, last time I chose to detour around a nine-mile section of the river downstream of Cowombat Flat—from Cowombat Flat to Poplars Camping Area. It's the only part of the river I didn't get to see. So, before I begin the Darling–Murray river system expedition, I need to see that final section of the Murray. I need to finish one journey before I begin another."

"I see", said Peter. "I admire your determination to complete your goal. And after that, what comes next?"

"After that, I come back here to your place to pick up Dave's kayak," I replied. "I'll strap it to the top of my rental car and drive north to the source of the Condamine River, about 80 miles west of Brisbane. I'll find someone willing to store the kayak for a few weeks, until I begin the river part of the expedition. And then, I'll return the car to Hertz at the Canberra airport. If it's possible for you to pick me up after I drop off the car, that'd be great."

"Consider it done," said Peter without hesitation. "And then?"

"And then, I'll need someone to drive me and my bike from your place to the village of Thredbo at the base of Mount Kosciuszko. I'll stay at the local hostel, spend a day hiking to the top of Kosciuszko, hike back down to the hostel, and then begin the 900-mile bicycle journey to the source of the Condamine, which, of course, is the beginning of the Darling–Murray river system. After about four months, if all goes well, I'll arrive at the Southern Ocean. I'll then rent a car in Adelaide, bring Dave's boat back here to your place, drive over to Sydney, and fly back to Canada."

"Sounds like an awesome adventure!" said Peter. "We're happy to play a small part in it. Once you figure out what day you'd like to go to Thredbo, Gemma will be glad to give you a ride. She might even join you for the hike up Kosciuszko! Until then, here's a key to the back door. Feel free to come and go as you please."

I thanked Peter and Gemma for offering a ride to Thredbo. Driving there would eliminate 120 miles of cycling, miles that I would have to backtrack without a ride. They were both avid hikers, bikers, and paddlers. They understood the futility of backtracking during self-propelled activities. If there was a way to prevent it, they strove to find it. Their knowledge of backcountry hiking in the Kosciuszko National Park region was extensive, as was their up-to-date knowledge of the gear needed to pull off a long-distance journey. They were always eager to impart wisdom they felt applicable to my undertaking. They wanted to be involved, and they now were. I also made a prudent point to thank them for their wonderful hospitality. They knew how to quickly help a stranger feel like a friend. And although they lived hundreds of miles from the rivers I planned to paddle, they were the first *river angels* of my journey. I was grateful for their presence in my life.

Perhaps the only drawback to staying at the Dodds' home was the fact I had no cell phone reception, which meant I had no Internet connection. The town of Queanbeyan was a 15-minute drive away, so I found myself there for large parts of each day, sorting through last-minute logistics and food purchases before departing for the Murray source. During my first visit to Queanbeyan, the day after I arrived at the Dodds', I discovered several things that put an instant damper on the trip and threatened to jeopardize the whole expedition.

First off, I needed to return The Red Beast to Hertz and exchange it for a smaller, less expensive vehicle. With all the expedition gear now stored at the Dodds' house, the SUV was no longer needed. When I arrived at the Hertz counter at the airport in Canberra, they told me I would be better off keeping the SUV rather than exchanging it. The rates were about the same. The staff were happy to extend the contract for another 20 days. They also pointed out a problem with my credit card. The security deposit charged to the card at the Sydney airport (where I picked up the car) had cleared, but for some reason the charge could not be applied to the rental extension in Canberra. The staff suggested I contact my credit card company and resolve the issue ASAP. I agreed and left the airport wondering what possibly could've happened to the card to cause the problem. It didn't take long to find out.

I drove back to Queanbeyan, found a quiet parking spot next to a city park, opened an Internet browser on my phone, and began to slowly unravel the mystery. What I discovered nearly gutted me. I sat transfixed, staring at the text on the tiny screen, wondering if what I was seeing was real. As I scrolled through a list of recent credit card transactions, I found several that were not supposed to be there. All of them were large amounts. Added together, they had nearly drained the account dry. As I mentioned earlier in this book, I was able to secure a few thousand dollars from my father to help fund the expedition. The rest of the money came from the Aquapac sponsorship. Somehow, I hoped to make that money last for six months. If I needed more money, I would have to ask my father for it, and considering how much he'd already given me, receiving a "No" from him was a definite possibility. So, when I saw that the balance on my card had suddenly plummeted, I felt sick to my stomach. My thoughts went immediately to an unfortunate endpoint: the expedition would be cancelled due to lack of funds, which meant I would not be able to achieve my paddling goal before taking my life. That was an absolute downer. The thought of suicide, and the grand scheme created to ensure its success, were my reasons for being there. To leave without dying meant failure, and failing was never part of the plan. Death was something I welcomed, but it had to arrive when *I* wanted it, when *I* decided the time was right. That's how I remained in control. Being in control of my life, and my death, gave me a sense of power. That power kept me alive. The striving for death, for suicide, for an exit of my own design, kept me moving forward. If anything interfered and prevented that from happening, I would not only be one unhappy motherfucker, I would also be a failure. *And*, as I said earlier, failing was not part of the plan. Somehow, this fucking mess needed to be rectified and I was the only one who could do it. As if the stress of the past week hadn't been enough, I now had to deal with this shit. Needless to say, I was fucking *pissed!*

So, where did the errant charges come from? Well, it turns out I was charged for the rental car I'd booked online in Chicago and never picked up in Sydney. After a series of frustrating phone calls, I discovered that not only did the company charge me for the entire reservation (seven days of rental fees, plus insurance fees), but they also charged me for *not* picking up the vehicle. And because the charges I was viewing on my phone were in Canadian dollars, none of the amounts matched the Australian dollar amounts

I'd been charged. I had to constantly convert dollar values while on the phone with a company I hated having to call in the first place. To complicate things further, I had unknowingly reserved the car via an online rental company based in the fucking *UK*! After calling the rental car company in Sydney to find out why I was charged for a car I never picked up, they told me I would need to call the UK company in order to apply for a refund—and not a *full* refund, mind you, but a *partial* refund.

In the end, I managed to get the charges reduced by only a few hundred dollars. As a way of keeping my money tied up in their business, they offered me a small amount of credit which could only be used on vehicles rented through their website. I wasted no time telling them what I thought of that idea.

"After this fucking fiasco, do you *really* think I'm going to rent another vehicle from you people?!" I shouted over the phone. "I want you to do two things: refund my money, and GO FUCK YOURSELF!!!"

And because that ordeal wasn't enough to send my stress level through the stratosphere, another ordeal arrived right on time to complete the job.

While scrolling through my recent credit card transactions, I discovered that additional charges had been applied to my card by an unfamiliar business. After a lengthy chat with my credit card company, I was able to piece together that I'd been double-charged for a hotel room in Shellharbour, Victoria—a room I never slept in! Not only did they charge me a sizeable fee for not showing up to claim the reserved room, they also charged me for the room—*twice*! These new charges, along with the rental car company charges, drastically lowered the available balance on my credit card, leaving me with no access to the money I sorely needed to finish the expedition. Needless to say (but I'll say it anyway), I was fucking *pissed*!

A phone call to the hotel in Shellharbour netted me some disappointing news. I was told that because the room reservation had not been cancelled within the allotted time, a charge had been initiated for the full amount (two nights, plus a cancellation fee). Those charges could not be refunded. The fee for the two additional nights had been charged inadvertently, so they offered to refund that amount. Of course, credit card refunds typically take four to six weeks to finalize, which meant that the money initially allocated to expedition expenses was now wrapped up in unexpected credit card charges. I hadn't put aside money for emergencies. There was no financial back-up plan. If the money ran out, that's it—trip over. It was a gamble from the beginning and I knew the inherent risks. I was operating on less than a shoestring budget. If I got lucky and no major catastrophe occurred, I could probably pull it off. But two major financial catastrophes had already taken place. The expedition hadn't even begun and it was already on its last legs. If the credit card refunds took longer than three weeks, I would have no other choice than to cancel the expedition. The best course of action, I proposed, was to push on with the expedition plans and hope that the refunds were processed ASAP.

Back at the Dodds' house, Peter and I pulled Dave Cornthwaite's sea kayak off the wooden wall rack in the garage and placed it next to a pile of camping gear. I wanted to pack the boat with everything I intended to take on the expedition to test its storage capacity. At 17 feet in length, the Wilderness Systems Tempest surely had plenty of room in its hull for gear. The hull space had served Dave well during his Murray descent. He was pleased with the boat's performance.

Many sea kayaks come equipped with foot-operated rudders. In theory, the rudder helps with the boat's steering and tracking capabilities. (Tracking refers to the boat's ability to go in a straight line.) The Tempest came equipped not with a rudder, but a drop-down skeg. For those unfamiliar with kayak vernacular, a skeg is similar to a fin on the bottom of a surfboard. It does basically the same job as a rudder, except it doesn't turn side to side. It remains stationary vertically. There is no need for foot controls—as with a rudder—because the skeg doesn't move. A retractable skeg (or *drop-down* skeg) retracts into a recessed slot in the rear storage compartment.

This provides a paddler the option of paddling with the skeg up or down.

Now, I've seen many boats with retractable skegs, but I'd never given much thought to where the skeg goes when it's retracted. I was actually surprised (and disappointed) to find that the skeg goes *inside* the boat when retracted. I know that probably sounds strange. Like, where the *fuck* did I think it went? It's embarrassing to admit that I thought it, uh, kind of disappears when retracted. Seriously! Well…it doesn't disappear. As I discovered when I pulled off the rubber hatch cover and peered inside the rear storage compartment, the narrow slot into which the skeg retracted inconveniently created a vertical partition in the compartment. This presented me with a big problem. I'm used to having an open-concept rear compartment that I can easily stuff with large drybags full of gear. The partition forced me to repack my gear into smaller drybags and then strategically position those bags in the compartment. It also meant that the gear would need to be packed into the compartment the same way every time. That, to me, was an inconvenience. It made me miss my old Necky Eskia sea kayak and its partition-less rear compartment. (The Eskia had a rudder system.) It also made me realize why Dave had stacked so much bloody gear on the Tempest's front and rear decks during his Murray River journey. There wasn't room for it in the boat! With all that aside, I still managed to get my gear in the kayak. It wasn't easy and I didn't enjoy doing it, but it worked. The effort, however, left me disappointed with the Tempest. It was already giving me a headache and I hadn't even paddled it yet!

Another thing that bothered me about the boat was the sponsor stickers on its hull. Cornthwaite had worked hard to amass a variety of sponsors for his Murray expedition and had plastered the boat with brand stickers to show support. He'd also spelled out his website address in vinyl lettering on both sides. Aesthetically, the Tempest was still very much Dave's kayak. If I was going to use *his* boat for *my* expedition, the stickers and lettering would have to go. I didn't want people assuming that I was somehow associated with the brands on the stickers or asking me who "DAVECORNTH-WAITE.COM" was. I don't mind promoting Dave's cause, but not during *my* expedition. That's just wrong and very confusing. Besides, I brought my own website address lettering and a bunch of Aquapac stickers to plaster on the boat. I needed to personalize it, just as Dave had done years prior.

In all respects, the sticker thing should not have been an issue. Dave and I had an online conversation about it. He was fine with me removing the stickers. But when it came down to taking a razor blade to them, I just couldn't do it. It didn't feel right to deface the kayak. The Tempest was Dave's and it would always be his. It would never be mine. I was grateful to him for letting me use it, but it would always be what it was: a hand-me-down.

There's always been a one-sided competition between Dave and me—one-sided meaning me silently competing against him in my head. I've been living in his shadow for a long time, or at least that's how it feels. Correctly put, I created the shadow and I chose to stand in it. Dave has never given me any reason to dislike him, but I resent him anyway. In my head, I've compared myself to him for years. Through hard work, he's amassed a sizeable following of admirers who support his adventurous lifestyle. They buy his books. They attend his talks. They buy tickets to his Yestival (an annual festival inspired by his successful Say Yes More and YesTribe projects). He's created many successful—and some not so success-ful—ways to make money from adventuring.

Conversely, I've been successful on a much smaller scale. Peo-ple seem to like what I do. I get the odd speaking engagement (when I seek it out). I've had plenty of sponsorship interest over the years. (I've been doing this "adventurer" thing for 20 years.) I've sold books. I've organized a 25-date book tour in six U.S. states. I've found ways to convert adventure into money. I'm happy with my accomplishments, but not as they compare to Dave's. Dave, it seems, is in a league of his own. Perhaps there is no need to attempt to attain what he's attained. Perhaps it's not possible, given that his success and the path he took to achieve it are entirely his own. I am not capable of replicating that, even though it has been a driving force for many years. It's been said that comparison is the thief of joy. I would be a happier man by heeding that advice.

Back in 2009, I was introduced to Dave online via a mutual contact in Australia. Dave and I had been exchanging emails with Rowen Privett, an Australian paddler who shared his Murray River experiences with us prior to our respective source to sea kayaking expeditions on the Murray. Dave, as I discovered, was a former graphic designer who had made the leap to self-propelled adventurer. He had two impressive feats under his belt: skateboarding the length of Britain and skateboarding across Australia—both firsts. His website was impressive as well. It was modern, clean, and colourful. His graphic design experience had obviously been put to good use. I didn't have a website at the time, but definitely wanted one after seeing Dave's. I didn't want him to be the only paddler on the Murray with a website. I was trying to make a name for myself too. I needed to make a splash somehow. Having my own website would allow me to highlight my past accomplishments, and a blog would give me an opportunity to share my adventure with others.

When I checked out Dave's website, I was jealous. When I saw his list of sponsors, I was even more jealous. I wondered why I hadn't been able to achieve his level of success. Had I not been applying myself enough? Was I shunning the media too much? Did I need to lighten up and invite more people into my journey? Back then, I was not on Facebook. I didn't have a YouTube channel or a Twitter account. Those things came later. The decision to branch out into social media was directly influenced by Dave. In many ways, I followed his example. I paid to have a website created (ZeroEmissionsExpeditions.com—now defunct). I sent out dozens of sponsorship proposals. Some companies bit the bait, but most did not. Nevertheless, my efforts yielded results. But those results could not compare to Dave's. His website was nicer. He had more sponsors. He did media interviews. I didn't measure up to him on many levels. Nor did I measure up to my own expectations. I was disappointed in myself and resentful toward Dave. I was grateful for the teaching, but bitter for learning the lesson.

During my kayaking descent of the Murray in 2009–2010, I numerously encountered people who had met Dave during his descent. "There was an English bloke here a few months back," they'd say, "doing the same as you. His name was Dave. Dave Cornthwaite. Do you know him?" "Yes…I know him," I'd reply, secretly sneering at the mere mention of his name.

All the way down the river I heard Dave's name. It drove me fucking crazy. The mayor of Swan Hill (a riverside town in the state of Victoria) had given him the key to the city. (The key to the bloody *city*, no less! Sheesh!) Months later, during my own river journey, I strolled into Swan Hill and, quite by chance, met the city's mayor in a camera shop he owned. After explaining how I'd come to arrive in his city, the conversation turned to how a certain Mr. Cornthwaite had also paddled into Swan Hill. *Oh, joy…* I thought, secretly rolling my eyes (without actually rolling my eyes, of course—didn't want to offend anyone). The mayor went on to recount the whole key-to-the-city ceremony. I listened with little interest, nodding where nodding felt applicable. I'd been relegated to second fiddle again. Forever stuck in the shadow of Dave Fucking Cornthwaite. Poor fucking me. All the way down the fucking Murray River…"Dave, Dave, Dave, Dave, Dave." I was *so* fucking sick of hearing that name!

But it didn't end there.

It happened in Memphis during his Mississippi River SUP descent in 2011. And again in 2012 during the lead-up to his Bikecar expedition. And again during our SUP descent of the Wolf River in early 2012. And again during his 1000-mile swim down the Missouri River in that same year. "Dave, Dave, Dave, Dave, Dave."

And now, in Australia—staying at his friend's home, packing my gear into the same boat he paddled, using the same Aquapac drybags he'd used on many of his expeditions. (In fact, he was the person who got me the Aquapac sponsorship in the first place!) All this, fucking *all* of it, was somehow connected to him. Standing in Dave's shadow. Again. *Always.* Fuck… After all this time, after everything I'd accomplished on my own terms, I was still placing myself beneath him.

Perhaps the saddest part in all this was the fact that I intended to use his kayak to end my life. Dave's goodwill was actually contributing to the downfall of his friend, and he was none the wiser. No one was. How would it affect him when he learned of his friend's suicide? How would his involvement with me affect his business dealings? Would he approach his adventuring friends—especially those prone to depression—more warily? Would his trust in people falter? Would his trust in himself falter? How would the staff at Aquapac react to the news? Indeed, how would *anyone* react to the news?

Despite this pent-up resentment, I still possessed a need to take Dave's kayak for a paddle. I clung to the notion that somehow my credit card fiasco would untangle itself and I would be able to move forward with my mission. Paddling Dave's boat gave me hope at a time when despair seemed to dominate my days. I was treading a treacherously slippery slope and I was very aware of my unstable footing.

"Did the authorities ever recover the body?" I asked.

Peter Dodds shook his head. "No," he replied. "His body was never found."

I sat silently across from Peter at the Dodds' kitchen table. I was lost in deep, dark, depressive thought.

Don't ask him, I said to myself. *Don't ask him if it was a suicide.*

Peter had no clue about my intent to take my own life. Or did he? Did he see a sign? Did he catch a verbal slip? Did I possess a predisposed personality trait that shaped suspicion?

Why would he tell me a story about a young Canadian male who ventured into the Australian Alps backcountry never to be heard from again? Why would he tell me that? Why now? Why here?

A chilling fear crept over me as I raised my eyes to meet Peter's. His face was calm, emotionless, soothing. I mirrored his serene look as my hypothermic paranoia began to consume all rational thought.

I'm shaking! I said to myself, panicking. *He can see me shaking!*

He knows! He has to know! How can he not *know?! How can he sit there and say nothing?! Is he hoping that the gist of his story strikes a nerve in me? Is he hoping that I'll confess my secret intent?*

The unnerving silence lingered impatiently like death itself, eagerly anticipating the moment of ultimate release, the pivotal moment when sanity exits and madness moves in.

Fuck! I shouted, inwardly. The expletive rattled around my brain like a pea in a whistle. *Fuck him! FUCK HIM! He knows! He knows! He...*

The pause arrived abruptly and unannounced. For one short moment, the pea came to rest.

Wait...! What if that story is untrue? What if he fabricated that whole thing for my benefit? Would he do that? Would he seriously do that?? Is he trying some weird-ass reverse psychology on me here? Has this crafty optometrist pulled the proverbial wool over my eyes?

> *Speak to me in words prophetic,*
> *make their impact quake my doubt.*
> *Leave me with a truth courageous,*
> *a pithy thorn that won't pull out.*

And in that fleeting instant, the rational mind resurfaced, cleaving a new persona and pitting it strong against the scathing inner cynic. It's been said that confusion leads to enlightenment. If that's the case, what does enlightenment lead to?

I'll tell you what it leads to! It leads to truth! It leads to undeniable actuality! This man, this kind man seated across from you has taken you into his home and offered assistance as any friend would. He's not fucking with you! He's not out to get you! That story about the Canadian who got lost in the wilderness...that story had nothing to do with you. He told you that story to illustrate the risks involved in backcountry travel. He knows the risks. And he knows you know the risks. Did that young guy commit suicide? Maybe. Or maybe you projected yourself into that story. Maybe your emotional turmoil coloured the facts. Maybe you need to check back into reality and join the rest of us. Maybe you need to stop taking everything so god-damned personally!

"Do you want to take Dave's kayak for a test paddle today?"

The sound of Peter's voice startled me, jolting me back to the present moment. My body was still shaking. My hands were cold. My neck and shoulder muscles were tight. I realized I'd been staring blankly at Peter's face this whole time.

"There's a lake about 10 minutes from here," he said. "It might be good to see how it handles."

I nodded, wordlessly.

"Good," said Peter, calmly. "I'll back the truck up to the garage and we can load the boat."

The kayak performed well on the calm lake. I sliced the paddle blades through the water as Peter took photos from the shore. The drop-down skeg did its job, proficiently pointing the boat in a true line while the rhythm of the paddle strokes helped subdue my negative inner voice. Fifteen minutes on the water, however, was not enough time to convince me that Dave's kayak was the ideal choice for my expedition. The skeg's partition in the rear hull would be a daily bother. I could be sure I'd curse it a thousand times by the journey's end. I'd also need to strip the boat of its sponsor stickers. The thought of defacing it didn't sit well with me. The boat had character. Its unique personality was a reflection of Dave, not me.

Despite my grumblings about reluctantly existing in Dave's giant shadow, I was grateful for his generosity. He was allowing me use of his watercraft. The boat was certainly capable of getting the job done efficiently. It had proven its worth during Dave's journey down the Murray, but I felt it had no part in mine. That realization, and the subsequent resignation, weighed heavy on me as Peter and I loaded the dripping kayak onto the truck rack. Options were few. I had no interest in fishing for prospective sponsors at the 11th hour. The thought of drafting and distributing sponsorship proposals made me ill. My hopes hinged solely on the credit card refunds. If that money arrived soon, I could probably buy or rent the boat I needed. If the money was delayed greatly, no boat would be forthcoming, and no journey either. The truth of those words made me doubly ill. Factors were piling up against this expedition and I felt it teetering on the verge of collapse. Fear and doubt had seeded their discontent in my mind. The stress related to the Aquapac sponsorship was paramount. Although Aquapac hadn't asked me to provide more than a small selection of merchandise photos and mentions in social media, the self-assigned pressure related to that inherent obligation tore at my insides. I was imploding. Downfall was inevitable. Anger, sadness, and guilt were ever-present and overbearing. For the camera, I smiled. For my future, I wept.

Peter and Gemma stood facing me in the shadowed coolness of their large garage. Bikes, boats, motorcycles, cars, and a hundred other recreational playthings surrounded them. Their love of the outdoors, and the methods by which they interacted with it, were on full display. There was an indescribable orderliness to their stuff. A great effort had gone into shelving and organizing their possessions. It spoke loudly of focus, an element sorely absent from my worried mind. A sound commitment to their chosen profession had provided them with the means to travel. They explored in their downtime. In turn, their downtime became their uptime, a time of active rejuvenation. As they aged, they assigned themselves more uptime. They knew the importance of health. They also knew the importance of exploration, in whichever form it took. They knew that *doing* was more important than not. *Not doing* equalled inertness. *Doing* equalled risk. And risk equalled reward.

"Just so you know," I said as I stepped out of the Dodds' garage and into the grey summer drizzle, "there's an outside chance I might have to cancel the expedition."

Peter and Gemma seemed visibly confused by my statement, but neither uttered a word of judgement. Instead, they offered support in their special, soothing way, just as they had since I arrived at their home.

"If we can be of any help, please don't hesitate to contact us," said Gemma, smiling.

Peter stepped forward and shook my hand. His farewell was simple and pure.

"Good luck," he said. "We'll see you soon."

Peter knew there lurked a demon within me. He sensed the turmoil hidden behind my silent gaze. A mask I thought opaque had all the while been transparent, framed in fear and fabrication. Every good optometrist knows when to look past the lens. Truth is never tested, it's sought.

Those who took the time to see,
gazed full upon the honest me.
Those who chose to pay no heed,
watched their judgements supersede.

The road to the source of the Murray River ran south out of the peaceful pastoral region surrounding the Dodds' home. Towering gum trees rose from the roadside, their smooth, salmon-coloured bark contrasting favourably against the vivid background of green fields. Near the town of Cooma, New South Wales, the highway angled southwest and climbed into the foothills of the Snowy Mountains. Contrary to the rainy weather that plagued me the previous six days, the Australian summer sun made a glorious reappearance, bathing the lushly forested slopes in a warm afternoon glow. The need to wear sunglasses lifted my mood and produced a faint smile as I sped onward into the mountains.

While the Murray's source has little to do with the Darling–Murray river system, its location, mystique, and magnetism had called to me every day since I first sought it out in January 2010. The river's font, hidden deep in the Australian Alps of New South Wales, had curiously eluded me on two previous searches—once at the beginning of my 2009–2010 Murray River expedition and once at the conclusion of the same expedition, when I travelled back to the source specifically to locate it and to walk the untravelled nine-mile section of the upper river from Cowombat Flat to Poplars Camping Area. Sadly, not only did the source's location elude me that time, but so did the river walk. The hike turned out to be far more difficult than I imagined and, after only two miles of hard-won progress, I chose to retrace my steps and return to Canada. Traversing those unseen river miles, as well as finding the true location of the Murray's source, inspired me to return to the Australian Alps before embarking on the Darling–Murray expedition. I felt a very strong need to faithfully finish one expedition before beginning another. Last time, I failed in my attempt. This time, I was determined to right the wrong.

GPS coordinates for the Murray's source are easily found online. Anyone proficient with map and compass can pinpoint its location, assuming they don't mind walking dozens of miles off the beaten path to find it. Supposedly, a short metal pipe driven into the ground marks the spot. I say *supposedly* because I've never actually seen the pipe. I know I've been within a few hundred feet of it. Heck, I may have even tripped over it without knowing! Even with the aid of a GPS in 2010, I still fell short of finding it. Having a GPS this time, seven years later, would've been a big help. An updated GPS, tricked out with the latest software, would've practically ensured me a notch in the win column. Unfortunately, I'd somehow misplaced my handheld GPS one day before leaving Canada and hadn't the funds to rent or purchase one. Entering into rugged mountain terrain without a GPS seemed like an extremely dumb idea. I would be miles from any road system. It was doubtful I'd see another human. There would be no cell phone reception. There were no established trails along the section of river I planned to descend. I was entering into a proverbial dark forest that would only darken the deeper I proceeded. The inherent risks were high. The possibility of failing, higher. Still, the undying need to close the circle of the previous expedition drove me on. Even though a self-imposed death wish was the key motivation for this recent trip to Australia, I hoped that living through the next seven days would allow me to die by plan later. It's good to have goals. They help you achieve things.

And so, as I sped south toward the Murray's source, seated behind the steering wheel of The Red Beast, enjoying the warmth of the summer sun, I thought less about the tiny font hidden deep in the thick Australian bush and more about the stretch of hilly road that lay before me. I'd purposefully come this way to scout the highway between Mount Kosciuszko and the Dodds' home near Canberra. This 120-mile section would be the first part of a 900-mile bicycle ride from the foot of Kosciuszko to the source of the Condamine River, the first of five waterways in the Darling–Murray river system. This was to be a summit to source to sea expedition. Never before attempted. Perhaps never thought of, until now. My goal was to be the first. It's good to have goals. They help you achieve things.

The easiest part, it seemed, would be the summiting of Kosciuszko. That I'd done before, in 2009, at the beginning of my Murray River descent. Surely, the source to sea section of the Darling–Murray river system gave me worries. There existed the possibility of having to walk for hundreds of miles in dry riverbeds until I reached a flow I could paddle in. After that, who knew? There might be additional dried-up sections, requiring more portaging and creating more headaches. Or maybe the rivers would flood as they did in 2011, improving the daily mileages but increasing the risks. Whatever the case, I cringed when the thought of descending this river system by kayak arose in my mind. What made me cringe more, however, was the idea of riding a bicycle 900 miles from summit to source. The lack of proper training was sure to be a factor. I hadn't made training a priority, mentally or physically. I hadn't made it a goal. And that's too bad, because it's good to have goals. They help you achieve things.

Bike touring used to be something that came easy to me. It was a form of therapy. I rode to stay healthy. I rode to stay sane. I rode because it felt like the right thing to do. I've crossed two continents atop two wheels. I've tallied more than 15,000 miles on a loaded bike. I've climbed mountain ranges and raced across prairies. I've spun wheels in snow, ice, rain, hail, sleet, and sun. If one hill was

tough to top, I'd soon find a tougher one—it was the way of the
road. I muscled. I moved. I motivated. I maintained. I achieved
distance through tenacity. I gritted my teeth, cursed, and pushed
on. I never once gave up. Giving up was never part of the plan...
until now.

The road before me rose like a narrow black wall. It climbed
into a wilderness unseen, a crazy maze of contour lines and frightening elevation. Up it wound, like an uncoiled whip across the
pitchy landscape. Up to where the oxygen thinned. Up to where
the tree line ends. Up to where rock meets sky at the height of the
nation. The journey to this precipice was lined with trepidation,
intimidation, procrastination, and finally, resignation. In the end,
doubt won out. In the end, a shameful rout. In the end, a loss of
clout. In the end, nothing to tout.

Self-confidence—that faithful companion who supported
me through years of arduous self-propelled travel—quickly disappeared as I piloted The Red Beast up the hilly highway to the
mountain resort town of Jindabyne. I pictured what it would be
like climbing these inclines under my own power. My lack of training had negatively impacted my self-assurance. Quite knowingly,
I'd neglected the very thing that might give me the edge I now
needed. All my energy had gone into gear preparation, expedition
logistics, bankruptcy proceedings, financial woes, and the unending chore of buoying myself through depression. I had worked
hard to get the bike properly tuned and tweaked. I took it for a 62-
mile test ride on Christmas Day (about four weeks prior). Everything worked fine. I was a little winded by the end of that ride, but
setting and achieving that distance milestone (62 miles = 100km)
helped me feel good about myself. I proved I could still ride 100km
in a day, something I used to do daily for weeks on end. But things
had changed. I wasn't nearly as fit as I was a decade ago. Emotional eating and a serious lack of physical activity had packed
on the pounds. I became car-dependent. Convenience trumped
health. Good choices were traded for bad, and the subsequent guilt
weighed heavy on me. Where once I thought myself more than

capable of carrying out a long-distance, self-propelled expedition, I now doubted my abilities. Giving up had never been part of the plan. But now, giving up seemed like the *only* plan worth considering. The financial woes I'd encountered in Australia had created a huge amount of stress. The situation with Dave Cornthwaite's kayak had been a disappointment. The uncertain condition of the upper tributaries in the Darling–Murray river system caused further worry. The Aquapac sponsorship obligation weighed heavy on me. Worst of all, giving up before I began would mean ditching my suicide plan. It would mean returning to all the shit in Canada that fuelled my depression. It meant failure. I didn't go to Australia to fail. I went there to die the way I wished. That wasn't failure. That was success. But moving forward with the expedition in my present state of mind ensured that stress levels would only increase, and I was already approaching my limit of manageable stress. *Getting on a bike and grinding up hills might just be the thing that pushes me over the edge,* I thought. *It might just be the thing that leaves me mentally shattered at the side of the road, crushed by my own incompetence.* Is that what I craved? Total annihilation? Total collapse? Absolute cessation? Did I crave failure and all its horrible, self-defacing side effects? The simplest answer is: no. What I actually craved was *easy.* I wanted things to be easy. I wanted an easy cycling route. I wanted things on the Darling–Murray to be uncomplicated. I didn't want the *hard* work. *Work* was okay, but, please, please, *please* let it be *easy.* I wanted my journey toward death to be an easy one. If I could tweak one more thing out of life, that would be it. But that's not how it played out. Life isn't easy. I hadn't made it so. I hadn't *chosen* to make it so. I'd chosen to make it difficult. And, of course, I got exactly what I didn't want. I got the *hard* way. *My* way.

Terminating an expedition is something every adventurer dreads. Doing so inevitably ensures that one's self-esteem will plummet, possibly to lows one has never experienced. Self-doubt. Self-defeat. Failure. Wholly and utterly incapable. Those are terms that are sure to repeat themselves in the mind of an adventurer long after the horrible resignation is given. And if one has gone through the trouble to publicly promote one's expedition, well, expect a flood of criticism from social media trolls. Expect to feel even worse when the world finds out you failed. Yes, you failed. You. Are. A. Failure. And it's not like you failed while trying. That, at least, would give you *some* credibility. No, you failed to *start*. You chose *not* to start. You chose to walk away and retain what little sanity remained. You chose to not push stress limits past manageable levels. You chose *easy*. *But*, you also chose *self-preservation*. You chose to live to try again another day. The self-preservation route may not sit well with everyone (especially not with the social media trolls), but there will be a few people who will understand. There will be people who have stood upon the precipice of insanity and backed away without leaping. They will be the ones holding the safety net. They will be the ones who offer support without criticism. They will be the ones who encourage you to live. They will be the ones who care. If unsuccessful suicide attempts produce anything for survivors, it's empathy. Those who are able to relate to the pain of others do so because they've been to a similar place. Their sufferings helped strengthen their resolve. Their sufferings, and all the pain they endured, helped make them better people—compassionate people, selflessly supportive and mindfully moral in action and words. Those are good people to have on your side when the proverbial shit hits the proverbial fan.

And so, I resigned. I failed. I quit. I terminated the expedition before it even began. It seemed better to not begin than take the risk of facing a complete meltdown partway through the expedition. The decision to quit left me feeling horribly sad and horribly guilty. My self-directed anger upped a notch, as did the ongoing depression. Minus the time I'd spent in good company with the Dodds, this whole trip had been a complete calamity. Here, within sight of the continent's highest peak, I'd reached a low point. Barring a premature death, or an in-depth interview with an Associated Press reporter (resulting in a derisive worldwide news story and the mass of social doubt and criticism that was sure to follow), things couldn't get a fuck of a lot worse. But, as is the case when life looks bleak and foreboding, an opportunity for redemption presents itself. Even if I'd counted myself out without taking a turn at bat, it still meant I had a part to play in determining the outcome of the game. It meant I could still salvage something from the failure. It meant I could pilot The Red Beast through the tight mountain valleys, moving ever upward and onward in search of the Murray's source. It meant I could walk those unseen river miles and cherish a victory long anticipated. Even if I couldn't begin the next expedition, nothing was stopping me from finishing the last one.

There are basically two ways to approach the source of the Murray on foot. One requires a person to traverse 30 miles of trails, starting from a trailhead a few miles southwest of Thredbo, a ski resort village at the foot of Mount Kosciuszko in New South Wales. I combined this route with paved roads and 4x4 tracks as part of a 107-mile circumnavigation of the Murray headwaters in December 2009 and January 2010. The circumnavigation was done on foot.

The second route requires a person to start from the south side of the Murray in the state of Victoria. A long drive on remote gravel roads brings you to a small parking lot two-and-a-half miles down Cowombat Flat Track. This track comprises part of the Australian Alps Walking Track, a 407-mile-long hiking trail that stretches from Walhalla, Victoria to Tharwa, ACT (near Canberra). Before a yellow swing gate was installed at the parking lot's north end, it was possible to drive a 4x4 vehicle to Cowombat Flat in Victoria, located about two linear miles from the Murray's source. These days, it's possible to do so only by self-propelled or animal-powered means, although the track still serves as a fire access road for emergency vehicles and National Park work vehicles.

Cowombat Flat, a large, open meadow set against a backdrop of majestic peaks, is gently bisected by the infant Murray, with the three-foot-wide river forming the fordable border between New South Wales and Victoria. Before the formation of Kosciuszko National Park, Cowombat Flat was favoured by cattle ranchers who grazed their herds in remote paddocks along the upper Murray.

The walking distance from the aforementioned parking lot to Cowombat Flat is six miles. I used this route to access Cowombat Flat and the Murray source area in April 2010 at the end of my Murray descent. I used the same route in January 2016 to access the same areas. My goals in 2016 were the same as in 2010: locate the Murray source and descend (on foot) the unseen, nine-mile section of river upstream of Poplars Camping Area. Here's how it all played out...

The two-day drive from the Dodds' home to the Australian Alps Walking Track parking lot took me through some incredibly scenic landscape. Barry Way, a partly paved mountain road that runs from Jindabyne, New South Wales to the Victoria border, provided amazing views as it paralleled the Snowy River and passed through the sleepy villages of Seldom Seen and Suggan Buggan. I overnighted along the Snowy on a tranquil sandbar (a short walk from the "Welcome to Victoria" road sign) and rolled into the aforementioned parking lot around noon the following day. After posing for photos with an enormous green walking stick (Australian insects are *so* badass), I filled my backpack with a week's worth of food and set off for Cowombat Flat.

A common thing people do before embarking on a backpacking journey is to strap on said pack and tote it around for a number of hours in order to get their body used to the forthcoming torture that they're willingly (and stupidly) going to inflict on themselves while on said journey. At best, a backpacking trip is a murderous endurance test undertaken by masochistic lug nuts unwise to the fact that carrying an additional 50 pounds on their back will undoubtedly increase the risk of injury. If you haven't physically prepared for such a taxing burden, then your body is sure to complain loudly and often.

Stupidly, I didn't prepare. It didn't take long for the bodily complaints to start filing in.

About halfway into the four-hour trek to Cowombat Flat, I removed my heavy pack and sat sweating at the base of a eucalyptus tree. Ochre-coloured dust—stirred up from the one-lane track—coated my shoes and white hiking socks. I peeled back the elasticized top of one sock and stared at the naked flesh beneath. After 30 seconds of transfixed fascination with hair follicles and leg skin, I realized I was fatigued. I chugged a few mouthfuls of water, mumbled some words of mild encouragement to myself, and gazed into the thick forest of gum trees. A short distance away, a snake moved slowly through fallen leaves on the forest floor. I lazily focused on the scratchy sound of its progress until my eyes closed and my head drooped. I was tired. Thankfully, the day wasn't wet or overly warm. Heat and humidity would've only added to the weariness.

It was only when I stood up and reached for my pack that the physical discomfort revealed itself. A searing pain shot through my right hip, causing me to jolt in the opposite direction as if to escape the pain. "Oh shit!" I shouted as I leaned heavily against the eucalyptus tree and took a few deep breaths to calm my racing heart. "This is *not* good at all." If I felt like this after only three miles of hiking, what might I feel like after 10 miles? An injury this early in the hike could very well be the beginning of the end for this backcountry journey. Would I fail in this attempt as well? Would fear of failure send me shirking back to the rental car? Would I defeat myself, or would I persevere?

After hobbling around for a few moments like an injured soccer player, the ache in my hip subsided enough to allow me to shoulder my pack. Movement, and not inactivity, seemed to be the healing influence.

Through roadside openings in the forest canopy, I could peer down into the steep-sided valley of the upper Murray River. In those moments, the sheer remoteness of the watershed was abundantly apparent. Over the next few days, I would be walking through the bottom of that wilderness, completely isolated from the outside world.

MAGNIFICENT SEVEN EXPEDITION

STAGE TWO

AUSTRALIA
Darling–Murray
River System
Summit To Source To Sea

South Australia

Queensland

New South Wales

Victoria

AUSTRALIA

Indian Ocean

Pacific Ocean

FINISH SEA

ADELAIDE

MELBOURNE

Wentworth

Darling River

Murray River

Bourke

Culgoa River

St. George

Balonne River

Condamine River

Source

BRISBANE

Tamworth

SYDNEY

CANBERRA

START SUMMIT

Mount Kosciuszko
[EL. 2228m]

N
W   E
S

Promotional poster for proposed
Darling–Murray expedition 2016.
Artwork by: Jeremy Bruneel

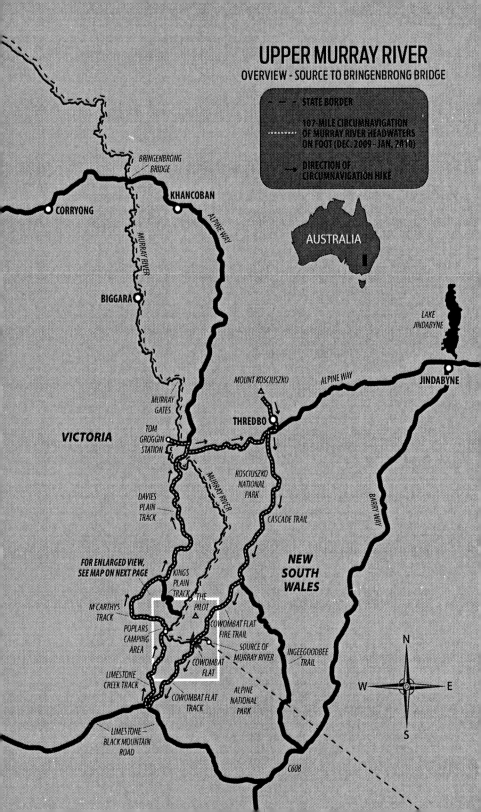

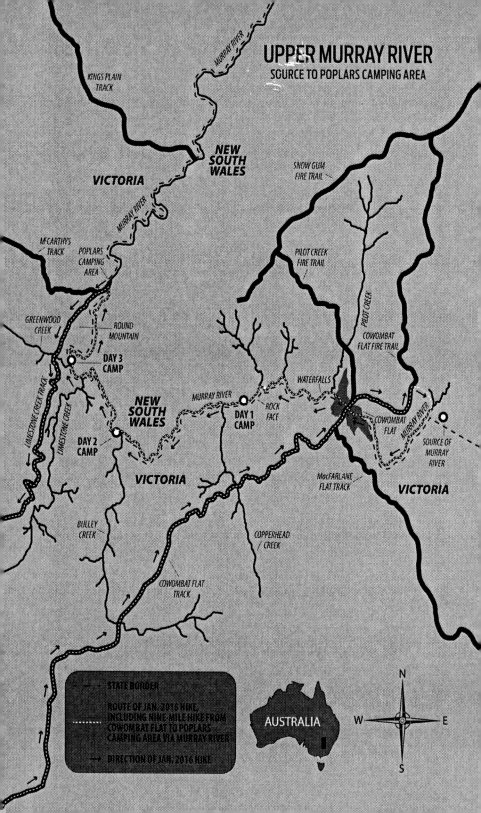

The gurgling sound of Mountain Trout Creek greeted me as I emerged out of the forest-lined gauntlet of the dusty track and onto the verdant expanse of Cowombat Flat. As the periphery mushroomed, a sense of relief flooded over me. Movement across this alpine meadow would be unhindered and non-linear. I could literally walk for a mile in any forward direction and still be able to peer back on where I'd been. Here, deviation from the established footpath is a welcomed option. A widened horizon means a widened opportunity to explore. Where the forest path had felt confining and rote, the meadow felt utterly liberating. This was a familiar place—a place I'd been to twice before. It's a place where summits stroke the sky with rocky fingers, where wild horses stomp hollow ground with unshod hooves, where the languid call of a distant crow sounds less like the foreign language of a common bird and more like the sing-song greeting of an old friend. Best of all, this sprawling oasis of stunted grass marks the hallowed birthplace of Australia's greatest river. Much of the continent, and many of its good graces, lay downhill from here. From this magic precipice, past worries and future fears are erased by the faultless clarity of the present moment. From here, everything seems possible. From here, everything seems *real*.

I stood silent and took in the spectacle before me. Craggy peaks towered over the forest to my right. To my left, gently rounded hills topped with thick stands of gums formed an undulating horizon. The late afternoon sun threw ample light and contrast on the blackened clouds that hung menacingly over the meadow. Something strong was brewing on high and I hoped its liquid yield would wait for sundown, or at least until I'd erected my tent. And then, quite suddenly, the whinnying of wild horses came to me on a gentle breeze. Their hoof-heavy movements were heard in the earth before their dark figures were spotted. They ran in spurts a half-mile distant, trotting across open meadow in packs of fours and fives before disappearing behind a clump of gum trees. When they quietly reappeared, one large male gave a loud snort in my direction. The others gathered at his side to curiously view me as I made my way toward them. Greys and tans and browns and blacks colourfully wove their way through shiny coats and luxurious manes. Lean muscles rippled when they walked and their strong necks relaxed gracefully as they bowed heads to drink from the infant river.

Littered across the meadow were the twisted remains of a Royal Australian Air Force DC3 airplane that crashed there in August 1954. Tragically, the plane's co-pilot was killed on impact. The other three crewmembers survived the crash. My mood was sombre as I snapped photos of a large severed section of the plane's wing, the weathered aluminum shell bluntly reflecting the afternoon sun. Tragedy, it seems, lurks even in the holiest of places.

Contrary to its name, Cowombat Flat isn't flat. It's actually a giant, gently graded gulley whose runoff feeds the upper reaches of the Murray River. At three feet wide and a few inches deep, the tiny river flows out of a wooded area to the north of the flat, partitioning the open meadow into two grassy sections before it enters a rocky canyon at the flat's west end.

I chose, as I had during my two previous visits, to set up camp on the New South Wales side of the river. A dinner of Minute Rice and canned beans satiated a gnawing hunger created by the afternoon's hike. As the gathering storm clouds squeezed out the last of the dwindling daylight, I crouched beside the murmuring stream and watched a cluster of dime-sized white moths flutter like frosty flecks in a shaken snow globe. Nature's animation— the rightful inspiration for any digitally-produced Disney spectacle—was now on full display. This scene, I noted, surpassed the trivial trappings of fussed-over camera positions and ritual frame-blocking. This scene was lit with truth and purity, two settings not found on expensive lighting equipment and top-shelf video editing suites. This was not entertainment. This was *education*. Here, on the roof of Australia, in the shadow of its highest peaks, near the source of its greatest waterway, a reminder had been wrought: that which Hollywood imitates, nature peerlessly defines.

From wonder comes bliss.
From bliss, gratitude.
From gratitude, acceptance.
From acceptance, peace.

The rain began around midnight. It wooed me to sleep and woke me six hours later. It peppered the tent as I ate my breakfast of oatmeal, brown sugar, raisins, and spirulina. It peppered the restless brumbies as they playfully cantered around Cowombat Flat in the dreary morn. And it peppered me as I emerged from the tent and filtered water from the nearby river.

Filtering water is one of my least favourite camping chores. The thought of repetitively forcing water through a ceramic filter encased in a stylized hand pump makes me cringe. It takes several minutes of pumping to produce a litre of drinkable water. Each downward push of the pump gets more difficult as the filter becomes clogged with sediment. Each push requires more force, as does each upward pull. Push. Pull. Push. Pull. Push. Pull. Push. Pull. I tire of it quickly.

There are, however, upsides to each down stroke. Having access to purified water in the backcountry is a necessity for every self-powered outing. Boiling water requires fuel, whether it be from a butane or propane canister or from a campfire. More boiling means more fuel, which means carrying more canisters or building more campfires. More canisters = more weight. More fires = more time. What's more, building a fire in the rain is never an easy task. I stopped having campfires decades ago. I'd rather spend my time relaxing in a tent than tending to a fire. At the end of an exhausting day, the last thing I want to do is gather wood and cook on a fire. *Bor-ing.* And what about all that smoke? Why would I run the risk of inhaling more toxins or putting more strain on my eyes? Forget fires. They suck.

Iodine tablets, a lightweight alternative to boiling, seem to have dissolved into obscurity. I haven't heard of anyone using them in years. Who wants water that tastes like rust? Who wants to digest another man-made pill? Forget pills. They suck.

So, that leaves water filters as the most logical and efficient way to purify water in the backcountry. There are numerous models to choose from. For the most part, they are lightweight and durable. They can be used hundreds, if not thousands, of times. Most come with some sort of filter—charcoal and ceramic are the most common. My Katadyn filter, which comes highly recommended by the World Health Organization, utilizes a cylindrical ceramic filter. The ceramic section of a new filter is about 3/8" thick. When used repeatedly with sediment-heavy water, the filter will clog and the pumping action becomes sluggish and laboured. Cleaning consists of abrading the filter with a scratch pad (a green pad used for cleaning dishes works fine). Of course, each pass of the pad diminishes the thickness of the porous filter. My Katadyn came with a C-shaped aluminum gauge for checking the thickness of the filter. When the gauge passes easily over the ceramic, it's time to replace the filter. Seeing no need for the gauge, I stowed it away years ago and stopped carrying it on outings. I continued to abrade the filter after nearly every use, and, as one would expect, the thickness and integrity of the ceramic membrane continued to degrade. The trouble is, I neglected to consider the consequences of my abrading actions. I'm a big fan of low maintenance camping equipment. The lower the better. But, as one would assume, ignorance and laziness go hand in hand. When responsible maintenance wavers, unfortunate consequences prevail. When shit gets overlooked, it usually comes back to bite the ass from whence it came.

And so, as I begrudgingly knelt beside the infant Murray on that soggy January morn, pumping purified water into a plastic bottle, I thought nothing about responsible gear maintenance or the increasing amount of pressure required to force down the filter's plunger. *Nothing*, that is, until a loud POP! pealed forth from the filter following a particularly strenuous down stroke. Water gushed through the filter at amazing speed. *Too* amazing, actually—like, at a speed I hadn't seen before. I pulled the plunger and depressed it slowly. The action took no effort to complete. No pressure. No chore. The action was *too* simple, *too* easy. *Something's wrong*, I said to myself. *Something is* very *wrong*.

I cautiously unscrewed the filter's plastic outer case and watched the untreated river water within spill onto the ground. I slid out the ceramic membrane and turned it over in my hands. What I saw on its flipside made me grimace. An overabundance of pressure had blown a thumbnail-sized hole through the side of the ceramic membrane. It was only then that I realized the membrane was less than 1/16" thick. All those years of abrading with a green scratch pad had taken a toll. I hung my head in defeat. The filter was irreparable, useless. A very curt expletive leaked out from between my sneering lips and hung in the air before me. It was a reminder. The consequences of my ignorant actions quickly revealed themselves. I had brought only enough fuel to cook food. I didn't have enough to boil water for drinking. With no dry wood (thanks to the rain), there would be no campfires. Boiling water, it seemed, was now no longer an option. The solution? Drink directly from the river. And the risk of that? Contracting a waterborne disease. Wild horses and other large mammals drank regularly from the river. They also shat where they drank. Parasites and pathogens from their feces could easily end up in the river, especially with the increased runoff caused by heavy rains. By choosing to drink untreated river water, I was significantly upping the risk factor of this journey. Add that to the fact I was already struggling mentally and physically, as well as venturing into remote backcountry without a GPS, and you have a veritable recipe for something to go wrong.

Clad in rain gear, I packed what little water I'd managed to filter into a daypack and set off in search of the elusive pipe-in-the-ground that marked the Murray's source. A 30-minute walk up the Cowombat Flat Fire Trail brought me to a small rock cairn on the trail's right side. I'd stumbled across the same cairn on previous visits in January 2010 and April 2010. At those times, I had a GPS in my possession. According to the GPS, the rock cairn marked the closest point the track came to the Murray's source, located about a half-mile distant. This time, however, I had no GPS. Pinpointing the location of the pipe would be like trying to find a needle in a hay field.

Just as I'd done during the first two visits, I followed a faint game trail until it petered out in the dense underbrush, leaving me to bushwhack east toward the source. Twice I saw a flash of black to my right and heard the heavy hooves of a nervous brumby stomp through the thick forest. Minutes later, I emerged into a large, open meadow that doubled as a pond during wet weather. The overnight rain had saturated its grassy surface. My hiking shoes sank ankle-deep as I squished my way across it. As suspected, the pond's outflow led me a few hundred feet to the east where it emptied into a narrow bog churned earthy black by brumby activity. Through the middle of this bog flowed the infant Murray, its narrow course less than two feet wide. It repeatedly dove underground, resurfacing as a clear, impatient gurgle, snaking its way between a gauntlet of gums and hardwoods. The spongy ground astride the stream was covered in thick moss and sprawling ferns. Basketball-sized tussocks topped with knee-high spiky grass dotted the landscape. According to information I'd found online, the Murray's official beginning lay upstream from this point, at a place where three tiny tributaries merged in the bottom of a gulley. If I followed the infant river upstream for a short distance, I'd surely come to this important junction and find the elusive pipe.

As it had since well before daybreak, a bothersome light rain continued to slowly drench the forest. My Gore-Tex rain jacket, saturated and useless after 90 minutes of drizzle, now functioned more as a heat seal, trapping body heat as I pushed through the thick, wet foliage. In a dense thicket of sinewy saplings 200 yards upstream, I came across orange flagging tape hanging lifeless from the spiny branches. *Could this be the source?* I asked myself, allowing my ears to listen for evidence of the three tributary streams that marked the true spot. Unfortunately, I heard only the infant river as it gurgled noisily in its tiny earthen trench. I pushed forward through the saplings for another 10 yards and searched the forest for more flagging tape. I found nothing. *Perhaps this is* not *the river, but one of the tributary streams instead,* I thought to myself. *Perhaps the source is actually* downstream *from here, not* upstream.

I glanced again through the forest ahead. The saplings leaned in on themselves like drunken wooden sailors supporting the weight of their stumbling brethren. Pushing forward into this claustrophobic morass seemed futile. The young trees would yield only to machete or saw, two tools I didn't possess. I made the decision to retreat downstream in hopes that the flow would soon merge with two others to form the Murray proper. In short, it didn't. Despite numerous forays into the bush on both sides of the stream, I found no other tributaries, and no important junction. Without a GPS, it was impossible to determine whether the stream was a tributary or the river itself. The only way to verify was to follow its course downstream. If I emerged onto Cowombat Flat after walking two-and-a-half miles downstream, then I would know for certain it was the river. If no obvious tributaries presented themselves during the downstream trek, I could deduce that the source lay somewhere upstream of where I currently stood. "And if that's the case," I said aloud, "I'll have to come back here this afternoon and do a second, more thorough search for the elusive pipe."

I followed the tiny stream as it snaked through the bottom of a 30-foot-wide, treeless gulley dotted with tussocks and carpeted with soggy moss. The gently sloping landscape on either side of the gulley was thickly treed, although I rarely found the need to enter this forest. Instead, I squished my way atop the rain-saturated moss and leapt across the narrow flow when the stream abruptly changed its course. Along the way, I saw no tributaries. The stream I'd seen all day was indeed the river. Its source, I deduced, lay upstream of my furthest venture. A second search would be necessary.

The gulley widened considerably as the Murray approached Cowombat Flat. The dark, undulating ridgelines of nearby mountains appeared above the treetops as I emerged onto the flat. Forest gave way to meadow as the horizon expanded and the familiar sound of hooves on hollow earth found my ears. Very soon after, my tent came into view. I'd come full circle by river and trail, but my trek was only half complete. Somewhere in the depths of the wet forest lay the Murray's source, and I fully intended to find it.

I ducked into my tent for a quick snack and a short respite from the endless drizzle, and then promptly began the 30-minute trek back up the Cowombat Flat Fire Trail to the rock cairn. Headlong into the forest I trekked, following the same faint brumby trail as before and bushwhacking the same dense stand of gums and hardwoods until I emerged into the same large meadow. I removed my daypack and left it in an obvious spot at the river's edge. Then I worked my way upstream, diving into the forest every 100 paces to look for evidence of the elusive tributaries. These forays often took me deep into the forest where wide glades carpeted with lush, ankle-deep grass sat serene and inviting. I stood unmoving for several minutes in each of those magical sanctuaries, mentally lost in the raw beauty of this riverine environment.

Evidence of human activity was limited to a small, fenced enclosure partly enveloped in creeping vines that sat several hundred feet from the river's left descending bank. I pondered whether a nearby pond had once been paired with the enclosure—the two seemed oddly related. Their purpose, however, never became fully evident. Time had made their purpose trivial and I found myself quickly abandoning the topic. Nor did it matter to the large colony of vocal frogs that called the pond their home. To them, the fewer humans they saw, the better.

I never again found the two pieces of orange flagging tape in the sapling forest. I never found the elusive tributaries or the mythical pipe-in-the-ground. An hour of searching yielded little more than a sense of disappointment. Somewhere in that dense forest was a tiny spring, the true beginning of the Murray River. It must've been only hundreds of feet from where I roamed. Without the aid of a GPS, my upstream trek proved futile. Four times in three visits I'd tried to locate the source, and four times I'd failed.

Frustrated and tired, I slogged back to my tent via the Cowombat Flat Fire Trail and cooked a hot meal of beans and rice. Dry clothes and a warm sleeping bag helped curb the displeasure of the day's defeat. The source of my misery had eluded me again, and it didn't help to know that the *real* test of my mental state—the definite *make-or-break*—lay *down*stream of Cowombat Flat, down in the depths of a foreboding canyon through which the maturing Murray ran loud and frothy. My previous attempt at walking the next nine miles of the Murray had failed miserably back in April 2010. Combine that with four failed attempts to locate the river's source and you're left with a whole lotta let-down. My batting percentage for completing anything on the upper Murray was a big fucking goose egg. With the odds stacked against me, I prepared myself for what lay ahead. Morning was sure to bring misery and disappointment in spades. Suffering would be the rule, not the exception. I had failed every test this short stretch of river had dealt me. But would I fail again? Only the river knew the answer to that query, and it didn't seem interested in speaking my language.

I woke to sunny skies and temperatures in the mid-60s, a much-welcomed departure from the soggy weather that plagued me for eight out of the previous 10 days. Less rain meant a shallower river, and a shallower river meant easier walking if I chose to trek in it, which I hoped not to. Besides the obvious disadvantages of trekking in wet shoes, walking in this section of the upper Murray presented numerous problems. For starters, the riverbed is rocky and often covered in algae, so it's incredibly slippery. Each footfall needs to be strategically placed, especially when carrying a heavy backpack. A tumble here could easily result in an unwanted injury or a potentially fatal concussion. The narrow river is also choked with natural debris, mostly in the form of fallen trees and log jams. No one maintains the river here. When trees fall across the upper Murray, they stay fallen. No one comes along with a chainsaw and hacks out the obstructive bits. During the seven days it took me to paddle the river from Poplars Camping Area to Biggara back in January 2010, I never saw a sawn tree. Indeed, the riverside forest upstream of Tom Groggin Campground (in Kosciuszko National Park) has never been logged. That section is as pristine as it gets. It is, without a doubt, my favourite stretch of the Murray. Virgin forests, wherever you encounter them, are always beautiful.

(I assume that raging spring flows wash away debris in the Murray Gates section [Tom Groggin Station to Biggara], so it makes sense that there is no need for maintenance on that stretch of river—although I'd hedge a bet some rafting companies likely pull a log or two out of the rapids to ensure a safer descent.)

Slippery rocks and fallen trees aren't the only obstacles on the upper Murray. As I discovered during my ill-fated, day-and-a-half trek back in April 2010 (the one where I had to turn back at river mile 4.5 because the terrain was kicking my ass), waterfalls, rapids, and steep-walled canyons are abundant. This *is* a mountainous area, after all. The river drops *four times* more in elevation in its first 78 miles than it does in its final 1500 miles. Long before it becomes the languid waterway dotted with houseboats and jet skis, the impatient Murray hurriedly tumbles over countless drops—some as high as 12 feet—and races past the base of towering rock faces. The river here is wild and untamed. It moves at a pace governed only by rainfall amounts and gravity. Walking in it, even in low water, is an option sought only when necessary. When you figure in the additional weight of a backpack and the instability it brings to the simple act of walking, *not* trekking in the riverbed seems like the smartest choice.

So, if walking in the upper reaches of the Murray is a dangerous pursuit, what is an adventurer bent on trekking it supposed to do? The answer to that would seem simple: walk beside it. Well, fact is, few things about the upper Murray are simple. Solutions rarely present themselves. Instead, they are sought. The key is to use what's already there. The river's course is already well-defined and unlikely to change. Over millennia, the Murray has carved a deep, V-shaped trough through the mountainous terrain. The steep slopes on either side of the river are home to a dense forest of gums and hardwoods. In areas where wildfires have ravaged the forest, stands of thick scrub, nearly impenetrable by hiking standards, are common. Large mammals, such as Sambar deer and wild horses, have forged footpaths through much of this terrain. My goal was to use these game trails to penetrate the forest. If the animals could do it, so could I. As I'd seen in April 2010, many of these trails ran parallel to the river and followed contour lines rather than running up and down the steep slopes. That meant easier hiking. As long as I could stitch together a plausible downstream route using these trails, I stood a good chance of getting to Poplars Camping Area before I ran out of food, of which I was carrying five days' worth— enough, I hoped, to get me through the challenging quest that lay before me.

At the western end of Cowombat Flat, about 500 yards from where I camped, the infant Murray ran headlong into a steep, 40-foot-high hill which abruptly changed the river's course. It was here that the Murray welcomed its first tributary, Pilot Creek. On this day, the creek's volume at the confluence was twice that of the Murray, effectively doubling the Murray's width from three feet to six. The flow and depth of both river and creek were clear, cool, and shallow.

When its length is traced back to its furthest point using a topographic map, Pilot Creek is longer than the Murray's first three miles upstream of the Pilot Creek confluence. The source of a river is often defined as the furthest point upstream from its mouth. Based on that equation, Pilot Creek should, by rights, be renamed "Murray River." Beginning on the steep western slopes of The Pilot (el. 5944 feet), Pilot Creek flows approximately four miles before merging with the Murray. Curiously, Limestone Creek—located just upstream from Poplars Camping Area, my exit point on this trek—is longer still. Limestone Creek's course can be traced back 20 miles from its confluence with the Murray, thereby making it longer than the first 10 miles of the Murray. Perhaps Limestone Creek, and *not* Pilot Creek, should be renamed "Murray River." (It's worth noting that Limestone Creek and Pilot Creek are shown as *intermittent creeks* on Australian topographic maps. This means they flow occasionally, like after a heavy rain, and are typically dry or near-dry the remainder of the time. *River sources* are typically defined as springs, streams, creeks, rivers, lakes, or other waterways/ bodies of water that have a continuous flow.)

As I stood snapping photos and recording a short video at the junction of Pilot Creek and the infant river, I failed to notice that I'd inadvertently disturbed a nest of biting ants and that a hefty number of the little black beasts were ascending my white socks with bad intention. Their searing bites came quick and plentiful as they reached the unprotected flesh on my calves. I wasn't ten minutes into the trek and already I was feeling the unwelcome sting of the upper Murray River anti-gods. They had it in for me. I was sure of it. Was there something downstream I wasn't supposed to see? Was this section of river supposed to remain unexplored and mysterious to me? Was the sight of white socks turning black with creeping ants supposed to scare me back to the comfort of my rental car, or maybe *all* the way back to the mollified safety of an insect-free Canadian winter? Surely this was a test, one of those trigger tests that slam into one's brain unexpectedly, clearly designed to disturb a well-rooted complacency and induce an animated dance of defiance. So, dance I did, almost throwing myself into the river to wash the beasts away, and then quickly remembering that I wanted to keep my feet dry as long as possible to, you know, ward off the inevitable foot rot and fungal stench that was sure to occur in the following days. Getting your priorities straight goes a long way when descending remote stretches of rivers on foot. Ants, as it turns out, have their own set of priorities, one of which is to ensure that warm-blooded predators and daft adventurers are sent packing when the entrance to their underground home is disturbed. Tiny mandibles in significant numbers provide all the deterrence necessary.

Downstream of the Pilot Creek confluence, I passed a river gauge housed in a large corrugated pipe embedded in the riverbed. A concrete water control structure resembling a tiny dam sat to the pipe's right. It wasn't clear whether this apparatus was still in use.

Strengthened by the additional flow from Pilot Creek, the Murray poured itself past the base of a craggy-faced hill and over the first of two sizeable waterfalls. A wall of rock on the river's right side forced me to carefully scramble along the opposite bank, taking care not to tumble into the plunging water. The highest of these waterfalls was about 12 feet. It was no Niagara Falls, but still quite substantial when compared to the nearly complete absence of animated water on the 1500 miles of lazy river downstream of Biggara.

While researching the upper Murray online in 2009 and 2015, I never once came across a mention of waterfalls. One would think that such a significant river feature would be highlighted in any discussion of the upper river. Truth is, finding *any* pertinent info about the river upstream of Biggara was a complete bust. I credited this to the fact that few people, if *any*, had ever seen the upper Murray, let alone descended it on foot or in a self-propelled watercraft. I went in blind in 2010. I had little idea of what I would encounter. Those who searched online for upper Murray River info after the spring of 2010 probably stumbled across my account of my paddling descent in 2009–2010. (The account, some of which appears earlier in this book, can be accessed on my website, rodwellington.com.)

Part of the reason why I wrote this book was to shed light on this beautiful section of Australia's greatest river. I feel it has been overlooked and underappreciated. Perhaps that is why it remains mysterious and magical in my mind. Few have witnessed the jewel that is the upper Murray. Fewer still have written about it. Even fewer still return time and again to study its course and search out its font. Rivers are like drugs. Once they get in your blood, they rarely leave. They make for good addictions, as long as you don't overdose on them.

Mike Bremers, an avid hiker and paddler who calls Canberra, Australia his home, is one of a small handful of people who have seen the upper Murray up close. In 2013, Mike and two friends backpacked 44 miles from the Murray's source to Tom Groggin Campground. Their goal was to follow the river's course as closely as possible. However, due to rugged terrain on both sides of the Murray near the Limestone Creek confluence, they chose to plot a shorter, more direct route to Poplars Camping Area, the site of their first night camp. Doing so allowed them to bypass the river's course, but it also prevented them from fully experiencing a section of the Murray I intended to trek. Their hike to Poplars Camping Area took 12 hours. It was, according to Mike's written account, a very strenuous affair, as was the rest of their eight-day trek to Tom Groggin Campground.

An expanded version of Mike's trip report was later published in *Wild*, an Australian outdoors magazine. In his article, Mike mentions discovering my Murray River Summit to Source to Sea Blog Archive *after* completing his hike. Making reference to both my blog and the challenging section of the Murray upstream of Tom Groggin Campground, he writes: "(Wellington's) account of this section of the river would not have given much hope of an easy walk." Around the same time as the *Wild* article came out (March 2015), Mike contacted me via email to inform me that he believed I was the first person to descend the Murray from summit to source to sea under my own power. I thought that was a pretty cool distinction. It also helped explain why it was so bloody difficult to find archived accounts of other people's descents when I was planning my 2009–2010 Murray expedition. In this excerpt from his 2013 account, Mike Bremers describes his own difficulty in finding accurate information about the upper Murray River.

> The problem with planning this walk was the lack of information. My First Edition (1979) 1:100,000 Jacobs River map shows a tantalising "Foot Track" that leads from the Cascade Trail down to the confluence of Tin Mine Creek with the Murray River and from there the track closely follows the Murray downstream on the Victorian side to Tom Groggin.
>
> However, we did not know of anyone who had walked this track and it did not appear on later maps. Also, with respect to the Upper Murray, the July 1982 edition of "it" (Canberra Bushwalking Club Newsletter) stated:

"There are few tracks in this area. Fishermen's tracks continue for some way up the river from Buckwong Creek. An old 1909 Mines Department map shows a mining track along the river from Tom Groggin to 'Pendergast's Old Hut' on Limestone Creek, but there is no trace left of it." Furthermore, the only report of anyone travelling along the river from the source to Tom Groggin was a party who walked and liloed in several stages in the 1980s, taking about a week following the river down to Tom Groggin. On their final day, they followed a track along the river from Tom Groggin Top Flat down to Tom Groggin but, since that was 25 years ago, we did not know if the track still existed. For their first two days, downstream of Round Mountain they needed to pull their lilos through the shallows, progress was slow, the water was cold and campsites were difficult to find in the thick scrub. (N.B. *Lilo* is Australian slang for an inflatable pool mattress. This group went on to descend the flatwater portion of the river in a motorized watercraft.)

After our trip, I found that Rod Wellington, a Canadian, had walked and mainly rafted down this section of the river as part of his source to sea expedition from December 2009 to March 2010. His account of this section of the river would not have given much hope of an easy walk. (Rod is the veteran of many expeditions and recently paddled the Missouri–Mississippi river system from source to sea.)

Even later, I read *Crossing the Ditch* by James Castrission, which is his account of paddling across the Tasman Sea with his mate, Justin Jones. Their first expedition in kayaks was with friend Andrew on the Murray from source to sea in late 2001. In it he briefly describes how, walking below Cowombat Flat, they became "surrounded by bluffs in scrub that was near impenetrable" so they surfed their packs down the rapids in freezing water for three days. All their gear got wet including their sleeping bags and matches, so they spent the nights shivering in wet thermals and needed to resort to "spooning" each other to keep warm.

Other Murray paddlers who start their journey from the source tend to walk to and from the source from Dead Horse Gap via the Cascade Trail and the Cowombat Flat Fire Trail, which generally runs parallel to the Murray but about four kilometres (two-and-a-half miles) to the east. There is good reason for this as explained by Josh Jones when he and Ro Privett enquired at Tom Groggin Station during their quest to paddle the entire Murray River.

This is where we sought further advice on the upper Murray between the source and Tom Groggin and learnt that three groups have tried to hike this section and have dismally failed.

Fortunately, when we started our walk we were not aware of these horror stories from the well-known adventurers that had preceded us.

It's worth noting that Mike Bremers has also kayaked the length of the Murray in sections, starting from the Bringenbrong Bridge near the town of Corryong, a common launching site for those paddling the Murray. In December 2017, Mike and three others hiked from the Murray's source to Poplars Camping Area, and then paddled to the Bringenbrong Bridge in inflatable kayaks. Mike and his daughter, Amanda, co-wrote *Murray–Darling Journeys*, a comprehensive book chronicling over 400 self-powered journeys on rivers in the Murray–Darling river basin. The book was published by Vivid Publishing in 2017.

In November 2012, Australian adventurer, Chris Hayward, became the youngest person to solo kayak the Murray. He was 18 years old at the time. Although Chris didn't begin from the source (he put in at the confluence of the Murray and Swampy Plain rivers, approximately 90 river miles downstream from the source), he did manage to paddle all the way to the sea and had a heck of an adventure throughout. Just 13 months later, Chris, hungry for more river-related action, decided to again tackle the Murray's length, this time embarking on a sea to source to summit expedition, something no one had ever attempted. His plan was to trek the final section of river on foot (from Hume Dam to the source, and onward to the summit of Mount Kosciuszko). Needing advice from someone who had been to where he wanted to go, Chris conferred with me about logistics. I provided him with a map showing the walking route I took to bypass the section of river between Cowombat Flat and Poplars Camping Area in 2010. I'm happy to say he followed the route I proposed and successfully reached the source and summit in May 2014. The word *difficult* would not even begin to describe Chris' expedition. He took an already challenging adventure and went firmly against the grain by going *up* the Murray. Where some people see obstacles, others see opportunity. Chris Hayward proudly belongs in the latter category. I have mad respect for that kid.

As impressive as Mike Bremers' and Chris Hayward's accomplishments are, their routes still hadn't closely traced the Murray's course in those mysterious nine miles between Cowombat Flat and Poplars Camping Area. Someone had to tackle that section and properly document their journey. I chose to be that person—a self-appointed guinea pig with a bad habit of wading neck-deep into the unknown.

Below the beautiful waterfall section downstream of the Pilot Creek confluence, I stuck to the river's left descending bank (Victoria side). The bedrock was pockmarked with dips and holes, adding to the challenge of remaining upright while lugging a heavy backpack. Mustard-coloured moss and knee-high bushes of dark green and tan thrived in areas exposed to full sun. Sweat poured from my brow and stung my eyes as I plodded downstream. I took little comfort in the fact that the *real* work was just beginning.

One hundred and fifty yards past the waterfalls, I came across a significant turn in the river's course. The steep, canyon-like terrain doglegged the Murray to the right. Rather than scaling the canyon walls, I opted to get my feet wet. The clear, cool water rose to my groin as I slipped my way over algae-covered rocks. I leaned heavily on my walking staff to keep balanced. Progress was slow and tedious.

Beyond the canyon, the riverbanks flattened and thick foliage lined the water's edge. Fallen trees obstructed passage, their unmovable bulk often spanning the width of the river. I emerged from the stream and moved more efficiently on established brumby trails on the Murray's left side. These trails pushed up and along the sloped bank, riding the gentle contour lines and weaving amidst a plethora of gum trees. Several times, I found myself carefully scrambling over and around rocky outcroppings 100 vertical feet above the river. The passage of animals (likely horses) had reduced the surface of the game trail to gravel, necessitating me to focus hard on my footing. Far below, the Murray roared white through numerous sets of rapids. The sound of rushing water was constant throughout the day. When possible, I dropped down to the river, elbowing my way through the thick scrub and stooping to scoop cupfuls of unfiltered river water to drink. I knew the inherent risks of such an act, and hoped I wouldn't pay dearly for it later.

Progress on the game trails was inconsistent at best. Paths would peter out for no reason, leaving me to bushwhack hundreds of feet before discovering another one. At one point, I spied two brumbies standing calmly in a small clearing beside the river less than 50 feet away. One horse was completely white—an albino brumby, beautifully unique. A four-foot-long brown snake basking on the trail in a slice of sunshine startled me out of a walking daze. Brown snakes (or *browns*, as Australians call them), are notoriously poisonous. After that encounter, I saw snakes *everywhere*. Every curled leaf, every fallen tree limb, every long, slender shadow on the forest floor resembled a snake. I wrestled with my overstimulated imagination as it tricked me time and again into thinking I was surrounded by perilous reptiles. The fear, unfounded or not, never fully subsided. It made me hyperaware and ultra-paranoid—two mentally taxing states that too easily distracted me from the beauty through which I was passing.

After four more hours of strenuous hiking, and only two miles of downstream progress, I stood at the base of a massive rock face that towered nearly 400 feet above the river on the Victoria side. The sight of it was disheartening, demoralizing, dismaying. I seated myself on a smooth river rock and glanced up at the imposing behemoth.

"So, old friend," I said in a weary voice. "We meet again."

Back in April 2010, I'd stumbled up to the same rock face in very much the same state of fatigue. My strategy at that time was to cross the river to the New South Wales side and push up through the thick scrub, working my way downstream along the contour lines high above the river. An hour of toil netted less than a half-mile of progress. The scrub—regrowth from recent forest fires—was nearly impenetrable. At times when a rare opening appeared, I caught glimpses of the imposing rock face as well as a large, treeless meadow where the rock wall ended. The meadow was less than a mile distant, but seemed *ten times* that distance when factoring in the potentially massive effort required to reach it. Exhausted and exasperated, I decided to throw in the towel. At the pace I was moving, it would've taken days to complete the river section and return on foot to my rental car. My food rations wouldn't last that long. Stupidly, I'd only brought three days' worth. What I envisioned as a fairly uncomplicated backcountry hike had become a life-threatening pursuit. I didn't feel like dying at that time—I had others things to do. I recorded a heartbreakingly honest video confession, and then hiked two miles back upstream to Cowombat Flat, where I spent the night. In the morning, I trekked another six miles on Cowombat Flat Track to reach my rental car. The seven unseen river miles between the rock wall and Poplars Camping Area would remain a mystery for another six years.

But now, with much effort and much determination (as well as more food), I had returned to the same spot. This time, there would be no turning back. This time, I would unlock the mysteries of the upper Murray.

With considerable effort, it seemed wholly possible to scale the rock face's western end and emerge atop the wall. Not knowing what the terrain up there was like, nor what the descent to the far-off meadow would encompass, I opted to walk in the river.

Raging water tumbling over an unseen drop soon forced me out of the river and onto the New South Wales bank (river right). I pushed my way through the thick riverside scrub, badly scratching my arms and legs on thorny blackberry vines and the spear-like limbs of young saplings. Game trails of any kind were non-existent. Progress was horribly slow. When the scrub became impassable, I took to the river once more, stumbling downstream like a drunken shore-leave sailor in search of his ship.

I managed only one mile of progress in three hours of arduous hiking, but that minor yield had landed me at the canyon's far end. Large boulders, the products of some ancient rockslide, lay strewn along the riverbed, causing the Murray to drop noisily over a series of rapids. I ditched my backpack at the river's edge and scouted the banks ahead for a suitable camping spot. Minutes later, I happened upon an established brumby trail on the Victoria side. I followed the trail for about 100 yards until it emerged from the forest onto a treeless slope, the same slope I'd seen from a distance six years prior. Etched into the grassy slope was the unbroken continuation of the brumby trail. My eye traced its path for more than a half-mile as it paralleled the river bend and eventually disappeared into a stand of gum trees. Here, the river rounded through the bottom of a deep, V-shaped trough. A dense forest of Dr. Seuss-like gums—their leafy green heads mounted on sinewy bodies of stark-white limbs and trunks—lined the steep slopes on the New South Wales side. Thankfully, the Victoria side was bare. It was the first open area I'd encountered since Cowombat Flat. There would be no bushwhacking here.

Happy with the overdue arrival of some potentially easy hiking ahead, but knackered from the efforts of the day, I decided to make camp at the river's edge. I found several flat, scrub-free areas beneath thick canopies of shade trees. As evidenced by smatterings of horse droppings, brumbies typically retreated from the day's heat in these shaded areas. Curiously, I hadn't seen any resting areas or trails during the half-mile-long rock face section. It led me to speculate that the horses might not migrate past the rock face. Those on the upstream side of the rock face might very well live out their lives without ever going downstream. The same could be said for horses living downstream of the rock face. In any case, I was glad to have the imposing obstacle behind me as I set up my tent next to two large boulders at the river's edge. Here, the Murray tumbled noisily over a three-foot-high drop as the sun-lit rock face loomed in the background. Unknowingly, I disturbed a large ant colony while gathering rocks to anchor the tent's guy-lines. The angry insects streamed out in every direction, many of them carrying maggot-looking larvae in their mandibles. The scene made me cringe and I retreated to an ant-free area upstream to record a video chronicling the day's events. In it, I talked happily about my optimism for the morrow. With the established brumby trail less than 100 feet away, the thought of an easy start to tomorrow's hike helped lift my mood. Hopefully, the trail would continue downstream and my mood would stay buoyed.

Some notes from my journal on this day:

Progress today: about two-and-a-half miles. Saw snake two inches thick in this section. It was grey/brown and was sunning on a rock. It slithered away. First snake on the whole trip. It was a reminder to watch my step in the forest. I'm making noise on the ground with my walking stick in order to alert snakes of my presence.

Series of eight steps (or drops) as the river passes rock face. It was very difficult walking in the river at this point. Tedious.

Cool breeze. Heard what sounded like thunder earlier. Could've been a jet. Blue sky is gone. Now cloudy. Hope it doesn't rain. I am at the bottom of a steep slope and there's a good chance water will pool here. Loud cicada or frog sounds at dusk. Hard to tell because of noisy rapid I'm next to. Not cicadas, but some sort of

> crickets. Saw them at Cowombat Flat. Got within a
> foot of one. The noise was shrill. It hurt my ears. It was
> underground. Small holes in ground where they live.
>   Saw a big brown spider on a rock. Almost put my
> hand on it. Took photos.

Several times throughout the night I woke to claps of thunder and lightning flashes. Rain poured down for what seemed to be hours. The storm raised two valid concerns in my mind as I lay awake in my dry tent. The first was the fact that forest fires in this region of Australia are often the result of lightning strikes. The last thing I needed was to be trapped in a bloody forest fire! Second, this latest deluge of rain—it had rained nine out of 11 days since I arrived in Australia—would surely raise water levels in the river and surrounding creeks. I had waded through waist-high water many times during the first day's trek. If levels increased, walking in the river would become a dangerous pursuit. So far, the bottom of my backpack had escaped any wettings. On this day, though, that might change.

Thankfully, I was greeted with clear skies and warm temperatures the next morning. The foliage, however, remained saturated and I received an unwelcomed wet-down as I pushed up through the thick scrub to reach the brumby trail.

I expected progress along the exposed trail to be quick and unhindered, but given the fact that I was 60 vertical feet above the river with nothing to break a fall, I harboured a numbing fear that I might slip or trip and roll down the treeless slope to the river below. Once this fear took hold, progress slowed. I focused hard on each footfall and moved cautiously along the brumby trail until it re-entered the forest where the river horseshoed to the southwest.

Passage through the forest brought shade and surer footing. The trail remained well-defined as it skirted a steep, treed slope. Far below, the river raged onward, rushing noisily over numerous drops.

A half-mile past the previous open area, I entered another. This one was much flatter. In many spots the grass had been worn away by brumby activity, leaving only patches of dry, dark dirt. According to Trevor Davis, manager at Tom Groggin Station, ranch owners often drove their cattle up into these flats decades ago to graze during the summer months. It's hard to say whether they reached this remote flat, but the area certainly seemed well-suited to that purpose. It would also be an ideal place to set up a temporary structure (tent, tipi, yurt) equipped with solar panels. Admittedly, getting all that stuff in there would be a huge chore. I also noted that this open area could accommodate a helicopter landing during a search and rescue operation. Hopefully, there wouldn't be a need for that.

The unnamed tributary creeks I encountered on river left were dry troughs, each about four feet deep. All of them had vegetation poking up through a carpet of brown gum leaves littered on the creek bed. Copperhead Creek—the most significant drainage I encountered, located just prior to the second open area—had a trickle of flow in it.

I entered a third open area about three-quarters of a mile past the second one. Passage through the forest between these open areas was swift and straightforward and I was happy about the headway being made. This area, like the others, had plenty of evidence of brumby activity. Sun-bleached horse bones (or perhaps cattle bones) lay scattered about. A small brook, dry on this day, drains the area during seasonal rains.

During my brief exploration of this third open area, a storm moved through the river valley. Thunder boomed and lightning flashed as I recorded a video describing my findings. I put away the camera and donned my Gore-Tex jacket as rain began to fall. Suddenly, the air temperature dropped about 15 degrees and a barrage of grape-sized hail poured down. (It was certainly the first time I'd been hailed on in Australia—at the end of *January*, no less!) The hail storm lasted about three minutes before switching back to rain. It had now rained 10 out of 12 days since I arrived in Australia.

Beyond the third open area, the brumby trail traversed high along a steep and densely forested slope before it disappeared completely. The ease of the morning's trek was replaced with arduous toil. Bushwhacking became the order of the afternoon. I moved prudently from tree to tree, gripping them tightly as I slowly made my way along the steep slope. Two hundred vertical feet below, the Murray raced through the bottom of a V-shaped valley. The river deepened by the minute as rain continued to fall.

Before breaking camp that morning, I'd chosen not to carry water in my backpack. I wanted to keep weight to a minimum. Like the day before, I planned to drink straight from the river when access allowed. However, due to the rugged terrain, I hadn't been able to access the river for almost six hours. My urine, when it flowed, was dark yellow. Dehydration was becoming a concern. I resorted to licking rain from the waxy surface of leaves and funneling the runoff from the sleeves of my Gore-Tex jacket into my waiting mouth.

At 3:30pm, after six-and-a-half hours of hiking and about two miles of progress, I stopped to rest and reassess my situation. I recorded a video while sitting in the teaming rain. Accessing water and finding a flat place to camp were the main topics in the video. What I failed to mention, however, was my growing concern surrounding the inability to pinpoint my location. Without the aid of a GPS, it was impossible to know exactly where I was. I'd given up counting creek draws and matching them to my topographic map, mainly because most of the creeks weren't on the map. I didn't feel lost, but I also didn't know where I was. That last fact was indeed troublesome, especially when factoring in the importance of knowing the location of Poplars Camping Area—my exit point on this trek. At my current pace, I would likely arrive at Poplars the following day. But if I wasn't aware of my location as I neared Poplars, I might inadvertently walk right past it, especially if I was on the New South Wales side of the river (the opposite side from Poplars). I made a promise to myself that from here on out, I would cross the river only when necessary. If I stuck to the Victoria side, I would surely stumble across Poplars at some point—it was simply a matter of time. In the meantime, I rested and tried in earnest to calm my worried mind.

The warm rain fell like water from a thousand faucets—solid columns of liquid silver streaming down from an unseen source. No two streams touched in the windless afternoon. The rain simply fell silently until it splashed upon foliage, upon rock, upon water, upon wood, upon mud, upon me. The lush forest received the wet kiss and drank it deep, deep into a fertile consciousness stripped clean of labels, deep into a place undeveloped by human conception, deep into a oneness that cradled my loneliness like an unrequited lover cradling hope. Beyond dawn lies light. Beyond dusk lies less light, but light nonetheless.

I sat unmoving at the gnarled base of an immature oak and watched the rain run glistening down its rough bark—tiny rivulets cascading over a vertical landscape, each depression a wooden valley filled with a forest of moss and clinging mites. Upon the plateaued precipices clung spiders and beetles and ants of all sizes. They eyed me safely from a distance, a wary distance given to those who entered their home unannounced. They spied me a thousand times over as a million of me stared back. It was a numbers game, a game I'd never win.

> *I was not their Noah.*
> *Nor was this their ark.*
> *Nor were they the pairs that spread*
> *their seeds into the dark.*
> *No mission lay at hand for them.*
> *No plan they had for me.*
> *And yet this flood that now besets us*
> *will somehow set us free.*

Leave it to dry Australia to deluge me with surprises. This was my third visit to the continent, and this was definitely the wettest of the three. The rain began just hours after leaving Sydney and stayed with me for 10 of the first 12 days. Each downpour dampened the mood of the trip. Each soggy weather forecast seemed like a giant middle finger thrust in my direction. Australia always had an or-

nery knack of doling out challenges. I'd overcome all the challenges
that came before, but this time things were different.

Even the mighty stumble.
Even the mighty fall.
Even the mighty, each hard of hearing,
must heed resignation's great call.

Before me lies a deep depression, an ancient scar upon an ancient
landscape. It is V-shaped, its steep sides lined with thick forest and
thicker mystery. At its bottom runs an infant river, jovial and unbridled. This river, named Murray, descends from meadows and
mountains and alpine sublime. Its font lies in a place treaded by
few, carpeted green with grasses and regally rimmed with white-
barked gum trees. A short metal pipe, driven into the earth to mark
the river's source, is the only evidence that a human has been here,
evidence that someone else has sought this sacred treasure. Beside
the pipe, cool, clear water emerges from the landscape, beginning a
1578-mile descent to the sea. This stream will cascade over waterfalls and squeeze between rock walls. It will pool and pass its time
until it resumes its journey. Its flow will increase as the rain lingers
on, drenching the steep valley slopes with turbid runoff.

This river lies where life begins,
the life beneath the funnel.
But to reach this life and prosper wise,
one must traverse a darkened tunnel.

In these hills roam *brumbies*, wild horses who know not the meaning of fences or saddles or iron shoes. These elusive beasts feast on
verdant flats and quench their thirst with river water. They spend
years running and grazing and breeding on the same familiar acreage. Aside from sickness and an occasionally fatal snake bite, their
existence is seemingly stress-free. Time, it appears, is their only
predator.

Their coats and colours vary.
Their bodies, angular and lean.
Their paths are etched into the earth,
but they are rarely seen.

In order to walk through this hilly land of brumbies, one must think like a horse. Here, there are no trails forged by humans. Here, the forest, and all of its riotous vegetation, forms a dense maze through which creatures of simple thought pass. Here, a human must quiet his frenetic mind and follow leads left by animals who chose efficient passage, their course based not on travelling the shortest distance between points, but instead a path whose obstacles are cleverly acknowledged and avoided. Fallen trees are skirted rather than straddled, as are boulders and rocky outcroppings. One must traverse the contour lines rather than climb the slopes. One comes to realize that horses, like rivers, find their way with little effort and little fear. In short, they walk the path of common sense.

Three more hours of painstakingly brutal bushwhacking brought me to a point of desperation. I needed water. Nine-and-a-half hours without had no doubt done some unseen damage, not only to my physical state but my mental state as well. I hadn't applied much common sense when deciding *not* to carry water earlier that day, but I also had no idea then that accessing the river would be nearly impossible without a major effort. And so, a major effort was enacted.

I carefully picked my way down the impossibly steep slope, down through the saturated foliage, down past the faint remnants of old brumby trails, down past stands of charred gums and eucalyptus trees, down, down, down to the river below. Finally, I popped out of the wet scrub and stood slack-jawed at the absurdity of what lay before me: a large, flat bed of gravel and sand. Surely, this was the only sandbar for miles! Surely, this was the only *flat* spot for miles! "What are the chances of finding this?!" I shouted as I dropped my pack. I smiled and moved quickly to the river's edge. Without hesitation, I cupped my hands and drank from its clear, cool flow.

Rain hammered my tent all night. During a pee break in the wee morning hours, I sprinted across the sand and gravel to check the level of the river. It had crept up noticeably, but was still more than 25 horizontal feet from my tent. I planned for an early departure and hoped the Murray wouldn't swell to my doorstep before I left.

The morning brought clouds, but thankfully no rain. The rejuvenated river, swollen to eight feet in width, sped wildly white between rocky banks just spitting distance from my tent. For now, I'd eluded the coming flood.

A quick scout of the river downstream revealed what I half-expected to see: rocky terrain and dense scrub along both banks. The Murray here was pinched into a tight valley. Traversing it anywhere near the river would require more effort than I was willing to expend. The alternative was a familiar one: ascend the steep slope and continue bushwhacking downstream. The plan was to stay on the Victoria side, as I'd done the entire day previous. Doing so meant that I would encounter Limestone Creek about two miles downstream from where I camped. Limestone Creek's outflow effectively doubles the volume of the Murray and would be the largest tributary I'd encounter. The Murray/Limestone Creek confluence was one-and-a-half miles upstream from Poplars Camping Area. Like the confluence, Poplars was on the Victoria side (river left). If the day progressed well, there was a good chance of arriving at Poplars by nightfall.

My biggest concern, of course, was missing the Limestone Creek confluence if the landscape forced me to the New South Wales side of the river. Although it seemed unlikely that I might somehow miss such an important confluence, the denseness of the forest, and especially the riverside scrub, made such an oversight possible. An even bigger concern was the possibility of missing the entrance to Poplars Camping Area. Having a GPS would've eliminated the stressful guesswork. Many times throughout the day, I cursed my bad luck at having lost my GPS before leaving Canada.

Bushwhacking was a painfully tedious affair, as it had been during the previous two days. The brumby trails had long died out, leaving me to fully adopt a horse's mindset and stick to one contour line running parallel to, and high above, the river. I side-stepped fallen trees and clambered my way up, down, and around rocky outcroppings.

When, after two-and-a-half hours of toil, no sign of Lime-stone Creek became evident, I started to wonder if I had somehow passed it the previous day. So began the evil second-guessing that begot the unshakable fear of not knowing where I was. I can't adequately put into words the feeling of standing alone in a veritable jungle somewhere in the wilds of alpine Australia and not being able to match the surrounding landscape with what appeared on my topographic map. I would've had better luck hurling a dart at the same map to determine my location. As luck would have it, I was completely out of darts.

I never learned how to use a map and compass. I never saw a need to learn. I can't tell my location based on constellations, mostly because my night vision is so poor I can rarely see stars anyway. Buying a GPS was probably one of the best gear purchases I ever made. Knowing where I was at any given moment had given me reassurance to trek into some very remote areas of North America and Australia. But when my GPS went missing just days before departing for Australia, I highly questioned whether I could pull off this backpacking trip without it.

It's pretty much impossible to get lost on a river journey. As long as you stay within sight of the river, and know approximately how far you've ventured upstream or down, you'll likely have a good idea of your present position. If you proceed downstream, you'll eventually end up running into a major tributary or maybe a road system. Referencing those things to what's on a map should be something even the daftest adventurer could do. And if you become *completely* bewildered, you can always go back the way you came.

If I'm able to follow my own bloody suggestions, why then did I harbour such a gripping fear of not knowing my location? How did I allow such a fear to manifest and mature into an injurious disease that kept me second-guessing myself at every bend in the river? As if the physical stress wasn't hard enough to deal with, I now had an overbearing mental load to carry. Unfortunately, there was no one around to help bear the burden, no one to point fingers in the right direction, no one to offer practical suggestions. There was only me—the man who'd come to this country to kill himself. I was down under with a death wish. Was this dangerous foray into the bush in line with how a suicidal person engages in risky behaviour? Was I hoping to die out here, alone and depressed? Had I pushed the world away for the final time? Was I beyond the tipping point? Was I somehow already dead?

The fact that I felt an indescribable fear of not knowing where I was, coupled with a longing to eradicate that fear by finding Limestone Creek and, further on, Poplars Camping Area, told me I wasn't dead, nor numb, nor dumb, nor desperate. I simply hadn't walked far enough. I simply hadn't reached my destination. I hadn't accomplished what I went there to do.

The sound of rushing water filtered its way through the thick forest and drummed its lyric-less song upon my sweaty ears. A break in the trees revealed a deep, sloping depression far off to my right. It was a drainage, but which one? I'd been adamant about keeping the river to my right as I skirted along the steep slope high above the Murray. The terrain had dictated that I keep to the Victoria side. The idea of crossing the river had never crossed my mind. But now there were two flows, two impatient toddlers hurtling themselves down this ancient landscape. Their insistent chatter seemed of equal volume. Somewhere in the green depths below, their paths would cross. One would yield. One would not. Somewhere down there a merger was ongoing. It was my job to find it, photograph it, and move beyond it.

I slowly picked my way down the steep, forested slope until a rushing creek came into view. As I parted the last of the thick scrub that lined the creek banks, I felt a waft of cool, moist air on my face and stood next to what I hoped was Limestone Creek. I stooped and drank from its shallow flow. It was cold, much colder than the Murray. Looking downstream, I could see the banks were choked with dense scrub. It was time to get my feet wet.

Using the tall grass and shrubs along the creek's right bank to steady myself, I tottered downstream for about 100 yards before encountering a large, rocky outcropping that doglegged the creek to the left. The change of direction, as well as a slight drop in elevation, shot the creek across a smoothly sloped rock shelf and over a 12-foot drop. White water splashed noisily off a jumble of logs lodged at the base of the drop. Over millennia, the creek had carved a tight sluice into the rocky outcropping. This sluice resembled a tiny canyon with smooth, vertical walls. Beyond the logjam, the flow tumbled over a four-foot drop before resting briefly in a small pool. Unseen below the pool was a sizeable waterfall. I guessed its height to be 30 feet. Owing to the rugged terrain, I wasn't able to access what must've been an impressive cascade. Its dominating presence would only be heard on this day.

I took an hour atop the outcropping to air out some damp gear beneath the cloudless blue sky. The sun felt good. I snapped dozens of photos from this precipice and recorded a few videos. I even smiled a little. Unbeknownst to me, moisture had infiltrated the lens of my GoPro camera, rendering every photo from this day blurry and distorted. Videos were equally affected, with the audio for each recording stripped entirely.

From atop the rocky outcropping, I could see the Murray's course 60 feet below, speeding onward from my right to meet the outflow of Limestone Creek. When my gear was dry, I climbed down to this confluence of creek and river.

On this day, there was a small island overgrown with trees and bushes just a few feet downstream from where the two waterways merged. Limestone Creek's flow was parted by the island, forming a side channel that ran along the left side of the island and merged with the Murray at the island's downstream point. The creek's other channel flowed shallow across a rocky bed, joining the Murray on the upstream side of the island. With the additional flow from Limestone Creek, the river's width increased from eight to 12 feet. Even with the recent rain, each waterway at the conflu-ence was shallow, clear, cool, and eager. Clumps of knee-high grass grew here. One clump housed a large spider and hundreds of her tiny offspring. The scene was cringeworthy and I wondered how many critters, poisonous or not, I'd failed to notice while trekking along the river. It is thoughts like these that keep people glued to television sets in comfortable living rooms, unwilling to set forth on an adventure.

With only one-and-a-half river miles between Limestone Creek and Poplars Camping Area, I was certain I'd finish at Poplars on this day. The thick riverside scrub and rocky terrain, however, kept me completely in the river after the confluence. Progress was slow and tedious. I used my walking staff to steady myself as I slid over algae-covered rocks and cautiously gripped grass along the right bank, hoping not to find more spiders. Unfortunately, I found *doz-ens* more!

Despite the unsettling abundance of creepy crawlies, unseen or not, views of the landscape definitely didn't disappoint. After an hour of light rain, the clouds cleared, bathing the river valley with brilliant sunlight. The canopies of towering gum trees glit-tered gloriously green against a stunning backdrop of blue sky and candy-floss clouds. Even the rocky banks, partially cloaked in a carpet of mustard-coloured moss, were curiously contrasted taupe and shadow black as the tea-tinted Murray swept past.

When four hours of fatiguing river walking failed to bring me to the doorstep of Poplars Camping Area, I began to worry. *A lot.* The familiar fear that gripped me the previous day was back with a vengeance. I simply didn't know where I was! Surely, I'd passed Limestone Creek earlier in the day. Surely, I'd made more than a mile of progress since leaving what I believed to be Limestone Creek. *Surely,* I thought to myself, *I must be very close to Poplars.* But I couldn't be sure. I couldn't believe. Without some definite proof, I couldn't be certain of anything when it came to verifying my location. A question ran through my mind as the panic set in.

Did I somehow miss the entrance to Poplars? I fucking hope not! That would be a seriously grave error if I did! FUCK!!

Not knowing. Not believing. Not trusting. Somehow, I had to get my mind around the fact that I'd been unable to cover one mile in four hours, or even *nine miles* in *three days!* Somehow, I had to convince myself I wasn't going to die in this alpine jungle, or go *insane* trying to exit it. I wracked my brain for any key signs that would indicate where I was, perhaps a landmark I could match to my topo map. Did I round any significant bends in the river after Limestone Creek? I couldn't remember any. Did I see any tributaries? Just one: Greenwood Creek. But I didn't know for sure whether it *was* Greenwood Creek. All I knew for sure was that I'd be spending another night on the river, and maybe another *day* on the river. *At some point,* I thought to myself, *this* has *to end! I just hope it doesn't end in a rescue.*

I didn't like hearing myself say the "R" word. In my mind, *rescue* meant defeat. It meant failure. It meant outside assistance. It meant an end to self-sufficiency. It meant *giving up.*

My only tie to the outside world was a SPOT tracker, a small handheld device that connects to a satellite and allows others to see your location via a link to an online Google map. When the device is activated, it sends out a signal in timed increments (usually every 10 minutes) and places a waypoint on the aforementioned map and navigational coordinates in a sidebar. Those following an adventure online can view and track an adventurer's progress. Used in this fashion, a SPOT tracker becomes an entertainment device. Despite the inherent entertainment value, the device is marketed primarily as a safety beacon. Each SPOT device comes equipped with a 911 button. When pushed, an emergency beacon is sent to a central monitoring system which then relays the information to local authorities in the area where the beacon originated. A search and rescue operation is then commenced.

Although I'd been carrying a SPOT tracker each day during the upper Murray River hike, I hadn't set up an interactive Google map page through the SPOT website. Outside of my immediate family, no one knew I was in Australia. I hadn't broadcasted the fact on Facebook or any other social media. I hadn't approached any radio, television, or print media—a stark contrast to my 2012–2013 Missouri–Mississippi river system kayaking descent, during which I gave 35 media interviews and shared the adventure on numerous social media platforms. This time, my silence was intentional for one simple reason: if I failed to complete the Darling–Murray river system expedition—a concern I'd held from the outset of the planning stage—my subsequent embarrassment would be lessened if fewer people knew about it. Online ridicule, especially on social media platforms (YouTube and Facebook comments sections are the worst places for this) could be virtually eliminated if no one knew where I was and what I was doing, or *not* doing. For a person who has long-suffered from low self-esteem issues and a debilitating fear of judgement, the wide-open, overopinionated peanut gallery that is social media inundates me with unspoken anxiety. For these reasons, I chose to fly under the radar.

It pains me to no end to admit that this trip had been underwritten with failure from well before its beginning. Did I unintentionally infuse the expedition with a toxic stream of self-doubt and negativity? Did that same toxic stream kill the dream before it was realized? Suicide, my ultimate goal for this trip, was never about negativity. It was about going out on top. It was about dying with a gold medal around my neck. It was about dying *my* way. If no one knew about my suicide plan, no one could stop me. Secrecy kept me strong. It was how I remained in control of all aspects of the expedition. It was how I retained a sense of self-control and self-worth. Pressing the 911 button on my SPOT device would eradicate all the self-confidence I'd mustered over the past few days. Giving up was the absolute worst case scenario. Media would no doubt eat up the story of a foolish Canadian who stubbornly entered the Australian wilds without a GPS. Media would also make sure the story came with a lesson: "Stay glued to your television in the comfort of your living room. Forget adventure! It'll only make you the next online laughing stock."

Life was much simpler and less stressful when I didn't know everyone's business. I'm all for people having a voice, but I prefer the pre-social media era when I didn't have access to everyone's opinions. For me, social media has been a great tool for connecting with people who share similar interests and for sharing relevant information. I use Facebook to promote my books and my publishing company (Crow Books). I haven't the time nor interest in creating content for, and maintaining, Twitter, Instagram, and YouTube accounts. I already spend far too much time scroll-scroll-scrolling on Facebook, usually coming away with very little pertinent information. In many ways, it's a waste of time. On the other hand, having access to aspects of people's lives in a seemingly non-invasive manner gives me a sense of belonging.

I spend most of my time alone. I rarely talk to others, online or face to face. I *choose* to limit my human interaction. I'm shy. I live with a very real fear of being judged by others. The choice to be alone is just that: a *choice*. Choosing to be alone is one of the ways I simplify my life. The downside is, I miss out on many of the benefits of interacting with other humans. I limit the actions and emotions—pain, joy, sorrow, struggle, failure, success, love, anger, and fear—that help define the term *human experience*. When I compare myself to others, I find I tend to struggle far more, but experience love far less. Of course, I realize it's detrimental to compare myself to others. It's often said that comparison is the thief of joy. Quantifiable perspective, I guess, comes with a quantifiable cost.

In many ways, I view life as wholly unfair. I feel I should be exempt from experiencing life in such a blunted manner. Do I feel entitled to a happy, pain-free life? Absolutely. Do I believe such a life should come with little risk and little disappointment? Absolutely. Do I believe such a life should be handed to me on a silver platter? Yes, and no.

As a white male living in the western world, I have, in many ways, already won the lottery. Western society, through its centuries-old, fucked-up process of distorting human equality through the warped lens of religion, has determined that the white male is the pinnacle of human existence. Of course, that line of thinking is a farce. But the farce has been acknowledged and adopted, but not always accepted, by just about anyone who has stood on the surface of the earth in modern times. So, if I have already achieved some level of hierarchy among humans by virtue of being born in the right place at the right time, why then am I such a miserable fuck? The answer to that question must have something to do with my distorted take on *entitlement.*

As I mentioned earlier in this book, expectation and disappointment rule my world. They are two of the cruelest reality checks I know. If I *expect* entitlement, I'll always end up disappointed. And yet, through habitual behaviour that is probably perpetrated by spending far too much time alone—I'm addicted to the concept of self-pity—I've somehow normalized the self-sustaining belief that I am privileged to a pain-free life. Of course, I know this isn't true. I'm not entitled to a pain-free life any more than anyone else. The confusing and very damaging part of all this begins when I *forget* that I'm not entitled. Unfortunately, I forget that fact *a lot.* And on a larger scale, I'm not alone in this detrimental forgetfulness.

Entitlement, as many of you have seen and read, is a hot topic on social media. An older generation of online trolls loves to spout off about entitlement and how they believe it applies to one of their favourite targets: *millennials.*

The term *millennials* refers to an age demographic. As with the age demographics that predate millennials (Generation Y, Generation X, Baby boomers), no specific timeframe exists to help define the generation. Although the birth years of millennials often overlap with Generation Y birth years, 1984 to 2004 is generally accepted as a loose template to work with. A millennial can perhaps be best defined as "a person reaching young adulthood in the early 21st century."

I extracted the following excerpts from the sea of text that occupies the "Millennial" page on wikipedia.com. I chose these two excerpts because they contrast nicely and help broaden the definition of the term. I also really like the "16% more narcissism" statistic.

A 2016 study by SYZYGY, a digital service agency, found millennials in the U.S. continue to exhibit elevated scores on the Narcissistic Personality Inventory as they age, finding millennials exhibited 16% more narcissism than older adults, with males scoring higher on average than females. The study examined two types of narcissism: grandiose narcissism, described as "the narcissism of extroverts, characterized by attention-seeking behaviour, power, and dominance," and vulnerable narcissism, described as "the narcissism of introverts, characterized by an acute sense of self-entitlement and defensiveness."

In his book, *Fast Future*, author David Burstein describes millennials' approach to social change as "pragmatic idealism" with a deep desire to make the world a better place, combined with an understanding that doing so requires building new institutions while working inside and outside existing institutions.

The online trolls to whom I referred earlier often berate younger social media users based on the comments they've shared. Based on their disrespectful replies, the trolls tend to believe that millennials are spoiled brats living off their parents', or society's, bosom, thereby enjoying the benefits of a struggle-free life. This lifestyle, of course, contrasts deeply with their own, which, based on what the trolls choose to divulge about themselves, often involves having worked several decades in a series of shitty jobs they hated while steadfastly displaying to the world a stiff upper lip. "Suck it up, buttercup!" would be a politer version of the typically contemptuous comments put forth online by these callous trolls.

The trolls' derision, however, doesn't stop at millennials. Unfortunately, they've found a wider target for their unending hate, embracing and overusing a derogatory term that has surfaced in this unapologetic age of President Trump. The term, of course, is *snow-*

flake, and, as you'll read below, its etymology and usage has been conveniently corrupted to suit the trolls' self-serving intentions.

Online, the term is used by trolls and non-trolls alike. It's often possible to find lengthy threads in Facebook comments where, based on their *entitlement* to do so, trolls and non-trolls unrelentingly scorn the beliefs of others they have willingly labelled *snowflakes*. According to the trolls' unofficial definition, snowflakes often embody left-leaning political beliefs, are proud supporters of human rights, are more prone to taking offense and less resilient than previous generations, are too emotionally vulnerable to cope with views that challenge their own, and possess some general love and empathy for the natural world around them. What the trolls may not know, however, is that the term's history is deeply rooted in American racism as well as the anarchic rhetoric of a fictional literary character who intentioned to strip away his followers' sense of uniqueness.

Below are excerpts from a story at gq.com entitled *Why Trump Supporters Love Calling People Snowflakes* by Dana Schwartz. The story pointedly spins the derisive term back on the pronouncedly rightist group that profusely uses it, all the while encouraging the demographic at which the term is aimed to claim the word for their own. (The story was published on February 1, 2017.)

> The concept of a "snowflake" as a derisive term first entered the cultural zeitgeist in *Fight Club* by Chuck Palahniuk. (The irony of staunch conservatives using language popularized by an openly gay author who writes shock-value stories about debauched sexual experiences is overlooked.) "You are not special," Palahniuk's protagonist, Tyler Durden, told his herd of anarchists. "You're not a beautiful and unique snowflake. You're the same decaying organic matter as everything else."
>
> The term "snowflake" did have another slang application: according to Merriam–Webster, "In Missouri in the early 1860s, a 'snowflake' was a person who was

opposed to the abolition of slavery—the implication of the name being that such people valued white people over black people." The meaning has more or less swapped. Nowadays, someone with a Confederate flag in their profile picture is more likely to be the one calling someone else a snowflake.

If branding the political opposition with a nickname is a longstanding tradition, it's also one that almost inevitably backfires. A group united by an offensive label is still united: it's only a matter of flipping the name into a self-identifier. "Tory" and "Whig" are both political party names that rose out of insults. The "Sans-culottes" during the French revolution likewise re-appropriated an insult about their lack of britches into a point of anti-elitist pride. From queers to suffragettes to impressionist painters, terms meant to deride become a catchy point of pride, a snarky acknowledgement of appealing underdog status that galvanizes membership. People who thought Hillary Clinton was referring to them as "deplorable" put it in their Twitter names; women who related when Trump called Clinton a "nasty woman" responded by emblazoning the phrase on their t-shirts. The only way to fight back against an insult that doesn't mean anything is to reclaim it, to diminish its power by making that identity a point of pride. This is the life cycle of all identity insults, and "snowflake" is already reaching the end of that cycle.

There's a slogan among Trump protesters that's become increasingly common on protest signs. "Damn right we're snowflakes," the signs read. "And winter is coming."

Of course, the faceless nature of the Internet lends itself well to this anonymous derision. Rarely are the trolls paraded through the streets for the crimes they've committed. And make no mistake— these are very *real* hate crimes perpetrated on individuals who deserve no less than a lot of respect and support for voicing their opinion in a public forum. Doling heartless derision on a stranger for simply stating their opinion is simply intolerable. Having said that, try sitting through a House of Commons session at the Canadian parliament. It's thoroughly embarrassing to watch party representatives—put there via a corrupt system of *public voting*—berate each other, *and* get paid to do so! In many ways, I'm convinced that western civilization is *completely fucked.* It boggles my mind that I somehow generate enough optimism to move forward day to day. Perhaps my life-long choice to abstain from the voting process has something to do with it. I refuse to cast a vote for corruptness. And before you deride me for having a say in the matter—that whole "Don't complain if you didn't vote" bullshit—I'll take this opportunity to extend to you a not-so-subtle FUCK YOU! This is my book and I'll complain about whatever I want! If you want to complain, go write your own fucking book!

It was thoughts like these that populated (and polluted) my head as I lay awake in my tent thinking long about society's many shortcomings (as well as my own) and how they applied to hiking the upper Murray River. The possibility of giving up and sending out a rescue beacon would undoubtedly lead to an unwanted, and unwarranted, backlash. I didn't need the judgement. I didn't need the ridicule. I didn't need the stress. I didn't need the fear. I didn't need the paranoia. I didn't need fame and I didn't need fanfare. Those things, I hoped, would arrive post-suicide. *Let the media spectacle unfold later,* I said to myself. For now, the only thing I needed was to finish the damn hike without incident. For now, I simply needed peace.

  That night, I went to bed afraid of myself and afraid of the world. I was afraid of what the following day would bring. I was afraid of the *truth.*

I woke predawn to the sound of heavy rain hammering my tent. It had been raining non-stop for almost 12 hours. I unzipped the tent door and peered into the gloom. The river had risen noticeably. In less than two hours, I guessed, the sandbar on which I was camped would be submerged. I had to move quick.

Before tearing down the tent, I recorded a video. In it, I voiced my concerns about possibly requesting a rescue. My mood was sombre. I had the look of a beaten man. There remained, however, a hint of optimism in my voice, a dangling hope that I might somehow get out of this incessant quandary alive.

What follows is a transcription of that video, recorded January 31, 2016.

> Well, good morning. This is the morning of Day 4 from Cowombat Flat to Poplars Camping Area. This is taking a lot longer than I thought. I thought for sure I could do this in three days. I'm concerned at this point, because I'm not overly sure where I am. I'm not sure the big creek I crossed yesterday was, in fact, Limestone Creek. I trekked for several hours past that confluence—until about 6:30…so, maybe for four or five hours…five, anyways—to get to this point (Day 3 camp). I passed another large creek to the left which I thought was just a backwater or swamp or something, but it was actually flowing. It was a very lazy little creek. I say *little creek*, but it was three-quarters the width of the river. It was obviously draining something. That may have been Greenwood Creek.
>
> So, it started to rain well before I got here. It rained from about 5:30pm until at least 5:00 in the morning. It rained *all night*. *Hard*. The river has come up about 10 vertical inches. Now, I'm on a little sandbar here which is flooded at certain times of the year, and the water has come up *noticeably* overnight…which gives reason for concern because the river is deeper now—which makes it harder to walk in and harder to cross. It's flowing faster now. It's going to make the whole river walking experience much more difficult. Thankfully, this area, and the area I had been walking through for several hours, is mostly flat. Some areas have rocky outcroppings—not too much on river right, but on river left there have been more ups and downs and some

spots where I had to go around the outcroppings because they pinched the river and created a pool that I
couldn't get through.

It's really hard walking in the river with a pack
on because the rocks are really slippery. Every footfall
needs to be specifically placed before you can move on.
It's just tedious. It's very, very slow going. And then
there's always the possibility that I could fall and in-
jure myself...hit my head on a rock...knock myself out
and drown. And definitely the possibility of falling or
sliding into a pool with a full pack on and just *sink*,
basically. It's way different than walking the river with a
life jacket...or a boat where I could stable myself, and
just get in the boat if there was a pool—paddle across
a pool and then out of the boat and into a shallow area
where I could just be pulling the boat. Walking in the
river is completely different. At least then, I would have
a life jacket on and I would float, or even if I slipped I
would still be able to float. This is not the case with a
pack on. This has created a very dangerous situation on
top of a dangerous situation, and I'm getting very concerned about timing for this. This is taking a *long* time.
There's a concern in my head that I've gone past Poplars...which I've been very conscientious about staying
in view of that side of the river—which would be river
left, the Victoria side—in case there is an opening that
I would see. I've been to Poplars twice and there is a
definite opening there. So it should be visible if I'm in
the river, or even beside the river—on the right side—
where I can see the left side and be looking for an opening. Like yesterday...a hundred times looking over for
an opening and not seeing anything.

Now, when I got here I decided to power up my
phone to see, if just by chance, I could get a signal. It
gave me a GPS location on a Google map which I'm
very surprised it did, but it put me in an area just past
Greenwood Creek—which may have been that creek I
saw—and it showed that I was on a large bend, or just

approaching a bend, a big kink in the river downstream of Limestone Creek and close to a road network. Now, I compared that road network—it was highlighted, I couldn't zoom in very far…the phone was searching for a signal…it was showing no service, so it was very sketchy zooming in and out with the map—but I was able to get a road system highlighted on a satellite map and see that it matched, to some degree anyway, the road system that should be there…which would be McCarthys Track, Limestone Creek Track, and Macs Creek Track. Now, I zoomed out and managed to get a bigger screen and it showed the area south of here was definitely Limestone Creek. So, if that's accurate, and I'm hoping it is, I'm not too far, maybe one mile, maybe one-and-a-half miles from Poplars Camping Area. So, I have to be very diligent that I do not pass that opening if I see it today.

I'm gonna have a go at it for another eight hours today. It's getting down to critical time. I have two days of food left. I should've been done this by now. I still have 17 miles of walking to do when I get to Poplars Camping Area—to get back to my rental car. I've flirted with the idea—with all the dialogue, all the imagined scenarios that go with it—of firing up my SPOT tracker and pressing 911 for a search and rescue.

Now, I'd really hate to do that, especially if I end up being rescued *300 yards* from Poplars Camping Area, but it's getting to the point where there has to be a turning point, where I have to be like, "Okay, you've got X amount of food left, you haven't reached your destination yet, you don't know where you are, and you don't know how long it's going to take to get to that exit point." And there's one exit point past that, which is Kings Plain—there's a little camping area there as well. There's a very steep 4x4 track to get down to it, but it's certainly walkable. But it wouldn't take me back towards where the car is. It would be better to go to Tom Groggin camping area at that point and see if I could get a ride to Thredbo, stock up on food again, and then walk 30 miles back to Cowombat Flat, and then onward another six miles back to the car. That would just be crazy! I would do it, but, ugh…it would get me out anyway. You know, Kings Plain? Walking? That's still a long way. That's at least, maybe, two days—probably two full days from here, *at least*! I can't even imagine it. I walked it pulling the boat (in 2010). I pulled the boat most of the day. It took *all* day to get just past Kings Plain. Crazy.

So, I don't like to think about it too much, but I *am* thinking about it too much. There is a possibility that, after today, if I do not get to Poplars Camping Area… I'm basically gonna have one more day…so, today's Sunday…it's 7:27am…I would say that if I haven't reached Poplars by tomorrow night, that may end up being the turning point where I would spend the night and then the next morning I would reassess the situation and seriously think about trying to get a search and rescue. (In the video, I have a look of exasperation.) Hopefully all that would be avoided if I reach Poplars Camping Area today.

I'm worried. Very concerned. I've been through some nasty stuff. *Nasty* stuff! This is definitely the hardest hike I've ever be on. I've been on longer hikes, but nothing of this difficulty. This is a pretty extreme hike. I can see why very few people, if anybody, have followed the path I took so close to the river, or *in* the river. This is not recommended. This is some hardcore stuff. This is just…I…I can't explain it. I'm lost for words. (Look of exasperation.) I'm gonna sign off and get back to moving downriver. Ciao for now.

In May 2015, Laura Kennington, a British adventurer and speaker, began a personal quest to become the first female, and fourth person ever, to kayak the Volga River from source to sea. (Located in Russia, the Volga, at 2300 miles in length, is the longest river and longest *river system* in Europe.) Before she began, Laura courted numerous sponsors and promoted her upcoming journey on social media. She did what many modern adventurers and explorers do; she sent out press releases to numerous media sources and happily responded to interview requests. The subsequent media attention, both online and off, expanded an already sizeable audience eager to follow her journey. Unfortunately, that same attention also created numerous unforeseen problems, some of which led Laura to prematurely end her expedition after only six weeks.

The events that influenced Laura's decision stemmed from three distinct situations: 1) the expedition's widespread exposure via social media platforms as well as conventional media sources (Russian media embraced Laura's story), 2) the unrestricted sharing of her website address and SPOT tracker webpage link, and 3) her belief that her personal safety was at risk while on the Volga River.

According to a post on Laura's Medium blog dated June 27, 2015 (published post-expedition), an estimated audience of 20,000 had been reached during the first few days of the expedition, with many of those numbers in Russia. Even before embarking from the Volga's source, Laura had been inundated with more than 1000 messages. Most of the messages were offers of hospitality and assistance. Others, as she stated in the same blog post, were not so cordial. "A significant amount of the messages (both sent directly to me and those we happened to see on Russian sites) expressed very sinister intent and the attention didn't ever back off. It all added up to a level of risk and vulnerability that is too high to justify and we have been unable to mitigate it sufficiently."

In a blog post dated June 8, 2015 (published post-expedition), Laura described a late night encounter with a group of 10 people who arrived unannounced at her riverside campsite. She believed they found her location via her SPOT tracker webpage. Bearing gifts of food and drink, the group apparently roused Laura from her tent around 11:00pm. Despite her telling them she was uninterested in having guests at that hour, the group insisted on staying for another 45 minutes and left only after she promised to meet them downstream the following day.

Laura never met the group downstream. She halted her trip for several days, consulting with her support team in Britain in an effort to determine the safest way to proceed. A request to fellow paddlers was sent out in hopes that someone would accompany her on the river. When no offers were forthcoming, and having exhausted all other proposed options, Laura made the heartbreaking decision to end her expedition.

While researching Laura's story, I had to regrettably wade through scads of online criticism and rudely damaging comments connected to her truncated expedition. The points of view from several Russians were quite pointed, illustrating stories that conflicted with Laura's riverside account and espousing the solemn hospitality that Russians are known for. In the end, we can presume that a few bad apples blemished the reputation of a cordial nation while the western world watched from afar. With that said, it's also worth noting that it was the disparaging comments from the western world that made me cringe the most.

One of the few positive things to emerge from the expedition was Laura's enthusiasm to forge on and plan new self-propelled adventures. Later in 2015, she paddled 236 miles of the Thames River in England and bicycle-toured in Ireland. She's since gone on to succeed at several road-running adventures. She loves to share insights from her journeys with crowds across the U.K.

As of January 2018, Laura has not made a second attempt to descend the Volga.

British adventurer/author/speaker, Sarah Outen, rose to prominence by being the first woman to row across the Indian Ocean. That expedition earned her three Guinness World Records. She was subsequently elected Fellow of the Royal Geographic Society and made a Member of the Order of the British Empire (MBE). Her book about the journey, *A Dip in the Ocean: Rowing Solo Across the Indian Ocean*, became a bestseller in the U.K.

Not one to rest on her laurels, Sarah then embarked on a 20,000-mile circumnavigation of the northern hemisphere by bicycle, kayak, and rowboat. Her journey began and ended in London, England. Originally slated to take two-and-a-half years to complete, the expedition's duration was stretched to four years due to unfortunate setbacks and several spates of much-deserved downtime.

Sarah departed from London on April 1, 2011, first kayaking down the Thames River and crossing the English Channel to the coast of France, and then bicycling 10,000 miles across Europe and Asia to Russia's Pacific coast. Alternating between bike and kayak, she journeyed south via the remote Russian island of Sakhalin and made a plucky open-water crossing to Japan. She continued south by bike, pedalling 1000 miles to the Japanese city of Choshi where she readied herself for a rowboat crossing of the Pacific Ocean. Twenty-five days into the crossing, Sarah was forced to halt the expedition when a tropical storm severely damaged her boat. She was later rescued by the Japanese Coast Guard.

Her rescue made international headlines, provoking senseless criticism from armchair adventurers across the globe. Online comment sections were filled with immeasurable scorn. Sarah temporarily retreated from public view, taking nine months to mentally recover from the setback.

In a self-penned article for *The Guardian* (published post-expedition), Sarah explained how her mental health was adversely affected by her unsuccessful attempt to cross the Pacific. She also discussed the steps she took to heal from the ordeal as well as the important role of women in the adventuring world.

> The crash in my mental health after my first attempt on the Pacific in 2012 was frightening, debilitating, and one of the biggest lows of my journey. I had been plucked from my tiny rowing boat 600 miles off the coast of Japan, one month into my row, after a tropical storm raged for three days, damaging my boat too severely for me to carry on safely. Alone, in life-threatening conditions, with unknown outcomes is a perfect recipe for post-traumatic stress.

On coming home I soon found that I couldn't cope, with terrifying flashbacks ambushing my waking and sleeping hours, leaving me paranoid and feeling so un-like myself, with all my confidence gone. I cried all the time and felt paralyzed by the thoughts in my head, considering an early exit on more than one occasion.

My psychotherapist and GP guided me through; my friends stood by. One of the most powerful things was one of my sponsors telling me, "I believe in you, even if you don't believe in yourself at the moment." Mental health can be so tricky to talk about, but asking for help shed some light in my darkest times. I probably wouldn't be here without that support.

The portrayal of adventurers in the media is of-ten that of square-jawed, bearded males, stoical and invincible. Fifteen or so years ago, I was inspired by the documentary on Ellen MacArthur's Vendée Globe sailing race—the first film of a woman's journey that I could remember. Even today, if I ask folks to name some female adventurers on TV, it is MacArthur they talk about. And yet, ask someone to name a man in this field and most people can reel off multiple names. Women are out adventuring too on journeys just as challenging, exciting, and engaging as the beards, and it is often the inner struggle and emotional journey that is the most compelling.

In April 2013, Sarah relaunched her rowboat from Japan and land-ed in Alaska 150 days later. She described the Pacific Ocean cross-ing as one of the most gruelling sections of her London2London expedition. In the spring of 2014, Sarah returned to Alaska and kayaked 1500 miles of the Alaskan coastline to the city of Homer. She then bicycled across North America in winter, arriving in Cape Cod, Massachusetts in the spring of 2015. Six weeks later, Sarah embarked on the first-known solo rowboat crossing of the north Atlantic by a woman. One hundred and forty-three days into the journey, she made the heart-wrenching decision to abort the crossing because of potentially life-threatening conditions caused by a hurricane passing through her location—1000 miles west of the U.K. coast. That same day, she was rescued by a Japanese freighter en route to Montreal, Canada.

While waiting for the Japanese freighter to arrive, Sarah conducted her final "phonecast" from aboard her rowboat. In a recording of her satellite phone transmission (the 193rd "phonecast" update from the expedition), sadness and fear are noticeable in her voice. She has accepted the fact that this part of the expedition is about to end. It must've been emotionally devastating to withdraw from an endeavour in which she had invested so much time and energy. Nonetheless, Sarah managed to retain a sense of optimism, as evidenced in this insightful excerpt from her last phone transmission.

"This journey has taught me so many things, but one of the lessons it keeps driving home again and again is that you can have a plan, and that's great, but plans don't often go as planned. Often, that's when the magic happens. Often, it's an awful magic, but you just have to roll with it."

(As of January 2018, the final 1000-mile section of Sarah's Atlantic crossing remains uncompleted. It is doubtful she will return to the ocean to complete this section.)

Sarah's Atlantic rescue, like her Pacific rescue two years prior, was met with online scorn and criticism. But countering the callous comments were countless offerings of support and encouragement. It was obvious Sarah's journey touched the lives of many, provoking a vast range of emotions and heated dialogue.

Sarah went on to complete the final leg of her around-the-world journey, bicycling through southern England before kayaking down the Thames River to reach London on November 3, 2015.

Sarah Outen's epic achievement definitely places her in a league of her own, but her earthy, everyperson demeanour and boundless curiosity helps influence people's lives in unique and positive ways. Conversely, she would be the first to state that her life has been immeasurably enriched by the people she met during her journey.

A good example of this is illustrated in the same *Guardian* article mentioned earlier. In it, Sarah describes meeting a Chinese man named Gao whilst bicycling through Asia. On a whim, Gao, who had no cycle touring experience, decided to join Sarah on her expedition. Having been alone for most of her journey up to that point, Sarah welcomed the company. Together, they sweated their way over mountain ranges and through the Gobi Desert, embracing the challenges at hand and establishing a life-long friendship. Five weeks later, when the pedalling pair arrived in Beijing, Sarah asked Goa to summarize his adventurous introduction to bicycle touring. His answer serves as a simple reminder to the worrisome procrastinator in us all.

> When I asked him to express how he felt about the journey in three words, he said: "I am happiness." And his message to the world was: "If you want to do something, just do it. Don't worry about anything, just do it." A stirring message for everyone, I think, reminding us not to be held back by demons or fears or change or challenge or unknowns.
>
> Life is too short and precious not to dare to do and make the most of it. And, if demons and fears are getting in the way and threatening that life, then asking for help can be the bravest thing of all.

Sarah Outen's London2London expedition is chronicled in her book, *Dare to Do: Taking on the Planet by Bike and Boat*. A film about the expedition is slated for release in the autumn of 2018.

Adapting to change is nothing new for American long distance paddler, Traci Lynn Martin. In 2009, the neonatal intensive care unit nurse and mother of three was diagnosed with chronic rheumatoid arthritis. For a woman who has maintained an active lifestyle and loves immersing herself in nature, the news was shocking and disheartening. Despite this, Traci refused to let her ailment rule her life.

In 2015, Traci's mother passed away from pancreatic cancer. On her deathbed, her mother spoke with regret about things she had not attempted in her lifetime. Remorse, Traci decided thereafter, was something she wished not to cultivate in her life. She viewed life as a precious gift, full of wonder and possibility. She promised herself to make the most of each day and to pass along purposeful insights to those struggling with doubt and dis-ease.

Traci's name is well known to competitive paddlers throughout the American Midwest. She has competed eight times in the MR340 (a non-stop, 340-mile paddling race across the state of Missouri on the Missouri River), finishing in the top three four times as well as winning twice in the women's solo division and once in the mixed tandem division. Along with top place finishes in a host of other paddling races, Traci has wholly proven herself as a fierce competitor who strives hard to achieve each goal she sets. Stubborn tenacity and strict self-discipline give her a sizeable edge over the competition, while obsessive enthusiasm and endless training keep her out front of the pack.

It was her competitive nature that led Traci to the idea of circumnavigating all five Great Lakes in one calendar year, and it was her need to push past imagined limitations that led her to have a go at establishing a new Guinness World Record for the longest distance kayaked in one calendar year. She teamed with fellow racer, Joe Zellner, a formidable paddler in his own right, having won the MR340 and other paddling races many times.

It needs to be stated that the long-distance paddling community has, for many years, disregarded Guinness as the official record keeper for long distance paddling journeys. Paddling legends like Don Starkell, Verlen Kruger, Steve Landick, Bill Nedderman, Aleksander Doba, and Piotr Chmielinski, have all far exceeded the distances recognized as "records" by Guinness. As with any record attempt overseen by Guinness, ample proof must be provided. In the case of distance paddling records, the following criteria must be met in order for a record to be certified: a log book must be kept, witness accounts must be obtained, 15 minutes of video per day must be recorded, and a GPS log of the expedition route must be submitted. While some paddlers set off on journeys intending to keep track in order to establish a Guinness distance record, many do not.

In 2009, Freya Hoffmeister, an expedition paddler from Germany, circumnavigated Australia in a kayak. She paddled 8568 miles in total, all within one calendar year. For reasons unknown to me, the expedition was not recognized by Guinness.

While doing research prior to their Great Lakes expedition, Traci Lynn Martin and Joe Zellner determined that Hoffmeister's journey was the longest kayaking journey made during one calendar year. In order to best Hoffmeister's record, they created a paddling route that covered at least 8600 miles. The route included the circumnavigation of all five Great Lakes combined with a giant loop utilizing waterways in the eastern U.S. and Canada. Besides its daunting distance, the route also presented Traci and Joe with a major time-related challenge: ice on the northern Great Lakes (Huron, Michigan, and Superior) would necessitate a later start date, ensuring that no paddling would take place in January and February. There was also the possibility of limited paddling during the following December if winter arrived early. Essentially, they were attempting to paddle, in less than 10 months, the same distance Hoffmeister paddled in 11 months. Undoubtedly, weather would play an important role in determining the success of their expedition.

At the time (2016), the Guinness World Record for the longest kayak journey was about 4000 miles. Knowing that many people had paddled longer distances, but seeing Guinness' oversight as an opportunity to set the record straight, Traci and Joe decided to tout their expedition as a Guinness World Record attempt.

March 2017 was selected as a start date. Sponsors were secured. Media was courted. A film crew was hired to shoot a documentary about the expedition. News of their record-breaking attempt spread to all corners of North America via social media. Everything seemed on track. Everything was coming together. And then, in

July 2016, Traci paddled in what she considered to be her final MR340 race.

At age 49, Traci had accomplished nearly every kayak racing goal she'd set for herself. Her fireplace mantle was overflowing with trophies and medals. With a major expedition on the horizon, she looked at the 2016 MR340 as her last competitive paddling race. She may have been ready to retire, but she fully intended to show her younger competitors that a strong fire still roared within her. Her goal was to finish in the top three in the women's solo division.

A strong start put her out front of the other female kayakers and she remained in the lead as she reached the first checkpoint, 51 miles into the race. If she could maintain the same pace for another 24 hours, she stood a good chance of a securing a podium finish.

By the 70-mile mark, Traci's closest competitor, a woman half her age, was matching her stroke for stroke, drafting only inches behind her boat. From the riverbank, their kayaks appeared as one, as though they'd joined forces to defeat the others, striving for a tag-team victory over the paddling peloton that pursued them from afar. But teammates they were not. Their unison was illusionary, their fraternity, false. Their only link lay in their singular rivalry. One led. One followed. But both intended to win.

These are the kinds of moments Traci Lynn Martin lives for. The grit-your-teeth-and-grind-it-out moments. The heart-pounding, joint-screaming, grunt-inducing repetition as you pull, pull, pull yourself and your craft downstream, drowning in the oppressive humidity, cursing the summer heat, thirsting for ice cubes and shaded respite, fearing the horrid effects of sleep deprivation and exhaustion, getting dangerously lost in doubt and confusion as the inevitable hallucinations seize possession of your sanity. And all the while, you hear the ceaseless splash of the paddle blades as they slice through the river's surface, and smell the stench of urine-soaked spandex and reeking armpits, and taste the salty sweat as it flows over your upper lip and finds your tongue again. And again. And again. And again, until the taste becomes normalized, until it becomes *no taste*, until it becomes part of the exhilarating experience of racing atop a large, mighty, muddy river. And then the weather changes, and everything goes to shit.

Traci never made it to the 100-mile mark of the race. Her boat sustained irreparable damage when it struck a partially submerged wing dam during a violent thunderstorm. She and her kayak drift- ed helpless in the current until they were washed ashore by wind and waves. As tears and rain streamed down her face, she cradled her broken kayak against her body and waited for a rescue boat to arrive. Emergency assistance by race crews meant instant disquali- fication. Traci's dream of finishing strong in her final MR340 was over.

Devastated by the loss, she immediately retreated to her home in Lee's Summit, Missouri. She sought solace in the familiar com- fort of her living room couch and in the warmth of tea sipped from her favourite mug. She cried for what seemed like hours. Her body shook with emotional pain as she replayed the tragic events in her head. She began the race as a warrior, but she returned from it a broken woman.

When her phone rang that afternoon, she refused to answer it. When it rang again, she checked the number and took the call. A dear friend asked how she was and what she was doing. Traci made no attempt to mask her disappointment and frustration. Tears flowed freely. The conversation was saturated with sadness. Traci told her friend she didn't want to be at home, drowning in a god- awful sea of self-pity.

"What do you want to do?" asked her friend.

"I want to be in the race," said Traci.

"Then go back and finish the race," said her friend, encourag- ingly. "You have another boat. The race is far from over. You won't receive a medal, but you can still finish the race."

Her friend's supportive words became the catalyst she desper- ately needed. Traci and her support crew loaded up her other kayak and drove back to the MR340, back to a *different familiar*, back to the natural world she loved, back to the world that nurtured her in times of hardship and healing, back to the river that challenged her and watched her grow as a woman, back to the congenial embrace of her paddling tribe, back to a gaggle of novice paddlers that lagged far behind the race leaders but were still keen to finish the race in less than the allotted 88-hour deadline. They were kind souls who paddled at a pace that Traci found leisurely and warmly welcome, kind souls to whom Traci's elite paddling status meant nothing. To them, she was a stranger, a new addition to their friendly group. They stowed their paddles when the urge hit and smilingly drifted for long, unhindered minutes. They laughed when things were funny and they laughed when the air was hot with challenge. They laughed at the waves and the wing dams. They laughed at storm clouds and lightning and driving rain. They laughed at rainbows that spanned the verdant river valley when the downpours departed. They laughed at riverbank weasels and faraway bridges. Gone was the competitive pressure that came with every race Traci had paddled prior to this. Gone were the judgements, the expectations, the disappointments. Gone was the old Traci, replaced with a new Traci—a happier, healthier, humbler Traci. It seemed like a promising new start to the next chapter of her amazing life.

Of course, a new start meant new challenges for Traci. She had a falling out with her expedition partner, Joe Zellner, and the two went their separate ways. Joe, who had invested much time and effort in the project, teamed with his partner, Peggy Gabrielson, and embarked on a mission to become the first to circumnavigate all five Great Lakes in one year. He also chose to forgo the 8600-mile Guinness distance record attempt. Paddling the five lakes, at a total distance of 5800 miles, would be challenge enough.

Joe's ambitious restart presented Traci with a new conundrum. If she pursued her 8600-mile distance record, she would have to abandon hopes of paddling the Great Lakes in less time than Joe and Peggy. If she dropped the distance record attempt and focused on paddling only the Great Lakes, she stood a good chance of claiming the circumnavigation crown. Either way, getting an early start and keeping a healthy pace would be crucial to the expedition's success. Like it or not, in the short span of a few weeks, Traci's life had become a race again—a race that pitted two friends, two veterans of the MR340, against each other. They had now entered a grander race, a race with grander rewards and grander stakes.

After struggling through the shooting of a five-minute trailer to promote the expedition, Traci parted ways with the film director and crew. Creative differences were cited as the main cause of the split. Shot and edited at a cost of $10,000, the trailer helped attract additional sponsors and conveyed, in a simple manner, the gist of the expedition to the general public. Armed with a GoPro camera and a gung-ho spirit, Traci forged on alone. This was now her show entirely. Make or break, she was completely determined to give it her best shot.

Traci began her expedition in Port Huron, Michigan on March 9, 2017. Winter temperatures and strong winds made for a frigid start. Ice became an increasingly challenging factor as she headed north along the Huron shoreline, necessitating her to launch from ice-free areas and paddle miles from shore to avoid the shore ice. Doing so put her in incredibly perilous situations. Her ground crew had to continuously monitor her position via Traci's SPOT tracker, which relayed waypoints to an online map every 10 minutes. They also had to scout ahead for ice-free areas where she could land at day's end.

On March 24, near Grindstone City, Michigan, Traci's ground crew lost sight of her as she paddled a half-mile from shore. Due to weak cell phone signals, efforts to contact her failed. As she struggled with a malfunctioning rudder on her kayak and was battered by strong winds and three-foot waves, her crew called police and a search and rescue was initiated. Firefighters and members of the Huron County sheriff's office used an airboat (a propeller-driven craft capable of gliding over ice and water) to locate Traci. She and her boat were escorted back to shore. She was checked by medical technicians, but refused further treatment. Huron County sheriff, Kelly Hanson, spoke with Traci, discouraging her from making any further progress until the weather, ice, and water conditions became more favorable.

News of the rescue appeared on numerous TV and radio stations and in newspapers throughout southern Michigan. Online, the story prompted criticism and scorn from experienced Great Lakes paddlers and armchair adventurers alike. Comment sections on Facebook raged with angry debates. Some argued that Traci was putting rescue workers at unnecessary risk by being on the water in dangerous paddling conditions. Others fully supported her intentions, claiming Traci was a skilled kayaker, well-versed in paddling in adverse conditions.

Although it wasn't the type of publicity she may have hoped for, news of her rescue created a huge spike of interest in her expedition. Almost overnight, her journey went from a novel pursuit of adventure to genuinely riveting entertainment. As Traci spent her frigid days dodging ice flows, a polarized audience jeered and cheered from afar. Some hoped for failure. Others hoped for success. Both sides hoped for the chance to say, "I told you so!" A battle was being waged beyond the wind, weather, and waves. The online masses tuned to social media for the latest expedition update, the latest disparaging comment, the latest debate. What would be the final outcome? Would Traci prove her critics wrong? Or would the critics have their field day, successfully stomping out the female underdog from Missouri?

Fortunately, Traci's critics didn't have to wait long to unleash another round of rage.

On March 27, just 72 hours after the first rescue, she was rescued again.

A story posted on mlive.com detailed the events from that day. Excerpts from the story appear below.

> It was the second time the Huron County Sheriff's Office was called out onto the frigid waters of Lake Huron to aid Martin, a kayaker of more than two decades who's attempting to set both a Great Lakes record and a world record.

The first time deputies mobilized the airboat to aid Martin, it was a fluke, she said, a miscommunication with her team born of poor cell service out on the lake.

But three days after that, on Monday evening, March 27, the 52-year-old Missouri resident was in real trouble.

"With the amount of daylight left and the distance she would have had to travel before she could have come ashore herself, her chance of survival was virtually nil," said Huron County Sheriff, Kelly Hanson.

Martin agreed.

"There's no way I could have made it back," she said.

She had left Grindstone City around 7:00am Monday. Her goal that day was to cross the mouth of Saginaw Bay to Tawas City, about 35 miles away.

Ten hours after she left shore, Martin said, she realized she had been going in circles, was near Caseville—the eastern side of Saginaw Bay—and had 20 miles to travel before she could land again.

Her confusion was born of an incident earlier in the day, when her team noticed her progress tracker (SPOT tracker) and GPS equipment were interfering with one another, Martin said. She was told to turn the GPS equipment off and rely on the boat's compass.

Strong winds, she hypothesized, pushed the boat around and gave the illusion she was following the compass.

Hanson said Martin was treated on-scene but refused any further treatment.

The next time the sheriff's office is called to assist her, Hanson said, it'll be the last time she'll have her 19-foot kayak.

"With all due respect to the seasoned kayaker who had the courage and ambition to attempt such an accomplished goal, she was respectfully told that we will resort to confiscating her kayak or abandoning it in the water if another incident occurs under similar circumstances offshore of our county," Hanson said.

> The sheriff said U.S. Coast Guard officials are considering "deterrent options" as well.

News of the second rescue went viral, letting loose another avalanche of online scorn. This time, however, the criticism was far more impudently malicious. Traci made an attempt to set the record straight by addressing the issue in a story posted on piadvance. com. In the story, Traci made reference to the public's negative reaction to the March 24 rescue and added there were many inaccuracies reported in the media. These inaccuracies, she claimed, were compounded following the March 27 rescue.

> "There was a lot of miscommunication between myself and my ground support and miscommunication between my ground support and the sheriff's department," said Traci.
>
> "People (on the Internet) said I lied to the sheriff, that I told him I would not go back out. I was very careful with what I said to the sheriff. I agreed with him that the ice was bad, but I made sure I did not say I was not going to go back out, because I knew I was."
>
> Traci said there were many inaccuracies in the media, including the notion that there was a rescue.
>
> "It was a not a rescue (on March 24)," said Traci. "The story just got out of control, and when I tried to defend myself online, people got very hateful."

Following the second rescue, Traci returned home to Missouri to recoup and rethink. During this 11-day downtime, she abandoned the idea of establishing the 8600-mile kayaking record and focused instead on beating the more feasible *surf ski* Guinness World Record of 3823 miles, set by south African paddler, Gerhard Moolman, in 2002. (Surf skis are longer, lighter, and sleeker than traditional kayaks. They were originally designed in Australia for surfing waves. Often used as racing craft in North America, a surf ski was Traci's premier choice for the Great Lakes expedition.)

Adverse lake conditions, cold weather, and arthritic flare-ups were factors in Traci's decision to modify her expedition goals. She stated online that she simply couldn't produce the daily mileage necessary to break the 8600-mile mark in one calendar year. Even though it was only March, with another nine months still available for paddling, Traci had already run out of time.

As a casual follower during the early stages of her expedition, I was not aware she had abandoned her bid to top Freya Hoffmeister's distance milestone. That fact didn't come to my attention until much later. A browse through Traci's expedition website revealed three different distances being pursued. A banner on the website's homepage read "Just Around the Pointe – Traci Lynn Martin – 5800 miles" while the five-minute documentary trailer (also prominently positioned on the website's homepage) proclaimed an 8600-mile attempt. Elsewhere on the site, the 3823-mile surf ski Guinness World Record is mentioned numerous times. Unfortunately, these three conflicting distances later contributed to inaccurate statistics being used in several news stories. These discrepancies were later addressed by Traci in a Facebook post. In it, she stated, "The information in my documentary video is no longer accurate. However, I do not have the funds to have it updated and changed. I am not attempting 8000 miles anymore, nor am I paddling the St. Lawrence Seaway. I hope this clears up any confusion."

While the online criticism cooled during Traci's downtime, Joe Zellner and Peggy Gabrielson quietly began their attempt to circumnavigate the five Great Lakes. Like Traci, they started their journey in Port Huron, Michigan. They too encountered frigid temperatures and adverse lake conditions. Thankfully much of the shore ice had melted, making navigation somewhat easier and safer.

Traci returned to Lake Huron on April 8, eager to stay ahead of Joe and Peggy. She did just that, strongly pushing north along Michigan's eastern shoreline before rounding the apex of the state's lower peninsula and entering Lake Michigan. Curiously, she never crossed paths with Joe and Peggy.

Both the Martin and Zellner-Gabrielson expeditions settled into the daily routine of paddling when weather permitted and anxiously waiting onshore when it didn't. Both camps encountered violent summer storms and wind-generated waves in excess of six feet. More often than not, Huron and Michigan acted more like oceans than lakes. The extremity of their harrowing experiences was never lost on both camps. Each day, they were simultaneously challenged and humbled. Each day, their minds matured and their paddling skills increased. Each day, they moved a little closer to achieving their matching goals.

Long journeys are never free from setbacks. Other than weather-related delays, which kept them off the water for more than three weeks, Joe and Peggy struggled through many setbacks during their expedition. Among them was the unfortunate fallout from an accident involving their support vehicle. The tasks of finding a vehicle replacement and setting straight the insurance claims prevented them from making any paddling progress for almost five weeks.

On September 2, five months after starting their expedition, Joe Zellner and Peggy Gabrielson abandoned their quest to circumnavigate the five Great Lakes. They made it as far as Terrace Bay, Ontario on Lake Superior's north shore, having successfully paddled the western shoreline of Lake Huron, most of Lake Superior's shoreline, and the entirety of Lake Michigan's shoreline. Dejected, but rich with amazing stories from their journey, they returned home.

Time, it seemed, was now Traci Lynn Martin's only competition. Too much time on land spelled certain failure while talk of an early winter made paddling in December less likely. She needed to push hard if she hoped to finish before the predicted freeze-up.

On October 15, Traci landed in Port Huron, Michigan (her starting point six months prior), thus becoming the first person to circumnavigate lakes Huron, Michigan, and Superior in one calendar year. She went on to paddle the south shore of Lake Erie and portage around Niagara Falls. She entered Lake Ontario on November 27. Six days later, she was forced off the water in Toronto by an approaching winter storm, the first of the season. Temperatures plummeted to record lows—harsh, even by Canadian standards. Traci spent the next two weeks in Toronto watching the weather deteriorate. As ice formed along the Erie shoreline, she took to Facebook and posted a video declaring an end to her Great Lakes bid. In the same video, she shared that she'd cried while making the difficult decision to abandon her expedition, but also mentioned that she'd made a lot of great memories during her journey and had met a lot of wonderful friends. For Traci Lynn Martin, it had been the adventure of a lifetime.

During her 10 months on the water, Traci paddled 3582 miles, 231 miles shy of the surf ski Guinness World Record. She plans to repeat her attempt to circumnavigate the five Great Lakes in 2020.

In all the above examples, the adventurers mentioned had sponsorship obligations and chose to promote their expeditions through media platforms of all kinds, online and off. Each adventurer knew the inherent risks of making their journey public. Each knew the risks that came with the possible failure of an expedition. If an expedition fails, it will surely attract media attention and produce an unfortunate media-user backlash. It's also sure to affect the adventurer's relationship with their sponsors. Will the same sponsors choose to back the adventurer's next journey? Will future sponsors shy away when they learn about the incomplete nature of a past expedition? Will sponsors accept that failure, or *incompleteness*, is a very real and possible outcome to an adventure? No one likes to talk about it, but adventurers die every year while on expeditions. As a working partner, each sponsor must acknowledge the risks involved in each prospective sponsorship deal and have a plan in place to address media inquiries should an expedition end in failure or death. Likewise, each adventurer must gauge whether the inherent sponsorship obligations are equal trade for gifted gear and/or money. Without a doubt, big-name manufacturers possess huge networks of devoted consumers both online and at a retail level. To an adventurer promoting themselves as a brand, gaining access to these networks may seem like a sure-fire way to broaden an audience. For some, the mental weightiness of sponsorship obligations is an unwelcomed burden while on expedition. Rather than spending copious amounts of time courting sponsors, some adventurers have forgone the idea of sponsor involvement and instead choose to bear the expedition costs themselves. Obligation and responsibility go hand in hand. If an adventurer enters into a sponsorship deal, they should ideally live up to their end of the arrangement.

(With the exception of showing up at self-planned book tour dates, I tend to shy away from responsibility when in a working relationship. For that reason, I choose not to entertain sponsorship deals anymore. For me, the amount of effort put into securing sponsorship deals never equals the amount of support received from a sponsor.)

When an adventurer begins planning an expedition, they must be fully aware that they are committing themselves to a risky endeavour. First and foremost, they have an obligation and a responsibility to their personal safety. Any dealings with sponsors should be fully researched beforehand. All levels of media will have interest in the adventurer's journey and they will publish stories as they see fit. Online trolls will have their say. Regardless of whether they fail or not, each adventurer will have to deal with the consequences of their actions. Whether they like it or not, they will have to stand naked to a judging world.

In 2008, Nathan Welch and Mark Kalch completed their quest to descend the Amazon river system from source to sea, travelling 4150 miles in 153 days. Prior to that time, only six people had completed the journey. Their rafting adventure began as a three-person team, but two months into the expedition, team member Phil Swart withdrew due to illness.

With the descent of South America's longest river system under his belt, Mark set his sights on conquering the longest river system on each continent, a lofty goal no one else had ever attempted. The idea gave birth to his 7 Rivers, 7 Continents project.

North America was next on Mark's list. The Missouri–Mississippi river system, at a length of 3800 miles, had never been paddled from source to sea. Mark set a launch date of May 1, 2011. His Amazon success ensured sponsorship support from some of the biggest brands in the paddling world. As a self-described explorer and storyteller, ample exposure on social media ensured a broader audience throughout Mark's Missouri–Mississippi expedition.

I first learned about Mark Kalch in July 2011, while doing research for my own Missouri–Mississippi river system kayaking expedition. As described earlier in this book, I'd stumbled upon the idea of descending the longest river system on each continent whilst daydreaming at my landscape maintenance job in Vancouver, British Columbia. The concept was developed independently of Mark's. I did not steal or borrow his idea.

During my Missouri–Mississippi research, I discovered that Mark had suspended the launch of his expedition due to shoulder surgery. In a blog post dated May 31, 2011, he extended sincere apologies to all the sponsors involved in the expedition. A generous two-month healing period forced Mark to reschedule his descent to June 2012, the same month I planned to begin. Undoubtedly, this would create some friendly competition. At the time, Mark knew that the river system had yet to be descended from source to sea. Somehow, that important fact had escaped me. One of us was going to get the first descent. Had I known, I probably would've started my expedition earlier to ensure a head start. With my sights on a gold medal, and a headstrong obsession to attain it, things may have strayed far from the "friendly competition" envisioned earlier.

I'm not giving much away when I say I ended up with a silver medal. Despite the fact that he started from the utmost source just one week before me, Mark Kalch went on to finish the Missouri–Mississippi river system a full five months before me. We both travelled 3800 miles under our own power. We both achieved our goals. Our agendas, on the other hand, were much different. Mark's priority was to finish the river quickly. Spending time away from his wife and three children was perhaps the most challenging aspect of his expedition. He missed them dearly and went on to complete the journey in 117 days. By contrast, my expedition took 256 days to complete.

Throughout the first four months of my 2012–2013 journey down the Missouri–Mississippi, I was organizing a charity event scheduled to take place in October 2012 in my hometown of Chatham, Ontario, Canada. Endless hours were spent off the river delegating work to event volunteers, requesting and proofing graphic design images, and making sure local media was well-informed prior to the event. At the same time, I was also lining up interviews with media at downstream destinations on the Missouri. I drafted press releases and sent them off, performed numerous television, radio, and print interviews, and shared the journey on social media. I spent the entire winter paddling on the lower Missouri River and the lower Mississippi River south of St. Louis. Short days, long nights, freezing temperatures, low river levels, numbing fear, and several bouts of illness ensured that the expedition went on much longer than planned. After all the hard work, I still ended up in second place.

Prior to his expedition, Mark had been in contact with Norm Miller—a long-distance paddler then-based in Bozeman, Montana—regarding the best options for shipping a kayak to Montana. Norm explained that Bozeman was a three-hour drive from Brower's Spring (the Missouri's utmost source). He offered to store Mark's kayak until Mark arrived by Greyhound bus from Seattle. (Mark was living in Britain at the time and flew to the U.S. for the river descent.) The two of them then drove to the Missouri's source area near Red Rock Lakes National Wildlife Refuge in south-central Montana. Mark began his expedition on June 10, 2012.

By virtue of his own paddling expeditions, Norm Miller has gained the respect of paddlers worldwide. In 2004, he retraced Lewis and Clark's 1804–1806 westward journey, solo paddling the Missouri River upstream from St. Louis to Montana, and then portaging and paddling all the way to the Pacific Ocean. He's also paddled the length of the McKenzie River in northern Canada and the southern coast of Thailand.

In 2011, Norm created the Missouri River Paddlers Facebook page, the world's foremost resource on paddling the Missouri River. He also alleges to have coined the term *river angel*, a phrase allocated to riverside citizens who offer assistance to long distance paddlers during their journeys. He is well-connected to networks of fellow river angels along the Missouri and Mississippi rivers. Several well-known river angels, including Mike Clark in St. Louis and John Ruskey in Clarksdale, Mississippi, assisted Mark Kalch during his Missouri–Mississippi expedition. Norm Miller, Mike Clark, and John Ruskey (the latter two are river guides on the lower Missouri and Mississippi rivers) are also well-connected to Canoe & Kayak magazine, North America's largest paddling publication. Every August, the magazine hosts the Canoe & Kayak Awards, a ceremony that honours stellar accomplishments in the paddling world from the past year. In 2013, C&K created a new award category: Spirit of Adventure. According to the C&K website, the award is given "to the person or group who best embodies the spirit of adventure in paddling." In order to engage their online following, the C&K promotional team encourages social media users to vote for their favourite paddler (or team of paddlers) in each of the six categories: Male Paddler of the Year, Female Paddler of the Year, Spirit of Adventure, Expedition of the Year, Paddle with Purpose, and Lifetime Achievement. Award nominees are encouraged to engage their online followers in order to drum up votes for themselves. The nominee receiving the most votes wins their category. Sadly, like many online contests of this nature (the annual National Geographic Adventurer of the Year Award is chosen in much the same way), the competition essentially becomes a popularity contest. Those with the largest online fanbase are likely to collect the prize.

I'm not sure if his personal connections with Norm Miller, Mike Clark, and John Ruskey had any influence on him being nominated for the inaugural Spirit of Adventure Award, but seeing Mark Kalch's name on the list of nominees sure fanned the flames of jealousy and anger in my mind. He was, of course, nominated for his achievement of being the first person to paddle the Missouri–Mississippi river system from source to sea—the very same thing I accomplished, except that he crossed the finish line first. Dom Liboiron, a Canadian long-distance paddler, also received a nomination. Dom, who also had ties with Norm Miller in the early stages of his expedition, carried his dead uncle's ashes in a canoe down sections of the Frenchman, Milk, Missouri, and Mississippi rivers, starting in Eastend, Saskatchewan and ending in New Orleans, Louisiana. Although his story is indisputably original, wholly Canadian (as any canoe-related journey should be), and amazingly heartfelt, 2815 miles of Dom's route (from the Milk–Missouri confluence to New Orleans) matched *exactly* with the route I descended. Dom, Mark, and I were on the river at the same time and shared our journeys on the same social media platforms, yet one of us didn't end up on the list of nominees for Canoe & Kayak's 2013 Spirit of Adventure Award.

I don't know if I can adequately express in words how fucking cheesed off I was when I discovered I'd somehow been overlooked for this award while two fellow paddlers whose achievements I'd closely matched had successfully made the cut. The anger in my head was unyielding. I silently lashed out at Canoe & Kayak magazine, fully blaming them for the roaring resentment I felt. I had been unfairly snubbed and dishonourably humiliated at the same bloody time! It was like being trapped in some warped high school nightmare where everyone but me receives an invite to the year's biggest party. "Loser Rod doesn't get an invitation. He's not cool enough. He's an outsider. He doesn't deserve to share the same space with us."

Being excluded from hanging with the cool kids is nothing new to me—it's basically the story of my life. I often work hard and receive no recognition. If I wasn't so damned bent on achieving some level of fame in this bloody lifetime—if I was *humble*, for instance—none of this would matter. But I'm not humble. I'm fucking obsessed with myself! Therefore, when I actually accomplished something *huge* and received no recognition for it from North America's leading paddling magazine, I got pretty fucking cheesed off.

In an attempt to muster some support from an audience who'd followed my expedition on social media, I took to Facebook and asked them to cast votes for me in a slot named "OTHER" at the bottom of the nominees list on Canoe & Kayak's website. Even if I didn't stand a chance of topping the other contenders, maybe I could secure an honourable mention.

Of course, no mention was forthcoming. There was no interview request, no footnote of praise to be found anywhere. Something, *anything* would've helped soothe the wound. I got nothing but angrier, swearing to never have any future interaction with Canoe & Kayak magazine. It was a grudge I planned to carry to my grave.

Dom Liboiron went on to win the 2013 Spirit of Adventure Award. The win angered me, of course, but I also felt a hint of redemption based on the fact that Mark Kalch hadn't placed first for a second time.

Insult was added to injury when friends and fellow paddlers Janet Moreland, Brad Tallent, and Austin Graham were all nominated for the 2014 Spirit of Adventure Award. Janet Moreland— the third person, first woman, and first American to solo kayak the Missouri–Mississippi river system from source to sea—had deep ties with Mike Clark, John Ruskey, and Norm Miller (who joined her twice during her descent). Brad Tallent and Austin Graham, two American adventurers who paddled 3000 miles from the Gulf of St. Lawrence in eastern Canada to the Gulf of Mexico, received much praise for their accomplishment, but were unable to top Janet Moreland for the win. All three of these paddlers finished their expeditions in 2013, the same year I finished mine yet my name did not appear on the nominees list. (Dom Liboiron also finished his Frenchman–Milk–Missouri–Mississippi expedition in 2013.) This time around, my anger was less pronounced, but my disdain for Canoe & Kayak magazine was not. (It's worth noting that my name was mentioned in a C&K feature article about Janet More-land's Missouri–Mississippi expedition. It was nice to get a little recognition. Thanks, Janet.)

While we're on the topic, let's have a look at the winner of the 2015 Spirit of Adventure Award: Keith Lynch. Keith had a lifetime total of 60 minutes of canoeing experience when he set off from the headwaters of the Missouri River (near Three Forks, Montana) with hopes of paddling all the way to his home in Dallas, Texas. Norm Miller (there's that name again) took a vested interest in Keith's trip, even going so far as to recover a camera bag that went missing when Keith capsized on the third day of his journey. Norm later returned the bag when he travelled to Texas to congratulate Keith at the end of his expedition.

It's worth noting that Mark Kalch was also nominated for the 2015 Spirit of Adventure Award for his solo kayaking descent of the Volga River in Russia. (The Volga is Europe's longest river system.) The expedition marked the third descent in his 7 Rivers, 7 Continents project. As of January 2018, Mark is the only person to be nominated twice for the Spirit of Adventure Award, losing both times.

The winner of the 2016 Spirit of Adventure Award was none other than Dale Sanders, who, at age 80, became the oldest man to solo paddle the Mississippi River from source to sea. Dale is a well-known river angel based in Memphis, Tennessee. He and I were involved in the first continuous paddling descent of the Wolf River in northern Mississippi and southwestern Tennessee. The story of that challenging descent, as well as the unfortunate drama that un-folded before, during, and after the expedition, is documented in my second book, *River Angels*. The best way to sum up my relation-ship with Dale Sanders is to say there is tension between us.

Curiously, Dale has the distinction of having hosted the three previous Spirit of Adventure Award winners at his home in Mem-phis during their individual expeditions. Mark Kalch, Brad Tall-ent, and Austin Graham also stayed at Dale's home during their expeditions. It's also worth noting that Norm Miller was at the

Canoe & Kayak Awards ceremony in August 2016 when Dale accepted his prize.

Is it too much of a stretch to guess that Norm Miller's influence has impacted the outcome of each year's Spirit of Adventure Award? I know for a fact that Canoe & Kayak magazine contacts him personally every year to get suggestions for possible nominees. They know Norm has his finger on the pulse of the paddling world and his recommendations factor greatly in determining who gets nominated for certain awards, especially in categories related to long distance paddling. The same can be said for Mike Clark and John Ruskey. Is there collusion behind the scenes when it comes to the Canoe & Kayak Awards? Perhaps. Is favouritism involved? Definitely.

Okay, now that we've had a thorough look at the misery caused by my connection—or *lack* of connection—with Canoe & Kayak magazine, let's bring the topic back around to Mark Kalch.

In late 2015, Mark announced he would attempt a descent of the Darling–Murray river system in Australia from source to sea on a stand-up paddleboard, a feat no one had ever before achieved. In fact, no one had ever attempted to begin a paddling journey from the river system's utmost source—the head of the Condamine River at the foot of Superbus Mountain in the state of Queensland. Only one person had achieved something similar. In 2007, Australian paddler, Steve Posselt, paddled and portaged 1860 miles from Brisbane to the Southern Ocean via a majority of the Darling–Murray. For some unknown reason, Posselt chose to bypass the source area, thereby nullifying himself from a true source to sea descent.

Mark's Darling–Murray announcement came as a surprise to me, given that I too planned to do the same thing at the same time. It seemed like a flashback to 2012 when we were about to embark on our respective Missouri–Mississippi river system descents. This time, he kept things fairly quiet, choosing not to broadcast his intentions too much. I found his approach interesting, given that I too was keeping a low profile. Mark's priority, as it had been before, was to finish the descent quickly and return home to his family. He planned to launch from the source in early January, right in the middle of the Australian summer. The oppressive heat and lack of flowing water would add to the challenge. All five portions of the river system, from the Condamine River in southern Queensland to the Murray River in South Australia, passed through remote areas of the Australian outback. If sections of these rivers were low, one would have to walk instead of paddle. During Steve Posselt's descent, he spent six weeks walking 600 miles of roadways that paralleled the upper tributaries before he could paddle his kayak. By starting in the hottest part of the year, Mark and I knowingly ensured ourselves a challenging endeavour. For me, timing had been governed by my Aquapac sponsorship. Money promised by the company could not be released until the beginning of 2016. Because I planned to use the money to purchase a flight to Australia, a ticket could not be bought until January. By that time, Mark would already be on the river system. Catching him, as was the case with the Missouri–Mississippi in 2012, would be impossible. The first descent of the Darling–Murray was up for grabs and it looked like I was destined to collect another silver medal. Thankfully, by concocting the idea of doing a summit to source to sea expedition—certainly something *no one* had ever attempted—I'd found a clever way to one-up Mark Kalch. In the end, Mark might get the gold medal, but my silver medal would be decorated with extra bling.

All this stuff—from the silent competition with Mark Kalch to the Canoe & Kayak Awards debacle, to my wavering physical and mental health, to my suicide plan, to the unfortunate financial crises that threatened to end the upcoming expedition, to the weight of sponsorship and social media obligations, to the fear of online criticism, to the unrequited desire I felt for Kitty Pawlak, to my cyclic and burdensome reliance on my father—*all of it*, and a lot more, rampaged my brain during those painfully stressful days in January 2016. Somehow, I had to keep my head together and get on with the expedition. Somehow, I had to complete it. Somehow,

I had to do what no one had done. And somehow, I had to kill myself when it was all over.

During the time I spent at Peter Dodds' home, sorting through endless logistical puzzles and deciding whether or not to use Dave Cornthwaite's kayak, Mark Kalch was making progress on the Darling–Murray river system. While he was quietly making his way to the sea, I was quietly losing my mind. Everything seemed stacked against me. Failure, it seemed, lay just beyond the next sunset. If—and it was a *huge, looming IF* in those dark days of January—if I did somehow cave mentally and had to abandon the expedition before it even began, at least I could do *one thing* to buoy myself through the agony, *one thing* that would offer a shred of redemption if the seemingly inevitable downfall occurred. I could, at least, finish hiking the unseen nine-mile section of the upper Murray River. *That* was one very important thing Mark Kalch could not take from me. Unless, of course, I had to be *rescued*. *That* would spoil *every*thing.

How is it that it never occurred to me to check the GPS on my iPhone while recklessly trekking down the upper Murray River? After all the worry about not having a handheld GPS, I'd somehow overlooked the phone's GPS function. Well, that's not entirely true. I knew, of course, that the phone had a GPS, but I also knew I was dozens of miles from the nearest communications tower. Getting a signal in the middle of this alpine jungle was hopeless. I hadn't given much thought to using the phone's GPS because I figured that, without a signal, it wouldn't give me a location anyway. Turns out I was wrong.

Imagine my surprise when, on the morning of Day 4 of this nine-mile hike, I powered up my phone and, after a tense moment of nothing happening, a flashing blue dot appeared beside the Murray River about one-and-a-half miles upstream of Poplars Camping Area. I sat wide-eyed, staring in disbelief at the tiny dot as it pulsed on the screen. "It can't be!" I shouted aloud. "How...? It...it can't be right..."

As I uttered those broken phrases of doubt, the blue dot began to magically move to the left as the GPS recalibrated its position. It then moved further to the left and stopped. Then it zipped back to the right. Then moved up. Then down. Then it settled in the same place it had been, right beside the river. It pulsed and seemed to say, "You are here." But *was* I there? Was the phone correct? Could it be trusted? How was it able to accurately determine my location if it had no signal? Was it simply guessing? Was *I*? I figured that a guessed location was better than no location and compared the GPS map with my topographic map. If the GPS was correct, I was less than a half-mile from the closest road (Limestone Creek Track). If I wanted, I could choose to bushwhack north to that road and follow it down to Poplars Camping Area. From there, it would be possible to stash my backpack in the woods at the campground, hike back to this spot, and then retrace my steps back to the campground. At least then I would know where the campground was and how to get to it via the riverbank. As I pondered this idea a little more, it became less appealing. I didn't need to do more hiking than necessary, I just needed to finish. And the simplest way to finish was to plod downstream until I reached Poplars. If in fact I was only one-and-a-half miles from the campground, I would surely reach it by day's end. Throwing my distrust of mobile phone technology to the free-flowing river, I made the decision to press onward as quickly as possible.

The sky was baseball white and featureless when I left my riverside camp at 8:00am. Thankfully, the rain had stopped. The all-night deluge had swelled the Murray into an impatient, turbid mess. No more would I be able to see the riverbed rocks while walking in the flow. From now on, each footfall would be blindly placed, drawing out the struggle of trekking downstream.

The river had risen 10 vertical inches overnight. It was now cold and mean. My bare legs quickly turned pork chop pink as I sank groin-deep into the current. The dirt-laden water lapped at the bottom of my backpack as I tediously plodded along the Victoria bank. I cursed aloud repeatedly and gripped my walking stick tight, wedging it between unseen rocks in the river floor. At times when I felt it necessary, I poked the stick's tip past my numb toes for fear that a deep pool lay hidden below the surface. The last thing I needed was to slide into a neck-deep pit and get swallowed by the river.

My topo map showed that Round Mountain was just downstream on river left. The mountain's southern base formed a towering vertical wall that sank well into the flow. The wall ricocheted the river around a sharp, hairpin-shaped bend. The Murray here was a noisy, vicious beast, churned white with anger and oxygen. Walking in it was no longer an option.

I backtracked to the last of the calm eddies and carefully crossed the river diagonally to its New South Wales bank. The terrain was choked with blackberry vines, dense scrub, and forest. Thankfully, it was also flat. I picked my way along the riverbank, weaving between trees and sidestepping the thorny vines before plunging back into the cold stream when the scrub became too thick. At the upstream tip of a large, grassy island, a sizeable portion of the Murray spilled off into a side channel. I forded the channel and waded through the thigh-high grass, brushing dozens of gangly black spiders off my wet legs as I went.

Large rocks in the river at the island's downstream tip had impeded the rain-strengthened flow and created a deep pool. Leaning out into the river and peering downstream, I spied a rocky outcropping jutting straight up from the Murray's edge on the New South Wales side. Its presence would necessitate a crossing to the opposite bank. Owing to the river depth in this section, I disappointingly had to backtrack across the grassy island and through the gauntlet of spiders to an area of the Murray littered with small boulders. The river here was waist-deep and swift. As I moved slowly from boulder to boulder, dark clouds drifted into view, unleashing a drenching rain into the river valley. By the time I reached the Victoria bank, I was cold, soaked, and cranky.

Through a thin stand of gum trees, about 300 yards from where I stood, I could see the rocky slopes of Round Mountain rising from the forest floor. From the mountain's base to the river's edge, the terrain was completely flat—a floodplain. *If this rain keeps up,* I said to myself, *it won't be long until this area floods again.*

I slung my pack off, let it drop to the mucky ground, fished out my phone, and powered it up. It was time to check my position. If the GPS showed my location as a point downstream from where I camped, then I would know for a fact it was working properly.

Hunched over to protect the phone from the pouring rain, I held it close to my chest and waited impatiently for the white Apple logo to disappear. I knew the battery level was low. There was a possibility that the phone might not power up.

Waiting. Waiting. Waiting.

"Hurry the fuck up!" I shouted.

Waiting. Waiting. Waiting until the moisture on my red face started to steam.

"What the *FUCK* is with this phone?!" I barked.

Waiting. Waiting. Waiting...

After struggling through a lingering eternity, the phone's screen finally lit up. A thin, red line in the upper right corner of the screen indicated the battery was indeed low. The other corner showed "No Signal." I put a wet finger to the screen and swept right. The map screen appeared. I waited anxiously for the blue GPS dot to materialize.

Waiting. Waiting. Waiting.

"Oh, c'mon!" I bellowed. "This is ridiculous!"

I stared hard at the phone and willed the dot to appear. Finally, after a full minute of agonizing apprehension, the dot flashed on the screen, hovering over the same place I'd camped the night before, about a half-mile upstream. I rolled my eyes and exhaled.

"Fuck..." I uttered, disappointingly.

The GPS was locked on the same position. It hadn't moved. It couldn't confirm my present location.

"Why do I put any trust in this bloody thing?" I shouted as a rivulet of rain snaked over my grimacing face.

I yanked out the Aquapac waterproof mapcase that contained my topographic map. Rain speckled the clear plastic face of the mapcase as I held it in my left hand. I brought it close to the phone so I could compare maps. Nothing matched.

What the fuck?! I thought.

I'd specifically folded the map to reveal the area I was trekking through and had always glanced at the correct side of the map when looking at the mapcase. This time, however, I did not. *This time*, I was looking at the *reverse* side of the map, something I'd never done. No wonder nothing matched! Before flipping the mapcase to the correct side, a bolded place name caught my attention. There, in the middle of the map, miles south of my present location, was a stacked series of contour lines showing a prominent rise in the landscape with steep precipices angling away from its peak. Two words were printed in black typeface atop this scenic anomaly: RODS DOWNFALL. I shook my head and exhaled deeply.

"How fitting…" I muttered.

The rain poured down incessantly as the river noisily raced around a tight bend to my right. A dark, depressive mood settled over me as my optimism waned. It was almost time to give in, almost time to admit defeat.

I removed the SPOT tracker from my backpack and held it in my pruney hands. I eyed the 911 button.

This can all be over with one push of a button, I said to myself. *All the worry. All the fear. Gone. I can push this, sit down, and wait for help to arrive. No more futile guesses at my location. No more stress. This can all be over* now *if I want it.*

And then, without the slightest warning, the blue dot on the phone's GPS began to slowly move downstream, following the river's course, zigzagging from bank to bank, just as I had done. My gaze shifted from the SPOT to the phone. My eyes widened. My heart raced. I held my breath and stared hard at the screen. The dot drifted downstream a final time and came to rest at the river's edge, abruptly south of Round Mountain.

"Fuck me!!!" I shouted. "IT WORKED!!!"

Shaking with excitement, I put a wet fingertip on the screen and scrolled down. Poplars Camping Area quickly came into view. It was less than a half-mile downstream.

"YES!!!" I screamed, pumping my fist like a baseball pitcher after a hard-earned strikeout.

I slid the phone into its waterproof case, shoved the SPOT tracker into the hip pocket of my shorts, shouldered my back-pack, and sprinted across the floodplain in the direction of Poplars Camping Area. As I ran, I made a decision not to cross the river unless absolutely necessary. In no way did I want to run the risk of missing the opening to the campground.

A glut of fallen trees, bark-free and ancient, lay angled upon one another like collapsed columns in some remote Roman ruins. The melee seemed to spread forest-wide, so I dove in headstrong with little hesitation, squeezing under and between the wet, smooth trunks. Long-fingered limbs repeatedly snagged the dangling straps on my backpack, slowing progress significantly and causing me to curse loudly at the delay.

Knees were muddied and cheeks were scratched as I emerged from the tangled, wooden maze. Despite my foul mood, a desper-ate need to reach Poplars drove me onward. The end was near. I could taste it in the earthy air. It was the taste of *victory*.

Victory, however, would have to wait until I navigated around a huge rocky outcropping that rose vertically from the Victoria bank. The options for bypassing this obstacle were few. I could climb the beast or enter the river. Reluctantly, I chose the river.

Back into the swirling mass I descended, my left palm pressed flat against the wet rock for stability as my right gripped tight-ly around my walking stick. The cold, swift current pushed me downstream quicker than I preferred, forcing me to focus hard on each footfall. Remaining upright was critical here. A tumble in the chest-deep flow could be perilous.

After several tense minutes of stress-filled struggle, I rounded the outcropping and sloppily stumbled up the muddy bank. The flat, thinly treed floodplain was a welcome sight. I pressed on eagerly, quickly tromping through the low scrub as I kept the Murray on my right.

A half-hour later, with the floodplain now transitioning to a full-fledged forest, I spied a faint footpath shallowly cleaved into the thick foliage. My heart raced! I hadn't seen evidence of a trail in more than a day! Whether trodden by humans or horses, the path led somewhere, and I intended to find out where.

I'd taken only a handful of steps down the trail when I spotted something on the ground that looked completely out of place in this environment. It was stark white and unmoving. At first, I thought it was a dead animal, maybe a rabbit or a bird. As I cautiously approached it, the clump took on the appearance of a pair of white socks. It wasn't until I poked at it with my walking stick that I realized what it was: used toilet paper. Normally, discovering such a thing would curl my nose. Not on this day.

"Toilet paper!" I shouted. "That's awesome!"

I was never so happy to see used toilet paper in my life! The discovery meant two things: a human had been there recently and they'd likely travelled there on foot. The footpath, I surmised, was probably a crude fishing access trail. If my hunch was correct, the trail was likely connected to Poplars Camping Area.

A wide smile crept across my face as I pondered the significance of the toilet paper. A few simple sheets of soiled two-ply represented to me a *human* connection, a link sadly missing from my life as of late. In defiance of a world I'd written off as worthlessly fucked-up, I'd isolated myself in a remote area of the driest continent on earth with a warped, but heartfelt, intention of going out on top. In the process, I'd severed ties with those who loved me. I had practiced a selfish indulgence, a dying need to manipulate and control the final outcome. It was an opaque loyalty, unseen by all who gazed upon me valiantly and longingly. The worship was one-way, a union incomplete.

And then, quite remarkably and entirely unintentionally, I reconnected to that missing sense of humanness. A clump of white in a jungle sublime and dangerous provided the necessary catalyst. Someone's waste was someone's gift. It just goes to show that hope, faith, and happiness sometimes come wrapped in the strangest packages.

With the finish line in sight, I set off down the path with renewed vigour. A celebration loomed and I raced towards it. After only 20 steps, I spilled out of the saturated forest and into a large, man-made clearing, spinning around wide-eyed to see a circle of stones on the ground with the charred remains of a recent fire in its center. My wide smile grew wider as I realized that I'd seen this fire circle before.

"This is where I camped in 2010!" I bellowed as the realization joyfully sank in. "THIS IS POPLARS! I DID IT!!! *I FUCKING DID IT!!!!*"

Exhilarating shots of adrenalized happiness coursed briskly through my head and heart. Hoots, hollers, and frenetic fist pumps followed. I even did a little dance.

When the echoed remnants of my jubilant shouts finally faded into the forest, I stood silent and humble at the river's edge. Relief washed over me. The hardest part of the hike had ended. I was glad it was finally over.

A short stroll on the first vehicle track I'd seen in almost a week brought me to the opening I'd long been searching for: the elusive window to Poplars Camping Area. It was the one I feared I might miss, the one I feared I'd passed. Finally, I was on the inside looking out.

I took a long minute and gazed at the Murray as it tumbled white over a string of rocks that spanned between the banks. The river was swollen and rising by the minute. I'd been to this very spot two times prior. Each time, the river revealed to me a different face. Each time, it cloaked itself in unknowable mystery. No amount of time spent along its banks or immersed in its depth could untangle that mystery. Only the river knew of its past, present, and future goals. It shared no secrets, told no lies. It spoke in a language indecipherable. Its saga was impenetrable. Its wisdom, unfathomable.

What knowledge I'd gleaned from my time on the Murray came not from the river, but from how I saw *myself* in the river. The Murray was a mirror, and I didn't always like what it reflected. Its face was mine. Its manner was mine. Its wrath was mine. It tucked me into bed each night and woke me the following morning. It fed me and fooled me. It cradled and cooled me. I learned and relearned patience as the river raced ceaselessly onward.

I respected the Murray long before I laid eyes on it, but I respected it far more when I turned from its gaze a final time. More importantly, a newfound self-respect had materialized. For more than a decade, my sense of self-worth had been relentlessly rammed through a grief-filled gauntlet of misery and misfortune. It had been reduced to ruins and abandoned like a diseased carcass. But now, thanks to the Murray and its unremitting stream of challenges, my self-worth had been resurrected. It had found its voice, its place, its *purpose*. It had overcome every obstacle and was now celebrating a long-sought triumph. An old expedition was now complete. With providence and perseverance, there was still a chance to begin a new expedition, a longer expedition, the *final* expedition. Yes, I still had the Darling–Murray river system in my sights. The nine-mile hike down the upper Murray had refuelled my confidence and buoyed my hopes. If I could somehow stretch my lean bankroll across the next five months and rectify the unfortunate credit card charges (and get them refunded), then a full descent of the Darling–Murray seemed utterly possible. *Maybe the money's already been refunded,* I said to myself, excited at the possibility of a positive outcome. *Maybe things will work out in my favour. Maybe I can finish what I came here to do.* I held fast to that nascent sense of optimism as I readied myself for the 17-mile hike back to my rental car.

A short stroll around Poplars Camping Area revealed that little had changed since my first two visits in December 2009 and January 2010. A short dirt track, packed flat by vehicle use, connected two primitive camping areas containing three sites each. Camping at Poplars is free, as it is in many of the alpine regions along the upper

Murray, but getting there necessitates the use of a hardy 4x4 (if you didn't arrive on foot or by self-propelled watercraft). The campground has the distinction of being the highest point on the river accessible by vehicle. McCarthys Track and Limestone Creek Track—the only roads in—are steep, rutted, dusty, and difficult to navigate. Each track drops like a giant staircase down to the river. Long descents into creek draws are common, as are the subsequent climbs out. Rain can turn the ochre paths into mud pits, bogging down even the toughest 4x4. Progress is slow. Traffic is light.

The hike to my rental car took less than 24 hours and was, to put it succinctly, a veritable walk in the park compared to the previous three-and-a-half days. That's not to say it was easy. After the initial drizzle departed and the sun reappeared, the uphill trek became a bloody sweat-fest. Even the short sections of *downhill* were gruelling. Creek crossings were significantly flooded and I forded each one without removing my shoes. The blazing sun and warm temperatures ensured that my shoes quickly dried before reaching the next creek. To keep my mood light, I playfully jabbered aloud in a thick Scottish accent, humorously critiquing the terrible condition of the rutted track and commenting exaggeratingly on the natural beauty of the forest. I'd spent the better part of a week loudly complaining while hiking on the Murray. Now, with the trek nearing its end, honing a heavy brogue and a headful of witticisms seemed like a much healthier option.

When I reached the rental car midday on February 1, I craved three things: a tall glass of cold orange juice, a comfy bed in an air-conditioned motel room, and a swim in the ocean. The coastal town of Lakes Entrance, 100 miles to the south, would fit the bill just fine.

During my time on the Murray, I'd consumed about five gallons of untreated river water. My water filter, sadly decommissioned on the first day of the trek, spent the remainder of the hike at the bottom of my backpack. With no iodine tablets to chemically treat the water, or enough fuel to boil it, I resorted to scooping it straight from the river. Thankfully, I didn't get sick while hiking—that would've been disastrous—but I did have an uneasy feeling that I'd pay for it eventually.

My first two days in Lakes Entrance were spent getting well acquainted with the motel room's toilet. It was a nice toilet, plenty comfortable for long sits. When I wasn't perched on porcelain, I was crumpled uncomfortably on a bed of starchy sheets as the room's air conditioner laboured noisily through its cycles. The idea of ingesting *anything*, solid or not, never consumed my thoughts. Dehydration called collect and said it would be arriving soon. "If you drink a river, expect a drought," it said with a chuckle. My angry innards complained loudly. My mind vomited regrets. My craving for a tall glass of cold orange juice went the way of my incessant bowel movements and dwindling optimism. Simple pleasures once yearned for were now being urgently purged down a drainpipe of despondency. The Murray, it seemed, had arrived in Lakes Entrance in the foulest way possible.

I'd like to say that this unfortunate shit storm ended resolutely with the expedited evacuation of my bowels, but it didn't. Unbeknownst to me, there lay in wait another shit-filled sewer to cheerlessly trudge through.

After going more than 10 days in the mountains without Internet access, I was eager to learn whether my credit card debacle had resolved itself. If the charges had been refunded, it would open the door for the Darling–Murray expedition to continue, which meant my suicide plot could proceed as planned. If the refunds were still in limbo, I'd be forced to either hang myself from the motel room's shower fixture or return to Canada a broken man in the dead of winter. It was hard to determine which option was worse.

In between sprints to the toilet, I managed to get online long enough to access my credit card transaction history. What I saw there crippled me mentally. There had been no refunds. Nothing posted. Nothing pending. To say I was devastated would be an absolute understatement. In place of expected redemption and deserved victory, I was instead dealt a swift kick of unwelcomed reality. The tipping point had been reached. The descent into misery had begun.

Perhaps the most demoralizing aspect of abandoning a dream is the heart-wrenching loss associated with it. The crush of emotions that follows such a loss is often more sinister than what came before. Overwhelming sadness and self-imposed guilt seem to saturate every waking hour. Debilitating depression becomes the norm. Blame is sought, but soon retracted. None but the self is at fault.

A dream's demise, whether initiated voluntarily or not, marks the end of one life chapter and the beginning of another. This vital transition is, however, rarely embraced or promptly enacted. Instead, an incessant desire to wallow in a cesspool of sadness is propagated and practiced, perpetuating a ceaseless cycle of self-directed guilt and blame. How does a person move beyond these self-created obstacles of despondency? The simple answer is: they don't. No matter their level of indomitable resolve, the callous effects of past defeats linger long and hard. Every future challenge comes riddled with indecision and fear. Resignation is the only path forward.

The eastward drive out of Lakes Entrance was a lonely but beautiful trek down a two-lane coastal highway lined with dense rainforest. Clouds, drizzle, and downpours helped drag out my dour mood. I'd long grown tired of the dearth of precipitation I'd haplessly endured on this Australian visit. I pined for omnipresent heat and desert-like serenity. I needed drought in the worst way possible.

When the highway reached the country's south-eastern corner and curved north, I passed over pavement I'd ridden during my continental crossing by bicycle back in 2004. Grades steepened as the road snaked through the lush southern forests of the Great Dividing Range. As I piloted The Red Beast up the intimidating inclines, I found myself pondering the incapability of my present physical and mental states. I had really let myself go.

Years of depression and anxiety had led to habitual inactivity and emotional eating. Sugar-tainted products produced in faraway factories provided temporary escapism. Apathy became my drug of choice. Where once I bicycled on the mountainous slopes of western Canada, I now drove a characterless vehicle across the bland prairie of southern Ontario. Where once I strived for a distinctively active lifestyle, I now settled for mediocrity. Where once I craved difficult, I now craved easy. My love of comfort killed my ambition.

I hated the thickening layer of fat that had formed on every inch of my body. I hated when I touched my chubby belly and squeezed the excess flab between thumb and forefinger. I hated measuring my worth this way. I hated the shame I felt. I hated the self-imposed guilt I projected on myself. I hated the unrelenting anger and sadness that accompanied this internal degradation. I purposefully distanced myself from others in fear of their caustic judgements. My endurance and determination had withered. I wasn't the self-propelled powerhouse I'd been only a few years prior. I'd become less by becoming more. I was now just a shadowy shell, cracked and crumbling under the weight of its own misfortune.

Before embarking on this third trip to Australia, I never once gave thought to cancelling an expedition. Struggling toward the finish line always appealed more to me than quitting. In fact, quitting was never an option. Arriving at the destination was always the definitive motivator. The tedious journey to the destination was often viewed as a necessary evil, begrudgingly tolerated and rarely appreciated. Still, thanks to my manic persistence, every expedition I'd undertaken was successful. Never had I given up.

But now, as The Red Beast revved hard up the steep hills of southern New South Wales, I wondered how I'd ever managed to pedal through this unnerving landscape. My former self never balked at these intimidating blacktop ascents. He simply pointed the front wheel forward, grinding upward and onward to the distant hillcrest. Gone was that two-wheeled warrior. The excesses of recent years had trumped his resolve. His unwavering confidence had been sadly replaced with staunch self-doubt. With head bowed low, I'd regrettably given my resignation. Exit the Warrior. Enter the Failure.

With the Darling–Murray expedition now dead in the water, I quite unconsciously moved away from the idea of taking my own life. I say *unconsciously* because no forthright decision had been made. I didn't want to die, but I also didn't want to live. I wanted limbo. I wanted easy. To me, living was easy and suicide was hard—or rather, the challenging *path* to suicide was hard, especially the one I'd chosen to tread. The choice to return to Canada was based solely on the fact that I had failed in my attempt to kill myself. I wasn't able to die the way I wanted, and the loss of that dream saddened me deeply. I chose to relinquish control over death. I strove instead to make living as comfortable as possible. The hard road had been too hard. I needed easy. I needed a break.

The Red Beast's tires were still hissing wet when I pulled into the driveway at Peter Dodds' house. I was there to retrieve the remainder of my gear and to break the news that I'd officially cancelled the Darling–Murray expedition.

Thankfully, Peter and his wife Gemma passed no judgement as I shared my sad news. They wholly accepted and supported my decision without debate. I was grateful for their comforting neutrality.

"If you change your mind, please know we'll be here to help any way we can," said Peter, his voice warm with reassurance. "Don't hesitate to call."

"Thanks," I replied, smiling. "Your kindness is appreciated."

"What's your plan now?" asked Peter as he helped me load a heavy duffle bag into The Red Beast.

"Well, I didn't come to Australia to get rained on every day," I said. "I need to salvage something from this trip before returning to Canada. I'm going to drive west to the town of Yarrawonga in Victoria. It's right on the banks of the Murray River. I remember paddling through that section in 2010. Almost every bend in the river has a sandbar—the locals call them *beaches*. There are tons of places to camp. The weather forecast for Yarrawonga is calling for sun and temps in the mid-90s for the next seven days. I plan to dry out for a week or so. After that, I'm gonna swap The Red Beast for a cheaper rental car at the Sydney airport, and then head north to scout the first three rivers on the Darling–Murray. It'll give me a hands-on look at what I'll be up against when I return one day to finish what I never started this time."

"That sounds like a fantastic plan," said Peter as he shook my hand a final time. "I know you'll make the most of the time you have left here in Australia. Please keep in touch. Safe travels, Rod."

I'm happy to say that Yarrawonga did not disappoint. Nor did the string of beautiful river beaches dotting each twist of the Murray west of town. I swam leisurely in the warm river and walked slowly through stoic forests of gums and eucalyptus that lined the river-banks. The soothing, cyclical sound of a million cicadas serenaded me during the hot afternoons. Curious kangaroos visited my camp, as did two venomous brown snakes and a spider the size of my hand. Great gangs of cockatoos screeched their way from treetop to treetop, their riotous explosions of white and pale pink shocking both eyes and ears, turning the forest into a maelstrom of feather and fury. They always seemed to be under attack by an invisible foe, a giant, unseen predator that incited these flighty sirens to fill the heated air with a voluminous racket. Or perhaps the deafening display was part of some instinctual mating ritual, thus guarantee-ing that the loudest cock gets the lady. Whatever the case, I wel-comed the hush at nightfall as they settled in their evening roost, and garishly grinned when one or two met their screechy end in the chomping jaw of a hungry, nocturnal fox.

I spent a week in that balmy oasis. It never rained a drop.

The Sydney airport parking lot was its usual frenetic self as I pi-loted The Red Beast past hordes of jaywalking tourists and stressed-out lot attendants. I was there to exchange the Beast for a cheaper rental car and then promptly exit the madness before the afternoon rush hour descended.

The scene inside the airport was doubly frenetic. I weaved my way through the ambling crowd of newly-arrived zombies and approached the smiling clerk at the Hertz kiosk. It was the same clerk I'd dealt with three weeks prior.

"Welcome back, mate," he said. "How was your trip?"

"Trust me, you don't wanna know," I replied, shaking my head with earnest disgust.

The clerk's smile quickly dissipated.

"What can I do for you today?" he asked.

I explained my desire to exchange The Red Beast and waited while he checked to see what other vehicles were available.

"We've three possibilities for a replacement," said the clerk, "and I'll be happy to discuss those with you in a moment. But first, you'll have to arrange payment for the SUV you've been using. There's an outstanding balance of $1200."

The amount made me cringe. Cobbling together enough funds to pay the bill wasn't going to be an easy task.

"According to what I see here," continued the clerk, "there was an attempt to charge the amount owing to your credit card, but the payment never went through. A notice was posted on your file 11 days ago saying that the credit card used to rent the vehicle was invalid. Do you have that card with you today?"

"Of course," I answered. I withdrew the card from my wallet and handed it to him.

He slowly examined it.

"Is this a prepaid credit card?" he asked.

"Yes," I said. "Is there a problem with it?"

"Well…yes," said the clerk, frowning as he laid the card on the counter.

An awkward, silent pause hung uncomfortably between us while I waited for his explanation.

"There seems to have been a mix-up when you rented the vehicle from me back in January," he said. "I'm sorry to say this, but…I shouldn't have accepted the card in the first place. I mistook your card for an actual credit card. Prepaid cards can be used for payments, but not for security deposits on vehicles. The deposit amount was never successfully applied to your card. A Hertz representative tried to contact you several times on your cell, but the phone number was apparently out of service. It's a good thing you brought the car back when you did. We were a day away from reporting it stolen."

"*Stolen?!*" The word sounded even more ludicrous when *I* said it. I could feel anger welling up in my chest.

"Yes, sir. Stolen," said the clerk. "Hertz takes these things pretty seriously."

"But this was *your* fault!" I shouted, angrily pointing a finger in the clerk's direction.

"You're right," he said. "And I apologize for the misunderstanding. The deposit amount should've never been charged to your prepaid Visa card. I'm sorry this happened."

I took a long, deep breath and stuffed my anger inside where a thousand other such angers resided. The clerk, sensing my agitation and my effort to diminish it, gave me ample space before he spoke again.

"If you plan to rent another car today, you'll need a valid credit card for the security deposit. Do you have one you can use?"

"No," I said, sheepishly.

"Then I'm afraid I can't rent you another car," he said.

"What the fuck am I supposed to do with my gear?!" I shouted. My voice was angry, desperate, urgent.

"Perhaps one of the other car companies here in the airport will honour your card. It might be worth a try," said the clerk, optimistically.

"You don't understand!" I said, almost pleading. "I need to use a car to take that gear north to Brisbane. There's something very important I need to do up there. I can't leave the country until I do that. I *won't* leave the country until I do that!"

We locked eyes. One of us was going to win this battle and both of us knew who it was.

"I wish I could offer more help," he said calmly. "Again, maybe one of the other companies can assist you."

This time, I had no rebuttal. Sadness and disbelief had rendered me silent. Defeat had arrived swiftly, far more swiftly than I expected. In fact, I expected it *not* to arrive. I expected it to keep its distance for the rest of the trip. It had shown its face far too many times over the past three weeks and now its reappearance irked me to no end. Inside I was livid, but I doubt the anger showed on my face. Misery was the only mask I wore.

In that suspended, ugly moment of inconvenient truth and embittered reality, I hated my life. Humiliation was preceding resignation. A lengthening que stretched behind me, disappearing into the crowd of luggage-toting zombies. In front of me stood an impasse, every bit as imposing as the steep highway hills I chose not to ride or the great river I'd chosen not to paddle. The Hertz clerk was the unwavering gatekeeper and I was the weary traveller seeking uncomplicated passage. Unfortunately, my passage was being revoked and my character rebuffed. The tipping point was fast approaching.

"How would you like to settle the amount owing on the SUV?"

His question jarred me out of my woeful head and back into the hapless present moment.

"I'll pay with cash," I mumbled.

"Sorry sir, we don't accept cash payments at this location."

"Well, you better, because that's all I have," I said, insistently.

After a whispered phone call to the Hertz head office, the clerk informed me that a one-time payment of cash could be accepted. A trip to the nearest ATM cost me my place in line and I frustratingly had to wait while the clerk assisted a new customer.

The counting and recounting of cash took a nerve-grating infinity. Clearly, the clerk's trust in me had gone AWOL. When the counting finished, the clerk looked up and asked, "May I please have the key to the vehicle?"

"I'll drop it off when I'm done unloading the car," I offered.

"I'm afraid you can't do that, sir," he said, firmly. "You'll have to give me the key now and I'll accompany you to the car to retrieve your possessions."

I reluctantly slid the key across the counter.

"Thank you," said the clerk. I sensed a hint of empathy in his voice, perhaps knowing how hard it was for me to relinquish the key. He was watching a man lose control. He was watching a man surrender.

We silently crossed the parking lot together. As I sat sulking in the passenger seat, the clerk drove The Red Beast to a processing area, presumably where lot attendants would clean it. The clerk handed the key to an attendant, wished me well, and strode back to the airport. I was too despondent to reply.

I spent the next hour in a haze of anger, sadness, stress, embarrassment, and crippling paranoia. The weight of all the other indignities from the entire trip befell me and crushed my hopeful heart. Retreat was now my only option. Although I loathed the idea, I would have to return to Canada. The end had arrived prematurely. The tipping point had finally been reached.

Efforts to reschedule my return flight to Canada yielded no same-day options, so I was forced to book a seat on a flight leaving the following day. At first, I viewed this as hugely inconvenient, but it ended up being a blessing of sorts. It gave me the opportunity to end the trip on a high note. I decided to ditch my luggage at the airport's storage facility and grab a taxi to Bondi Beach on Sydney's southwest side. If anything would give me some satisfaction after the unexpected pummelling I'd just endured, it would be a long swim in the ocean.

The cab ride to Bondi took almost an hour and cost me $100. Ouch! As luck would have it, my prepaid credit card was declined, leaving me to fork over half of my remaining cash. The combination of car rental and flight rebooking fees, as well as the overpriced cab ride, had nearly drained my meagre funds. If another unexpected expense reared its ugly head, I would surely be sunk.

Fortunately, Sydney was enjoying its first hot day in weeks, which made swimming in the warm surf even more pleasant. Bondi's setting is amazingly and uniquely beautiful. The crescent shaped beach is hemmed with a densely packed neighbourhood of terraced apartment buildings, hotels, cafés, and endless restaurants, all of which somehow compliment the natural beauty of the arcing shoreline and whitecapped ocean.

An asphalt walkway, animated on this day with joggers, in-line skaters, and leisurely paced tourists, separated the tahini-coloured beach from a spotless emerald lawn that sloped up to the surrounding entertainment district. It proved to be an ideal spot to take in a dazzling sunset, with both sky and water lit lipstick pink and rose red. I didn't want it to end.

Fragrant wafts of pizza, pasta, pork, and pot drifted through the warm night air as I wandered the seaside streets in search of accommodations. I wanted this last night in Australia to be one of comfort and nurture. I wanted to cleanse myself and sleep in an actual bed.

After inquiring at a number of fully booked hotels, I found a vacant room above a posh-looking bar filled with neon lights, mirrors, and bad music. Curiously, there wasn't a soul in the place, save for a non-chatty office dweller keen on taking my money. Equally curious was the fact that my credit card was declined when I attempted to pay for the room. I'd purposefully put extra funds on the card to cover any unforeseen expenses and it bothered me as to why it was being revoked. As I forked over the remainder of my cash to the hotel clerk, I made a mental note to call the credit card company as soon as I settled in.

The hotel room was less than basic, the bed less than comfortable, and the view less than spectacular. The bland white walls had been streaked yellow by time, cigarette smoke, and sheer neglect. (I was glad I'd requested a *non-smoking* room.) Thankfully, the air-conditioner worked flawlessly and the shower doled out an endless supply of hot water.

I wasn't thankful, however, to hear that United Airlines had inadvertently double-charged my credit card for the return flight to Canada. The extra $300 charge had driven down the available balance to next than nothing. That explained why the card had been revoked by the taxi driver and the hotel. I was told the charge would be refunded in four to six weeks.

As I lay on the bed and wrapped my head around United's senseless blunder, I watched in gross amazement as a thumb-sized cockroach emerged from beneath the rumbling air conditioner and scurried diagonally across the yellowed wall. I sighed and shook my head.

"My problems are like cockroaches," I said aloud as the pest disappeared under the bathroom door. "Where there's one, there's sure to be more."

It was entirely fitting that the trip should end with such simple irony. The endless treadmill of inconsistency had become both cheerlessly predictable and frustratingly erratic. The enticing expectation of adventure and self-imposed death had led to disappointing resignation and a second chance at life. Somehow, I had to be grateful for the lessons and move on.

It was also entirely fitting that my intercontinental flight should land during the worst blizzard London, Ontario had seen in a decade. No point in breaking up a streak of irony!

I took three long days to acclimatize to the frigid temperatures and heaps of fresh snow. Sugar and sleep buoyed me through the transition. On the morning of the fourth day, I dug out the unfinished manuscript for *River Angels* (my second book) and began in earnest to complete it.

It felt good to write. It felt good to be busy. It felt good to have a goal. It felt good to work out the pent-up anger and disappointment I brought back from Australia.

Six weeks later, the manuscript was complete. Six weeks after that I was holding a printed copy of the book in my hand. A month after that, I was kicking off a 20-date book tour in the U.S. I was making it work. I was finding success on my own terms. I was giving myself a second chance. I was moving on.

I'd endured plenty during those four arduous weeks in Australia. I'd gone there with a desperate plan and returned with hopeful determination. For the first time in many months, I had a positive goal in my sights and I was determined to see its fruition.

I've never believed in fate, luck, or chance. I've always believed that success stems purely from diligence and dedication. The boulder reached the mountaintop because I pushed it there. It didn't arrive there by luck or circumstance. But even while labelling myself as ambitiously motivated, a question still lingers in my mind: if hard work and commitment lay at the root of success, why didn't I succeed in taking my own life in Australia? Some people might say, "Because things happen for a reason." If that's so, I still don't understand *the reason*. Is this book you hold in your hands the reason? Is sharing a positive message of hope and optimism the reason? Is simply being *alive* the reason?

If *reason* can be seen as an aim, a motive, a cause, a goal, or a purpose, then I can confidently state here and now that it was never my intention to write a book about this healing journey, or to share a message of hope and optimism, or to even be alive. I never wanted those things to transpire. And yet, miraculously, they did. Did something conspire to make those things happen? Was it predestined? Was it *fate*?

To me, *fate* implies that something beyond myself, something beyond this plane of existence, has somehow influenced the outcome of my intentions. I don't subscribe to that theory. Freewill, not fate, fires my engines. Investing in fate, luck, and chance seems like a senseless gamble in a world filled with concrete conclusions and provable facts. But what about the undeniably tangible truth that resonates from the hearts of *mystery* and *paradox*? Every one of us, during every hour of every day of our lives, places longshot bets on the unknown. Some bets pay out. Some don't. Even the hardest worker among us doesn't always succeed at pushing the boulder up the mountain. Sometimes the peak is never reached. Sometimes things don't go as planned. Why? I have no fucking idea. Maybe it has something to do with fate, luck, or chance. Maybe things *do* happen for a reason.

While putting the finishing touches on the *River Angels* manuscript in March 2016, I got word that Mark Kalch had abandoned his paddling descent of the Darling–Murray river system. He'd been at it for two months, paddling and portaging 620 miles through oppressive temperatures and low water levels before exiting the Darling River just upstream of the town of Bourke, New South Wales. With much effort, he'd descended the lengths of the river system's first three waterways (Condamine, Balonne, and Culgoa), but still had 1470 miles to go to reach the Southern Ocean.

As more information came to light, it was revealed that Mark had contracted a waterborne disease during his time on the aforementioned rivers. The illness left him debilitated, making paddling impossible. With no other options available, he used his SPOT tracker to send a distress message to his mother and brother in Australia. His decision to do so was something he'd agonized over for days before pushing the button.

Mark was subsequently hospitalized and diagnosed with leptospirosis, a form of meningitis. It was months before he fully recovered.

The news hit home with me because I'd become ill from drinking untreated river water on the upper Murray. Thankfully, the effects of my illness occurred well away from the river. I was able to recuperate in the comfort of a motel room and did not require medical attention. In hindsight, maybe it was a good thing I gave up my goal of descending the Darling–Murray and returned to Canada. If suicide didn't kill me, a deadly disease may have.

In an effort to better understand the extent of his illness, I sent Mark Kalch a list of questions via email. His answers, printed below, also shed light on the emotional pain he endured as a result of his decision to end his Darling–Murray descent.

RW: What date (approx.) did you start and what date (approx.) did you leave the river above Bourke?

MK: January 14, 2016. Started from the source. Took off the river a day's paddle above Bourke, around March 15, or the day before that.

RW: Was it devastating for you to pull off the river? You mentioned in earlier correspondence you felt "gutted." Can you unpack this feeling for me? How did the decision to quit impact you emotionally and physically?

MK: Oh yeah, it was a real bummer. Two years on, I am obviously over it. But if I recall that time period, it still gives me the creeps. It was such a tough descent because of the heat and lack of water and waiting for a big brown snake to get me! :) I am pretty good at just grinding through and was doing a pretty good job of doing just that. So, to get nailed by this leptospirosis really sucked.

RW: Did the feeling of loss grow stronger after you got home?

MK: Yeah, it was hard not to think about for a long time. You know circumstances dictate a lot of outcomes. I have four kids now (three at the time) and have, for the entire time we've had kids, disappeared for months at a time leaving Hol (his wife) to look after them despite her having a very hectic job. The decision to stop at that time and go home would not have even been an option for me if it was just me. Heck, I would have recovered at my mum's house right on the beach for however long it took—one month, two months, whatever—and then put back in. Piece of cake! Funnily enough, I would say, physically, it took six months (to recover). And mentally, who knows? Depends how you measure it. As I mentioned above, it still gives me the heebie jeebies! But life happens. Priorities change. What was more important to me—that less-than-desirable river, or my family? Ha! Easy answer. But I suppose, in a way, it made taking off the river even tougher. I had no option. Tell the kids and Hol I was going to stay in Oz until I was better? It would have meant maybe 10 months away (from them). Yeesh! These rivers aren't *that* important to me.

RW: When was the feeling most intense? On the river? In the hospital? At home after the expedition?

MK: The feeling of being pissed off for taking off? Probably two times. After I was allowed to leave the hospital, back at my mum's just staring at the waves, agonizing over what to do. And then, once I had returned home, for sure. On the river and in the hospital, I wasn't even thinking about it. It was kind of touch and go (at least in my mind!) for a while. I thought it could have been this kind of meningitis (he included a link to a story about naegleria fowleri, a brain-eating parasite). Fortunately, (it was) a different form. Defo primo conditions for it where I was paddling.

RW: How did you radio for help before you left the river? SPOT? Cell phone?

MK: Almost no phone reception out there. I agonized over using my SPOT even just for pick-up request from my mum and brother. But better not to be dead, I eventually figured. At about 5:00am, after a night of agony (I eventually collapsed during the night, half in and half out of my tent, lying on the ground. Oof!), I hit the pick-up button, waited 20 minutes, hit it again, and then 20 minutes later, (hit it) a third time. I figured getting three emails from me would let them know it was pretty serious. Would have helped to read the instructions, as after hitting that button it sends an email every two or three minutes, or something like that. Mum and my bro ended up with something like 43 emails! They thought I must have lost the plot.

RW: Who picked you up when you left the river?

MK: So, mum (being a mum!) was pretty worried and got on the phones and had my brother do the same. My bro contacted the SES (State Emergency Service) which is our all-volunteer service, but they said they only come out by request of police. With very patchy phone I had the day before, I told my mum not to contact police no matter what, but after 43 emails, I can't blame her. So, she did contact police in Bourke. They had my location from mum and got in touch with the farmer who owned the land. As the sun came up, I thought I would try to paddle on to where a road almost hit the river. I couldn't stand, so I sat down. I paddled for a few hours and was fading. I knew if I spent another night out there, I would have to hit the emergency button or maybe kick the bucket. Early arvo (afternoon), I heard a motorbike and spotted someone on the bank. I yelled out but they cruised on. I was pretty bummed. Luckily, he circled back and yelled out to me to pull over up ahead at a water pump. Thirty minutes later, he returned in his 4WD. Scott Mitchell was the land owner. I was pretty relieved to see him. He told me he was out looking for me. I said to him, "Mate please tell me it's just you and no cops or emergency services." He laughed and said, "Nah, they are on their way." Ha! Ten minutes later, two coppers and a 4WD from the SES turned up. Everyone was really chilled. They were just happy I wasn't dead. They had a woman get lost a week or two previous after leaving her car and they found her dead. Copper said he was happy he didn't go two-for-two! Coppers really great, said it was not a problem. If I told them I was all good, they would just turn around and leave me. (I asked) if they could take me into town. I got a lift with them into town and got a cabin at a caravan park. My mum turned up next day. She was pretty relieved.

RW: Where did you first visit a hospital after you left the river? Bourke?

MK: Yeah. Bourke hospital. I was still being stubborn, but mum obviously wanted me to get checked up on, and so did the coppers who we visited next day. So, I did. Here is short description from Instagram at the time:

Hey folks, I will try to give a quick little update on where I'm at currently. Longer version will have to wait.

Anyway, in short, I came off the river on Friday just above Bourke, NSW feeling pretty knackered, but okay (a story in itself). Saturday, at everyone's insistence, I went to the local hospital where they put me on an IV drip and did blood tests. Results said, "onset of renal failure and muscle damage." Rest for a week.

Rather than a week in the heat of the bush, headed back to coast. Sunday afternoon intense pain in my head so taken to emergency where I spent six hours and more blood taken, more IV rehydration, IV morphine, plus tablets. By 1:00am, felt ok to go home.

I was back at 7:00am to emergency, worse. Another morning, more pain meds, and docs scratching their heads.

Eventually, the guys from infectious diseases were brought in. I had a lumbar puncture, which doesn't hurt as much as you think, but still feels pretty creepy. They tested my spinal fluid and (it) came back (with) strange results. The thought then was leptospirosis. Have not heard more.

So, I have been admitted into the infectious disease ward. No one allowed into my room without mask, gloves, and apron. Have been given a few more IV antibiotics and more blood taken. Haven't seen a doctor since yesterday. Hospital is pretty boring eh?

I don't feel too bad, but (it) would be good to know what's up.

Amazingly, I am being treated for free only because I am a UK resident! A reciprocal deal. Been away too long and don't qualify for Medicare. Crazy huh?

Will keep updated when I can. Apologies everyone.

RW: Please describe the mental and physical effects of the illness.

MK: Well it was leptospirosis meningitis, so I had all the fun symptoms of that which are easy to find (online). Headaches, light sensitive, sore muscles. I was peeing a lot. Throwing up a lot. The head problems were probably the most painful. It felt like my head was going to crack open!

Like I said, in terms of recovery it took a long time. As you well know, after two months paddling you are usually pretty well conditioned and hard physically, but looking in the mirror, my muscles were like jelly. It was really odd. It was like messages to them weren't getting through properly.

Mentally, yeah, as above, it wasn't great. I thought about it a lot. Maybe if I had waited another day it could have ended worse. So, in a lot of ways I was happy with my decision. Again, better to crack some jokes with the cops than have them zipping you up in a body bag. Defo (definitely) more embarrassing in terms of skill and decision-making to end up with the latter.

RW: Do you feel your reputation was impacted negatively by your decision to abort? If so, how do you believe it was impacted?

MK: No, not at all. It was personal disappointment. I just grind out these trips. Nothing stops me, etc. I only care about what my kids think of me. Back then, and even prior to it, it was my just my kids and people like Norm Miller and Piotr Chmielinski and my peers, such as your good self, who I cared about their reaction. Only they know what goes into these things. People who followed me on social media have no bloody idea.

RW: Describe the stress related to sponsorship commitments and the commitment to posting regularly on social media. Did you see these things as burdens during the expedition?

MK: I think years ago, I didn't mind it at all. It was just a part of it. I kind of grew tired of working my ass off to get good ROI (return on investment) for my sponsors and being ignored, or just thrown more equipment when I really needed cash. Or even worse, after some big descents, being given the same gear that a rank beginner would be given by the same sponsor for their dinky charity paddle down a section of the Thames! Like I mentioned, even by 2016 I was well over it. Mostly due to the above, but also by the steady creep of professional social media folks whose expeds were pretty average at best, but with a good social media game, (they) could hype up things a lot. Really did my head in. I am overjoyed to be out of the scene.

~~~

She is the special one, the one that makes my heart beat faster. For more than a year, the memory of her stayed embedded in my daily thoughts. I pined for her. I let her go a hundred times and held her close a hundred more. During my time in Australia, during my time in Chatham, during my time book-touring in the U.S., I kept a love light burning, a beacon that saw me through many dark moments.

In November 2016, while seated in the passenger seat of my car, laptop on my thighs, hammering out the manuscript for this book, I reached out to Kitty Pawlak via Facebook Messenger. I felt it was time to share a secret.

Rod: I have a few things I need to voice.

I have liked you ever since I met you at The Minga a year ago. Even before you took off your coat and went to help Frances Jane in the kitchen. Even before Jody introduced us and we shook hands. It happened when I turned and saw you walk past the cash register. It happened when I saw your face, your hair, your smile. It happened when I noticed the quirky sway of your body—one that spoke of humour and confidence. At that moment, I could not look away. Nor did I want to. You weren't perfect, but you were perfectly you.

During the course of that evening, I fell into something...I'm not sure what to call it. It might've been love. Or obsession. Or infatuation. Or a pretty serious crush. Whatever it was, it helped me feel *alive*. It frightened me. It excited me. It angered me. It saddened me. It helped me experience a joy I hadn't felt in a long time. It also did one more thing, something I don't think I've ever experienced before. It showed me I was capable of compassion. It showed me I was not scared of committing. At one point, sometime between the library event and the concert (a span of two weeks), an overwhelming feeling enveloped me, in a good way. I believe it was compassion. I felt, from that moment onward, that if you were to fall ill, I would take care of you. Now, I've felt a similar obligation in past relationships (eg. girlfriend has the flu, I take care of girlfriend). But this feeling was different. It went beyond caregiving. It spoke of commitment and it reminded me how much I craved the feeling of committing to someone and them committing to me. I miss the union, the partnership, the intimacy, the trust, the reciprocal love I experienced in past relationships. But I don't want to repeat those experiences. I want to create *new* experiences.

I've been on an emotional rollercoaster since I met you, Kitty. I've been through peaks and valleys. I carried forward a hope that somehow you and I might explore a relationship together. At times, that hope, as well as a few other key elements, kept me alive. Several times, I discarded the fantasy of *you and me* in hopes of alleviating the pain of rejection if and when it came. And every time I discarded the fantasy, it reappeared. I learned I didn't want to, or perhaps could not, move on. I clung to one hope, and it pains me to admit that I still cling to it. There is something so undeniably special about you, something that effortlessly pierces my heart, something that returns each time I cast it away. And although those things hint at some deeper meaning (or feeling), I still can't define it. I'm not in love with you, but I do pine for you. Do you feel any of this when you think about me? Are you in a relationship? Are you looking? Are you planning to be in a relationship?

If you want to discuss this further, one on one, face to face, I'm willing to meet with you. If it's pretty cut and dry and you see no reason to meet, I'm fine with that too. I know your time in southern Ontario is limited and that there are several people you want to meet with. I respect that. Just let me know what you want to do. My schedule is flexible.

And lastly, from the bottom of my often chilly heart, thank you. Thank you for sparking a fire in me. Thank you for helping me experience new feelings. Thank you for helping me grow. Kitty, you are a truly amazing woman. Peace.

Kitty: I'm at The Minga for the craft sale. I've been really busy getting ready for it. If you would like to get together, I have a much easier time expressing myself face to face. You have a beautiful way of writing and can communicate on point. However, for me, I require the use of my hands, facial expressions, and sometimes theatrical performances. So, if we can make that happen, I would be interested.

Rod: Good luck with the craft sale! People be buyin' luv when they buy your creations. :)

I'm interested in hearing (and seeing) what you have to say. My schedule is flexible, so whatever is convenient for you works for me. I don't mind driving. Where and when shall we meet?

Kitty: I appreciate your honesty and willingness to open up to me. I value your truth. I am in a place where I need to take my time in matters of the heart. I would be interested in getting to know you. I enjoy your energy, presence, and adventuring spirit. I write this to you because as I get closer to seeing you, my anxiety is crazy and my fear is amping up. I need to be honest as well, that I need you to understand that the relationship (and I mean that in any sense of relationship, not just romantic) we can foster would have to be slow. I don't want to lead you on, and if you're in a rush, I cannot participate. I feel like this is causing my anxiety, and fear is caused by my previous relationship. I do not want to be controlled by these fears and that is why I would still like to see you and face those fears. If this is too much, I understand. Also, I was wondering if we could go for a hike or something outdoors instead of a café?

Rod: Yes, we can absolutely go for a hike. I will do a little research and see if there's a cool trail in the Cambridge area. (I'll get back to you in a few hours regarding that.) If you know of one, or have a favourite place in mind, let me know. P.S. It doesn't need to be near Cambridge. I'll bring a vegan treat from Eat What's Good (a Chatham restaurant). If you have any of your bags left, bring them. I'll trade you one for a copy of *River Angels*. :)

Okay, nerves. Sounds like you're anxious and nervous and fearful. So am I. I have no idea what's going to happen and I'm nervous as fuck. Thankfully, we have three things going for us: 1) we're both risk takers, 2) we're both courageous, 3) we're both a little loopy.

Okay, well, you're *more* than a little loopy. But that's okay by me. I like loopy. ;)

The fact that you do not want to be controlled by your fears, and you want to face them and grow from the experience, is a huge show of courage. That's fuckin' *rock star courage*, grrrl! High fuckin' five to that! And then there's this: you opened up, put your feelings into words, and sent them to me in a Facebook message. That takes courage. I honestly did not expect you to do that. Not because I didn't think you had it in you, but because I thought you'd save it until we talk face to face. You made yourself vulnerable. It wasn't easy, but you did. Thank you for sharing your thoughts. It shows there is an element of trust developing between us, which is good.

I do not feel that you are leading me on, and I am not in a rush. I can't put a label on what we're growing here, but I'm glad to be part of it. Peace.

Wild come the mountains.
Wild comes the sea.
A new continent will be created
when you bring your love to me.

"I'm pregnant."

She pushed the words at me like a toddler rejecting a plate of vegetables. A sad sense of desperation and anger lurked in her voice. It was obvious to me that she viewed her condition as inconvenient, unwarranted, aggravating.

Kitty Pawlak never wanted children. She was too free-spirited for that. She couldn't be burdened with the chore of raising a child when there were ocean reefs and exotic landscapes to explore. Besides, what kind of person brings a baby into this fucked up world?

Despite her storied history of promiscuity, Kitty Pawlak had tactfully avoided pregnancy through a dependable combination of well-timed pull-outs and astute observation of menstrual cycles.

Unfortunately, it only took one small explosion to eradicate years of practiced perfection. As my father would say, "There's a first time for everything."

With relative ease, she and I were able to pinpoint when and where it happened. The sex was steamy that night. She coaxed. I came. She drew me out and kept the truth to herself. She knew the timing was wrong. She knew the inherent risk. But she also knew how great that moment was for me. Afterward, she held me close and slowly kissed my neck. It was springtime. We were in love.

Kitty Pawlak never wanted children. She wept as she told me how she had consumed an herbal tincture in order to induce a miscarriage. When this didn't work, she resorted to punching herself in the stomach, When that didn't work, she had sex with me in hopes that vaginal penetration would induce what the other acts hadn't. Nothing worked.

Kitty Pawlak never wanted children. She told this to the nurse at the Morgentaler Clinic in Ottawa just prior to having an abortion. Still groggy from sedatives, she grimaced at the shaming shouts of pro-life protesters as she exited the clinic. Their placards—plastered with larger-than-life images of dead, bloodied fetuses—only exasperated the anguish of her self-inflicted guilt. The experience made her weep. She never wanted to take a life. To do so went against her spiritual teachings. In her eyes, she wasn't just betraying the unborn, she was betraying the universe. For weeks, her body had been at war with her conscience. Now, for better or worse, her body had won.

Kitty Pawlak never wanted drama in her life. She never wanted to be controlled or manipulated. She never wanted to feel as though she was walking on eggshells around anyone. She never wanted to be judged. She never wanted to second-guess herself. She never wanted to be told she was hated. She'd heard too much of that in her previous relationship.

Kitty Pawlak never wanted to commit suicide. She never wanted to twist a coat hanger around her neck until it almost choked away her life. She never wanted to abandon her suicide mission and collapse in tears on a cold linoleum floor. She never wanted to go through that awful episode alone. She never wanted to share that story with anyone. She never wanted anyone to know. She also never wanted anyone to have to go through what she went through.

Kitty Pawlak never wanted to be physically assaulted. She never wanted her parents to beat her when she was too young to defend herself. She never wanted a man to sexually assault her when she was a girl. She never wanted loved ones to verbally abuse her repeatedly. She never wanted men to misinterpret her words. She never wanted men to view and treat her as inferior. She never wanted men to speak for her. She never wanted men to dismiss her intelligence. She never wanted men to disempower her by explaining things she already knew.

Kitty Pawlak wanted to love and be loved. She wanted to dance and sing and laugh and eat really good food. She wanted friends and lovers and sunsets full of vivid colours. She wanted to swim in the ocean. She wanted her dog to sleep next to her at night. She wanted to give and receive smiles. She wanted to give and receive encouragement. She wanted to give and receive support. She wanted community. She wanted to allow time for yoga and meditation and books and thought-provoking documentaries. Kitty Pawlak wanted to heal. She missed being happy, healthy, and whole. She wanted her life back. She wanted to move forward.

I never wanted to physically assault Kitty Pawlak and I never wanted Kitty Pawlak to physically assault me. I never wanted to hurl insults at Kitty Pawlak and I never wanted Kitty Pawlak to hurl insults at me. I never wanted to threaten Kitty Pawlak's life, but I did—*repeatedly*. I never wanted to drive recklessly on a rural road in New Brunswick, searching for obstacles on *her* side of the road to ram the car into. Trees, guardrails, potholes, ditches, fences, farmhouses—they all flashed past as she ranted endlessly from the passenger seat. I didn't want her dead as much as I wanted her *gone*. I wanted her voice to cease. I wanted my stress to cease. I wanted this drawn-out road trip from hell to find its finish line. I wanted freedom from the feeling of being trapped. I wanted freedom from the anguish, the anger, the desperation. I wanted freedom from the bully she'd become, from the bully I'd become, from the bullshit our relationship had become.

I raced around tight bends and purposefully eased the steering wheel toward the gravelled shoulder, hoping this time the tires would slide uncontrollably on the loose stones and plunge us into a tree. The collision would be no accident.

She ranted. I listened. During the lulls, I provoked. Voices grew louder. Ugly intent freely festered. Fantasy lunged forward. In my mind, I saw my fist upon her chin, her teeth upon the ground, her blood upon my shoes.

The argument started as a resolution, a discussion about how to remove the eggshell-walking from our lives. Our shared anxiety was quickly killing us. Our volatile, all-or-nothing personalities made it impossible to get along. We were trapped in a cycle of dangerous competition, a power struggle without compromise. Despite our concerted efforts to seek out fair and proper solutions, ego always managed to interject and direct our hapless actions.

I proposed that we should speak our minds without fear of consequence, that our shared habit of holding back had interrupted the flow of good energy between us. Our initial back-and-forth showed promise, but soon the discussion was stalled by awkward silence. No further solutions were put forward. In my embarrassment, I kept quiet. Quiet and Kitty do not mix well. She is a potent tonic in and of herself. Her brand of firewater is lethal, illegal, immoral. She blinds the world with pure emotion and watches it burn with bad intent. She is feisty, defiant, unapologetic, rude, crude, intense, and immature. She is wholly *alive*, and *that* is why I had to kill her.

I felt no remorse about taking her life. This wasn't murder, it was *problem-solving*. It was purging. It was pure and necessary. It was for the good of us all.

You came into my life like a lightning flash,
all lashes and liquor and liquid veneer.

You offered me a stiff drink,
a mixture of some "me" think,
a shot glass full of sexual anonymity.

Ice clinked on crystal
and hair hung down low,
touching your waist like a whisper.

I found myself enamoured,
yet lost my self-composure
and asked you if you thought
ants were real creatures
or just six-legged dreams.

The outline of your lover
was chalked on the sidewalk
as we exited the bar hand in hand.

And the moon shone holy patience
through silver effervescence
and bathed a path for you
to share a tale.

You told me of that time
you squeezed into a rat trap
and traipsed through rooms
of deadly crumbs and corpses.

The maze led ever inward
and you stumbled ever onward,
confident that you alone
would emerge unscathed.

And in your bed that evening,
as your naked body slept,
I spied the sprouting of a tail
I'd somehow overlooked.

Rod: Adding to my blue mood is the fact that I'm not with you right now, and haven't been for a while. For over a year, you were a very important part of my life. Now you're not, even though you're very much on my mind and I spend a lot of time thinking about you. I don't fully know what went wrong and I don't know how to fix it. I'm mourning a loss. There's no other way to say it—I'm heartbroken. I realize what I've been feeling is part of the healing process, but it's damn painful to go through. I think if I had access to a magic wand, I would zip myself over to where you are so I could tell these things in person. I would ask you for a hug, and I would give you one if you wanted it. I wanted you so bad for so long. I really thought this was going to last for the rest of my life. Expectations and disappointments.

Kitty: You have said to me before, you understand why things didn't work. You understood that you pushed me away, at times being downright mean. You allowed your anger to take over our relationship. Your expectations were high on yourself and me. I lost patience with you. I don't want someone who is going to tell me they hate me then gives me no space. Your ego is running a lot of your life. You choose to take it out on others rather than recognizing your emotions and actions. I do hope you get through those things. You're a good-hearted person. You tend to mean well. Don't be so hard on yourself. Love yourself. Then, you can love others.

Rod: Yes, I had big expectations. It seemed normal for me to do so. It still feels normal to do so. My belief is such that I create an expectation and then try to manipulate the situation to meet that expectation. Most of my brain sees this as rational behaviour. Sometimes the manipulation is successful and the expectation is met. Sometimes I hit a roadblock. *You* are a roadblock, or at least *part* of you is a roadblock. Part of you wouldn't allow me to manipulate you in order for my expectation to be realized. I saw you as the ideal. You had the face, the brain, the hair, the body, and the attitude I was attracted to. But you were also incredibly defiant. You refused to be manipulated in order to meet my expectations. I wanted the ideal. What I got was *reality*. I discovered you were not who I imagined you were. I discovered you weren't interested in fulfilling my fantasy of you. When it became obvious—quite early on, actually—that you could not be manipulated, I began to lose interest.

Now, I should also say I was not always aware I was being manipulative. Much of that behaviour is subconscious. Most of the times we butted heads was probably due to me acting in a manipulative way subconsciously, and then me becoming angry because 1) I wasn't getting my way, and 2) you were showing opposition to something that I felt *needed* to happen. I likely appeared confused because my *need* (my *expectation*) wasn't being met—my *need* wasn't being realized. And so, you were seen as the enemy. Instead of being the princess I believed you to be—which you were—you were also a wicked witch. You were holding me back from realizing my dream of having a princess. With you, it was impossible for me to be a prince, or more correctly, a *manipulative* prince.

I'm sorry for forcing things on you back then. I'm sorry for confusing you. My mind is a scary place. I can be ruthlessly malicious. Maybe I should've been a soldier, or a hitman, or a used car salesman. (Actually, I'm a little too dumb to be a used car salesman.)

And yes, I endlessly engage in push and pull behaviour. Passive/aggressive. I love you and I hate you. I'll hug you and I'll kill you. It's all normal in my head. I am not proud of the fact that I behave this way. Doing so has contributed to my being alone. Forced isolation is the *push*. Me writing a Facebook message is the *pull*. I do this with everyone. It would likely be a lot less stressful if I changed this behaviour. It is manipulative and I probably wouldn't want others doing it to me.

Kitty: Yeah, that's definitely not the relationship I want. To me, a healthy relationship is one where both people are inspired by each other, inspired to be better, supported in their own choices. The funny thing is, I know I'm a good partner. Like everyone, I have faults. But I would treat the right person like gold, as long as it was mutual. Your expectations may have been met had you not tried to manipulate me.

Rod: True. But I will in no way claim sole responsibility for the souring of this relationship. The blame lies on both of us.

Kitty: Yeah, not so true, Rod. I may have been affected by your actions, but I did not at any time try to hurt you. The only reason we didn't work is because I wouldn't allow you to control me.

Even now, you're trying to manipulate me.

Rod: What's sad to me is that the last two days we spent together were really nice. They were an example of what every day could be like. I can remember what happened during those days, but I can't really pinpoint what made them special. We never talked about ending the relationship. We just knew that you were going out west and I wasn't. Your decision to move elsewhere and me not following you were decisive factors. I had no interest in moving to Nelson. I had no interest in following you. I find it sad that I had no interest. I guess it was time to go down a separate path.

Anyway, getting back to those last two days. In hindsight, it felt like spending time with someone who is going to die—you want to make the most of the time that's left. You died. I lived. And now I'm left with a big hole in my life. Those were two very good days. I'm glad it ended the way it did (on a high note), but living with the idea of how much promise those two days showed is very difficult.

Kitty: Exactly, you lived it like it was the last time you were going to see me. In that, you allowed things to be natural, allowed for me to be me and to step back from control. You were, at the end, who you portrayed to me when we first got together. It was organic, freeing and I actually felt love from you. It was when you let go of controlling me that the relationship was good. I was done, completely, at the end. You had treated me like an enemy, like a burden, like it was me who was hurting you. You hurt you.

And those first days and last are what I would bring to the relationship, and that's true because those were the only times you stepped back.

Rod: "And those first days and last are what I would bring to the relationship." I'm curious. What do you mean by this statement?

Kitty: I mean that you stepped back and let things be more organic, in the beginning you showed patience when I needed time. In the end, you allowed for love to shine through and you didn't try and manipulate things too much. I'm aware that you kept me there longer than necessary and that was a manipulation, but you didn't try to control the situation past that. When you control the situation, you don't allow for me to be seen in the relationship. The relationship then becomes you.

Moonlight on white nylon,
a corporate logo silhouette.
I've gone out past the seedy hotels
to see how lonely I can get.

One cricket in the distance,
one dove upon the wire,
one itch that never leaves my trigger finger,
one killer left to hire.

One shot, one hole, one bullet,
one vacant artery.
One voice upon a chilling wind
once whispered your name to me.

In dreams I roam an empty jail
and repeat my short roll call.
One name, one number, one person,
one blame I shall forestall.

A letter never sent:

> I was going to compose a long rant about how much
> I fucking hate you, but I decided to save myself the
> trouble. I'm sick of forcing the issue. I'm also guilty of
> forcing the issue. I can't tell you how much anxiety I
> feel before deciding to do *anything* related to you. Ever
> since I met you, I've been scared of alienating you. I
> live with this undying fear that I will say or do the
> wrong thing, and that the wrongdoing will lead to our
> *un*doing. I fear manifestations. I fear that if I refrain
> from telling you I like you and want to be with you,
> the oversight will lead to us separating. Ideally, I should
> just let things happen as they will, perhaps as they're
> meant to. But I also believe in the adage of "no input,
> no output." If I say nothing, nothing will keep right

on happening. If I say something, *anything*, my words will likely set change in motion, whatever that change may look like. Unfortunately, by taking action in order to create change, I also feel that I force the matter, perhaps even being the one who controls the outcome of a given scenario by initiating change in the first place. I hate like fuck that I feel guilty of being ambitious about our friendship and our relationship. I feel like I've mostly chased you, but you've rarely chased me. Of course, you would probably disagree. After all, it's in your nature to disagree. You seem to enjoy disagreeing with me and the world in general. Your disdain for me—which I believe stems from negative experiences with other people and not necessarily from me—is one factor that seems to hinder your desire to chase me. Or maybe you believe I'm not worthy of a chase. You don't know how many times in the past three months I wished to receive a message from you saying how much you miss me and would love to see me. Do you know how many times my wish came true? *Zero!* So, how the fuck do I interpret that? Well, I say to myself, *Written communication doesn't come easy to her. Maybe she's busy. Maybe she doesn't have a good phone signal today. Maybe she's seeing someone in Nelson and is not interested in me anymore.* And then, I get a Facebook message containing a photo of your vagina. (Or at least I'm led to believe it's *your* vagina.) I then get more naked photos and an explanation that you had a successful masturbatory session and you just wanted me to know I was directly linked to its gushing outcome. With that I'm left thinking, *Well, maybe she* is *interested in me. Just one problem: there are 2300 miles between us and that gap isn't about to close anytime soon. So, what to do? Should I take the initiative in October and drive to Nelson to talk with her?* Well, that never happened. No input, no output. And then the anxiety begins again. *Did I just waste an opportunity to be with her? What if I had gone? What if? What if? What if?* I keep what-fucking-iffing until I drive myself fucking crazy. What if I go insane trying to sort out this situation with you? Answer: Too late. I'm *already* insane. Fuck!

Sometimes I just want to chuck this relationship (or whatever the fuck it is) and walk the fuck away. But I don't. I force the matter. I create new expectations that are similar to the old expectations. And each time I do, I fall face-first into a pit of disappointment. Imagine that! But you know, I force the matter because I like you. I like that you are beautiful, sexy, smart, and witty. I force it because I want to have sex with you every day of the week. I force it because I think there's a possibility of us overcoming our shortcomings and finding happiness in our relationship. As I've mentioned before, I would like a constant touchstone in my life—someone I can send messages to every day and get timely and heartfelt responses in return. Someone I can share my deepest fears with, and listen intently when they do the same. Someone I can lean on. Someone who trusts enough to lean on me. I imagine you want many of the same things.

There are many things that need to change in order for us to be happy together. We need to change ourselves. You will need to alter or dispose of some traits, habits, and behaviours if we are going to proceed. The same goes for me. I'm willing to compromise on some things. Some things I won't compromise on. I imagine you will be the same.

And now, I want to come back to the idea of *making an effort.* As I write this, I'm in a forest in South Carolina. It's my first time in this state. It's 10:00pm. It's quiet. No distractions. No phone signal, otherwise I'd send this message to you tonight. More importantly, you are at your mom's house until Tuesday or Wednesday. In your last message, you mentioned you weren't sure how we might be able to connect before you return to Thunder Bay. My plan was, and still is, to check out some beautiful national forests in Tennessee, Georgia, and the Carolinas. If I left this area when

I received your message, I could've reached your mom's house by Saturday. But I didn't. I kept following my original plan. Why? Because it seemed like you didn't have much desire to see me. No input, no output. I've seen it a hundred times since I met you. You seem to have little or no interest in sending me a message that reads: *I'd really love to see you. How can we make that happen?* I would love it if you did! In my head, I say those same words a dozen times a day. In my head, I hear *you* say those words a dozen times a day. Why? Perhaps to manifest change. Perhaps to cling to the idea that I like having you in my life. Perhaps I need to force the issue. Perhaps I don't. If it was meant to happen, it would. Fate, fucking fate.

For three months, I've struggled to grasp what you mean to me. I still haven't figured it out. I haven't fully processed all the good and bad things that happened between us in the past year. Perhaps I don't need to. Here's what I *do* know: I create a lot of stress for myself and others (you, for example). I don't need to do that. I don't want to do that. I'm going to die at some point and I hope it's not from some self-induced cancer or complications from consuming too much Coca-Cola. My emotional eating patterns sicken me.

I won't see you by Wednesday. I feel guilty to admit it, but I'm actually enjoying each day in these southern forests. I have a reason to get up each day. I have no idea what I'll encounter tomorrow, but I know it will be beautiful. I am always steps away from suicide. When my world seems fucked and hopeless, death seems like the best option. I say to myself, *What's the fucking point in going on?* But being on the road brings new hope, a new chance at composing a new chapter. I've yet to finish my book. I've yet to release a truth to the unsuspecting masses. Doing so leads me onward. In some ways, you are fading from my sight and that saddens me deeply. I thought you were the one that would change everything. I thought you were the one who would save

me from me. And maybe you are, or *were*. You should
be the biggest light in my life, but you're not. That saddens me deeply. I wanted you more than anything else
this past year. In the end, I only have memories. For
me, memories are not enough. That's why I force the
issue. For me, nothing's ever good enough.

Steve French

Somewhere lightning is lighting up your eyes
and a humid breeze is pushing your thoughts around.
Somewhere a mosquito is balanced on your arm
and I am here completely out of reach.
Somewhere you are north of the border
and I am here below you,
perched on a low peak,
tongue-tied in double-speak,
at odds with my ambiguous behaviour.

Somewhere the moon is waxing nostalgic
and dredging up white waves from the past.
Somewhere you are making silly, silly faces
while someone points a phone in your direction.
And somewhere I wade through the apprehensive wake
of our previous spontaneous encounter.
You told me things I knew,
things that eventually came true,
things that were painful for you to go through.
You shared a gentle lie,
held back a stifled cry,
and made friends with those who betrayed you.

Central America held several secrets,
jewels uncut and raw,
the facets of which reflected a future westward trek,
a journey upon which you embarked alone.

And so a full year later,
our paths refuse to favour
a crossing or a meeting of the minds.
But my heart continues pining
for that elusive silver lining
that I hope, one day, you will find.

To the best of my knowledge, Kitty Pawlak is still alive. To the best of my knowledge, she is not pregnant. To the best of my knowledge, we are not a couple. To the best of my knowledge, we have no plans to get back together. To the best of my knowledge, my broken heart is healing. To the best of my knowledge, I will be okay.

~ ~ ~

On April 17, 2017, a nondescript, picture-less post caught my attention as I scrolled through my Facebook News Feed. The post had been posted to the Murray River Expeditioners group page, a place where people can share information and stories about paddling the Murray River. The page was started by Australian adventurer, Chris Hayward, who was mentioned earlier in this book.

> G'day all!
> I'm hoping I can get some help fact-checking.
> I'm currently 78 days into my SUP paddle down Australia's longest river system and I've just been asked by someone following the page (@sup4dca) if I'll be the first to paddle the length of the Darling River by SUP.
> Setting a record wasn't the plan and I've got no idea if I will be, but naturally it would be pretty cool to find out and would be a big boost for the fundraising side of the trip to add a record.

I haven't been able to find anyone online who has done it before, but I thought I'd check here along with some other spots as I'd hate to claim a false title.

Any help would be hugely appreciated!

Cheers,

Tom

I felt a bit blindsided and a whole lot jealous when I read the post. I had no idea someone was in the midst of paddling the length of the Darling–Murray. I'd been spending so much time with Kitty, I hadn't kept up with the goings-on down under. Maybe my time offline was a blessing in disguise, because I sure wasn't happy to read about someone claiming a first descent of the Darling–Murray. And what about Mark Kalch? I wonder how *he* felt about this riveting newsflash.

Tom Dunn, the 21-year-old Australian bloke who posted the post, went on to finish his SUP journey down the Darling–Murray, claiming a first descent in the process. A quick scroll through his Facebook page showed he'd encountered near-drought conditions in the expedition's early stages, much as Mark Kalch had. Fortunately, Tom's journey wasn't cut short by a waterborne disease. He also carried out his expedition in a noticeably different fashion than Mark.

As he had during his other source to sea descents (Amazon, Volga, and Missouri–Mississippi), Mark chose to carry all his gear on his stand-up paddleboard. Tom, on the other hand, utilized a vehicle and ground crew, leaving him to travel less encumbered. Whereas Mark slogged his way down the Condamine, Balonne, and Culgoa rivers, Tom, when the waterways became difficult to navigate, chose to walk roads parallel to them. Tom claims he walked or ran 560 miles before he was able to paddle continually to the Southern Ocean.

Make no mistake, it's not my intention to devalue Tom Dunn's accomplishment. I admire his unyielding persistence and his dedication to his goal. As evidenced by the following blog post from his website (whattomhasdunn.com), he is also very passionate about improving the health of Australia's rivers. With time on his side (he's only 21!), I'm sure we'll be hearing much more about Tom Dunn in the coming years.

The idea was to stand-up paddle board the length of Australia's longest continuous river system. The very source of the Murray–Darling basin to the mouth of the Murray, (a total of) 2330 miles. Before I started, I imagined paddling down a wide, winding river full of wildlife and water. What I got, instead, was something completely different.

A drought in Queensland made for a rough start to the trip. Forced to walk the first 560 miles of the trip was less than ideal and not what I imagined. But I couldn't make it rain, so I had to walk. I trudged through the riverbed searching for water I could paddle on. Initially, in the spots where there was water, gas bubbles and human waste made the river a foul mess. Eventually, when the riverbed became impassable, I left it behind and walked the roads and highways searching for water. In the middle of the summer heat, walking on the edge of the road, I drew plenty of attention. My own attention, however, was on the paddocks I walked alongside. I noticed that the cotton crops were doing well and nearly all the livestock paddocks had full troughs too.

It was good to see. Australia was built on farming, and I'm from a regional area myself. I know how bad things can be in a drought. But if this was truly a drought, how was there enough water to keep crops and stock going so well? The answer to that was in the river. Huge pumps lined the banks, manipulating the current and the water levels around. A few even managed to pull me back upstream as they sucked the water that was left from the already struggling river.

As I moved further downriver, I spent more time with locals. Everyone empathized with my attempt to paddle the length of the river system. A few even laughed. It was common knowledge that up here, in the upper reaches of the Murray–Darling basin, drought or not, there was never enough water. I was an outsider and this was my first visit to the region, but I couldn't understand how there was never enough water. As I reached the Darling River itself, I listened to the stories of how big and busy the outback towns used to be. I heard stories of the riverboats and paddled past their old mooring points, now so high and dry. Everywhere I went, people told me how towns were closing down. Whole towns were crippled by the lack of population as people packed up and disappeared from the bush. Droughts happened, but this was something bigger. Those that were still left in the towns told me why. "This river system is dying," (they said).

I don't know enough about the government water buy-backs, cotton farm water allocations, or the amount of water it takes to keep stock alive to give an opinion on the health of the Murray–Darling basin. I may have spent 113 days on every inch of the river, but it doesn't compare to the people who have spent their entire lives on the banks. These people, no matter if they worked for government water management, on a cotton station, or were stock farmers, (they) always agreed on one thing: change is needed.

I don't know the river, but I have met its people and they are scared. The river used to be a life source. But when it dies, it will kill all the communities on its banks too.

I'd love to be able to return in five or 10 years and paddle down the river I imagined. But unless something significantly changes, I think I may be the first and last person to ever SUP the length of Australia's longest river system.

Sign a petition to change the Murray–Darling Basin for the better at:

www.acf.org.au/murray_darling_petition.

On November 30, 2017, I was once again scrolling through my Facebook News Feed when another river-related post caught my attention. This one, posted on the Missouri River Paddlers group page by Norm Miller (who was mentioned earlier in this book), alerted the group to the fact that former group member, Mark Kalch, had recently completed his source to sea descent of the Darling–Murray river system. The news came as a surprise. (I didn't even know he was on the river!) I was happy to hear that Mark had returned to finish his expedition.

Behind the scenes, Norm asked Mark, (who is no longer on Facebook) if he could write a trip report for the other group members, many of whom met Mark during his historical descent of the Missouri–Mississippi river system in 2012, and again when he partook in the first Missouri River Paddlers Reunion in Missouri in 2015.

Mark's account, included below, details his struggles on the second half of his Darling–Murray expedition as well as his choice to forgo social media. (Expedition dates: First half – January 14 to March 15, 2016. Second half – September 4 to November 7, 2017.)

> G'day MRPers!
>
> I am no longer on Facebook, so Norm asked if I could give you guys a rundown on my last descent.
>
> As some of you know, I have an ongoing project to paddle the longest river on each continent from source to sea. I am pretty happy to have now completed four out of those seven—those being the Amazon, Missouri–Mississippi, Volga, and now the Murray–Darling in Australia, which I finished a couple of weeks ago.
>
> I had a crack last year (2016), but came up short. No water in the river didn't help, nor did contracting meningitis from the water that was in the river. In 51 days, I only managed to paddle and portage 620 miles, more or less, before I got nailed. I spent a couple of days in emergency, a week in the infectious diseases ward,

and I reckon six to seven months to come good physically. Longer mentally. I am not even convinced I am over it now which is odd. But I had to go back to that river.

At the end of last year, I decided to remove myself from the social media arms race and paddling for a living. I grew tired of having to regale everyone with my exploits in order to get likes and to keep sponsors happy. I saw too many folks with, to be honest, pathetic paddling and/or adventure CVs getting ahead by having a savvy social media game and being cavalier with the truth. Meanwhile, my friends with better stories to tell, and paddling/adventure resumes that would blow your mind, were being ignored—sometimes out of choice, but often not. I opted out of the circus. Life changes. Motivations change. For 10 years, paddling as a sponsored athlete was my thing. Now it's not and I am happy about that. Best move ever!

So, with altered motivations and having moved to Malawi with four young kids, I managed to get back out to Oz. I decided to do zero updates, blog posts, or social media for the descent. I avoided any media like the plague! It felt strange at first, but I got used to it. I still recorded the journey with photos and in my journal, as well as with my SPOT device.

The Murray–Darling is around 2095 miles in length, so a couple of hundred miles shorter than the Missouri. In many parts, it is being bloody generous to call it a river. The first 620 miles was a battle of portaging and occasional paddling. For the first time on one of my big descents, I used a SUP board. It was a canny choice. It meant that I could, when the water ran out, easily step off and drag the board as necessary, and then jump back on. In a kayak, it would have been killer to be constantly climbing in and out of the cockpit. I can't emphasize enough the grind this part of the river was. Perhaps it was this that made me question just what the heck I was doing as a paddler. Why paddle this river just to tick a box, instead of a river that I really wanted to paddle? Seemed a little crazy. So, after 51 days and 620 miles, I contracted meningitis, etc., etc.

I came back this year (2017) and put in where I took out, just above the town of Bourke in New South Wales. After just three days of paddling, I was ready to pack it in. But after a call with Hol (his partner) telling me to harden up (!), I was back on course.

Still on the Darling, I now had 932 miles of tinder-dry bushland in outback Australia to reach the Murray. Very often, the river ran with maybe an inch of water in it. Occasionally, weirs backed up the water which made paddling possible, but I knew I would pay for that on the other side of them.

I passed the occasional property homestead where I refilled with water and chatted to folk. A few times, I was put up for the night in shearer's quarters or an old caravan and fed dinner. Good people out there. I rescued a lot of sheep stuck in the mud! No matter what sort of day I was having, I couldn't paddle by one of the poor buggers. One day, I rescued five sheep and paddled 'round a corner to be confronted by a topless French girl sunbathing! We were in the middle of freaking nowhere. Quite the surprise for both of us.

Every single day, I was on edge waiting for the water to run out proper or to develop symptoms of meningitis again. It used up a hell of a lot of energy. I paddled, on average, 11 hours a day and covered only about 22 miles. No flow whatsoever. A grind for sure. Although, this average did slowly increase.

Finally, I reached the town of Wentworth where the Darling meets the Murray River and finally I could relax knowing there would be water to paddle. From the confluence, I had 517 miles to go to the ocean. Now, an 11-hour day of paddling got me on average 31 miles covered. Still minute compared to paddling on water that flowed. The Murray did not. I passed through 10 weirs with locks. The lock masters were super cool guys. It was almost as if it was part of the job to be a joker.

More towns on the Murray and more people. Holiday homes, fishermen, and speed boats appeared. Massive houseboats as well. I often wished I was on one of them.

The Murray doesn't just flow into the sea as you might expect. Instead, it opens into Lake Alexandrina which itself opens on to the ocean. Big winds only held me up for a day crossing the lake. So, in a very low-key fashion, I paddled by a couple of sand dredgers and dragged my board onto the sand. Descent done.

The Murray–Darling river system is rough. As a river to paddle from source to sea without portaging, it is impossible. Its flow is a hugely contentious issue in Australia. Mismanagement has resulted in a river that is in real trouble. Forget having a bad day's paddle when the people who depend on it for drinking water or irrigation are acutely affected. A real shame.

So, in summary: I used a 13' 2" Red Paddle Co. Explorer+ SUP board. I completed the descent in two parts. 51 days to go 620 miles and 70 days for the remaining 1473 miles. 121 days source to sea. It was slow going, considering the 3728-mile Missouri–Mississippi took me 117 days! As with all my descents, I carried all my own gear, food, etc. No support team to meet me each night, etc. As usual, I had porridge and black coffee for breakfast. Throughout the day, I munched on chocolate bars and muesli bars with occasional fruit. Dinner was pasta and tuna with Tabasco sauce. On my board, I could carry up to 14 days of food, but usually carried around 10 days. That, plus water and gear, made for a heavy load. I lost 22 lbs. on the paddle, more than I have on any other trip by far. To be fair, I began paddling weighing 229 lbs. and finished at 207 lbs. Back up to 220 lbs. now! Best gear used was probably my Alpkit tent, SPOT, Led Lenser headlamp, and my Kindle. My Benchmade folding knife was also brilliant—used on every descent from the Amazon 'til now. Ten years of hard use. Also, my 2GB iPod Nano, which has braved all the source to sea descents as well. Still going strong after 10 years too.

Was it my favourite descent? Not by a long shot. My attitude played a huge part in this. I just wasn't there properly mentally, which didn't help. There were plenty of parts of the river which were beautiful. Notably for me was from Wilcannia to Menindee on the Darling and from Wentworth to Renmark on the Murray.

It was more of a relief to reach the end of this descent after getting so sick last year. As for the 7 Rivers 7 Continents project, it goes on. I am far less motivated to complete it. Like I said, life changes. The project was a professional goal, something to put my name next to as a sponsored paddler. Now, who knows? I could care less about followers, media coverage, and accolades. Fortunately, I still love paddling big rivers, so it's still on the cards for sure.

Cheers

As an addendum to the above, I've included below another short Q&A with Mark Kalch.

RW: Was the prospect of a first descent enticing to you? Did losing that claim have impact on you? If so, how did it impact you?

MK: In Oz, it wasn't on my mind at all. Even by early 2016, I had lost my motivation for hyping up my descents and wanting to let people know how amazing I was. Knowing what sort of rivers the Condamine and Darling were, for anyone to claim a first descent on it, I think, is a bit ingenious. Tom Dunn walked about 560 miles of that river, and not really following its course. Having a support caravan the whole way, I suppose, might have affected his decision, but of that 560 miles of not paddling, it wasn't as if there was not water for paddling for 560 miles. No way. I had long sections where I had to drag a fully loaded board or long portages, but that was on the riverbed or beside. At some point, there is water to paddle even if just for a few kilometres. Not zero paddle-able water for 560 miles though? Two blokes paddled the entire river (after the 2012 floods) from the town of Condamine to the sea. Only possible because of flood waters. Apart from maybe more historical descents (will forward some amazing newspaper clippings from Norm about this Aussie bloke who paddled the Murray–Darling and the Missouri–Mississippi in 1954 and 1956!), that would have to be the closest to a full descent that I know of. Likely others too. But anyway, I digress. Good luck to anyone who in good conscience claims a first descent on that river. It is too strange a river to bother with such a claim though, I reckon.

RW: How did you change your approach to sponsors and social media prior to going back to complete the river system? Any other approach changes worth noting? (e.g. mental and physical changes, gear changes, a more relaxed schedule, did you leave more time for paddling?)

MK: I just didn't do any sponsor stuff or social media at all! I knew it would likely end up sponsorship suicide, but I decided to move on from doing these expeds full time or as a job. I was never much good at it anyway. It really had lost the magic because of social media and worrying about sponsors and trying to keep impressing them and trying to make money from it. My life has moved on. I still really love paddling and expeds, but into the future I will just do them like I did in Oz just now. Hopeful for a north/south or south/north of Lake Malawi in the next couple of years. Dang crocs and hippos are kind of oft-putting! Ditto for the Nile. Makes sense for me to be prepping for that first, but almost feel that the Yangtze is calling me more strongly. We shall see which comes first.

No other changes, really. My kit is dialled in. Physical dialled in. Mentally well. It's just that first 10 days on the river where your head has to adjust. After that, all good. Always miss the kids which makes things a lot harder. I still paddled a lot, probably 10–11 hours a day mostly. I like the grind!

Anyway, (your questions) were brilliant and just reinforce more to me that people have been doing cool stuff for years and that I have no desire to broadcast about it. This "no broadcasting" has come about by my negative view of it. Is it always bad, this Instagram, Twitter, etc.? No way. I met so many people in Oz who wanted to follow my updates from the trip who were bummed and perplexed that I would not be doing so. They were so interested and always saying that I should be. So, in that regard, maybe I should be. Who knows? The human brain, eh?

To learn more about Mark Kalch, visit his websites: markkalch. com; 7rivers7continents.com.

~ ~ ~

Fallibility is a motherfucker. So is humility. They're ego killers. They suck.

I never thought myself invincible, but I surely never thought myself incapable either. I spent decades doing awesome self-propelled adventures. I never believed I couldn't. I dreamed. I planned. I executed. I excelled. And then fallibility came along and fucked everything up. Not only did it shred my ego, but it also shredded my suicide plan. Not cool, fallibility. Not cool at all…*motherfucker.*

Living with mental illness fucking sucks. Wanting to kill myself fucking sucks. Suffering through depression fucking sucks. Feeling awkward in social settings fucking sucks. Fearing my way through patterns of paranoia in the workplace fucking sucks. Doubting myself fucking sucks. Being judged by others fucking sucks.

People have told me I'm obsessive and compulsive and depressive and repetitive. They've told me I'm manic and anxious and reckless and blind. They've told me I'm lazy and crazy and twisted and cruel. I've been called an asshole, a thief, a prick, and a cunt—all in one day! People have told me I overthink things.

People have told me medication will help my *condition*. They've told me it works for them, that their brain responds positively to pills produced by heartless pharmaceutical companies with greedy agendas. "Medication smoothed out my brainwaves," they've told me. I bet it did!

Fuck medication. Never used it. Never will. I don't want my brainwaves *smoothed* out. I don't want my reality neutered. I don't want LifeLite™. I want to experience *real* emotional pain, the kind that helps me grow. Sure, it sucks when you're trapped in it, but I think it's better to endure the anguish than to numb it with prescription meds.

There was a time in my life when I self-medicated. I used alcohol and recreational drugs to cope with an onslaught of stress that never seemed to recede. I worked shitty jobs, brought home shitty paycheques, and pissed the shittiness away *all* weekend long. And then, one day, I stopped…and everything got *very real*. That was in 1998, 20 years ago. Someone recently asked me, "Is your life better now than it was when you drank?" "No," I replied. "Nothing beats ignorance. It's the most blissful high you can have."

Fallibility is a wake-up call. It's reality *concentrated*. It can't be trademarked because it can't be mass-produced. It can't be mass-produced because it would kill the *fuck* out of everyone. That's why it only rears its ugly head occasionally.

Remember Charlie Sheen? Me neither. Remember when he did that interview on *20/20* and he said he had *tiger blood* in his veins? Me neither. Remember when he was *#winning*? *#MeNeither*. Remember when he did that stand-up comedy tour? Me neither. Remember when Charlie Sheen was *cool*? Me neither.

Remember TV? Me neither. Remember Ronald Reagan? Me neither. Remember mutually assured destruction? Me neither. Remember conspiracy theorists? Me neither. Remember Noam Chomsky? Me neither. Remember UPC codes? Me neither. Remember breast implants? Me neither. Remember colon cancer? Me neither. Remember Facebook without the annoying advertisements? Me neither. Remember old growth forests? Me neither. Remember the reason you got out of bed this morning? Me neither.

I didn't shave today. I didn't shave yesterday. Or the day before that. I've spent the past seven days parked in front of a computer screen, writing this *fucking* book. I'll be glad when it's finished. I'll be glad when someone hands me a $20 bill and I hand them the paperback version of this damned manuscript. I'll be glad when I can breathe fresh air again. I'll be glad when I can go out west again and climb a *fucking mountain*. It's been too long. I used to climb mountains all the time. And then fallibility came along and fucked everything up.

Remember when *fallibility* was a word you had to look up in the dictionary? Me neither. Remember that time when you *didn't* compare yourself to others? Me neither. Remember that time when you laughed all day because life was funny and wonderful? Me neither. Remember that day when you had no suicidal thoughts whatsoever? Me neither. Remember when that special person gave you hugs when you needed them? Me neither. Remember when your dead mother told you everything was going to be okay? Me neither. Remember that time when you went the whole day without crying? Me neither. Do you remember your dreams from last night? Me neither.

Fallibility is a motherfucker. It shows you that you are *not* what you thought you were. It cuts you down to the size you *are*. It makes you the person you *never* wanted to be. It force-feeds you the truth and watches you eat it. It flattens your fangs and fattens your lip. It knocks the chip off your shoulder and grinds it to dust. It grins while you wince. It laughs while you weep. It stays when you leave, and it's still there when you return. It is judge, jury, and *expeditioner*. It's the *evil* explorer. It's a *motherfucker*.

It's one thing to have fallibility come along and fuck up an extravagant suicide attempt, but it's quite another to have it interfere with a love relationship. Seriously. What the fuck is up with that???

My relationship with Kitty Pawlak was supposed to be the stuff of dreams. It was supposed to be the final relationship for both of us, or at least until one of us died, which probably would've been me, seeing that I'm 18 years older than her. Yes, *18*. It was pretty fucking awesome being a 50-year-old guy dating a hot, 32-year-old woman. I felt like I won the lottery. I was the luckiest guy around. But you know what they say about luck: *Luck never gives; it only lends*.

I threw everything I had into that relationship. I gave until it hurt. And then I gave more. Well, that's not *entirely* true. I gave, but I also took. I took *a lot*, actually. I didn't, like, steal from her. But then again, yes, I *did* steal from her. I stole some of her *shine*. I stole some of her time. I stole some of her trust. She put her heart in my hands and I cut it. I wounded the womyn warrior, the rebel, the defiant, feisty beauty, the one who vowed to compromise (and *did*, I should add—but not *enough*), the one whose eyes lit my darkened dreams, the one to whom I promised commitment. Yes, I cut her. Deep. Deep enough to sever the tether.

In light of the #MeToo and Time's Up movements, in light of the oppressive self-guilt, in light of my loneliness, I contacted Kitty Pawlak via Facebook Messenger in January 2018 to pose three pertinent questions.

> **Rod**: Do you think I suffocated your self-expression? Do you think I had a sense of entitlement when it came to having sex with you? Do you think every question I send you is a form of manipulation?

> **Kitty**: Why are you asking all these things? Are you working on things or obsessing?

Rod: These are all serious questions and I hope to get serious answers.

Kitty: Yes, but why are you asking?

Rod: Yes, I'm working on things. And yes, partly, I'm obsessing. I'm attempting to understand your side of the story. In light of all the Hollywood (and elsewhere, for sure) allegations of sexual misconduct, it got me thinking (or perhaps, at times, *obsessing*) about my behaviour and how my behaviour affects others.

Kitty: Yes, you took away some of my shine. I had to deal with you and your issues, and then I was exhausted. I didn't have anything left for myself. As for sex, absolutely. When I couldn't have sex because I was having those serious pains, you treated me differently, indifferent, unkind. You wouldn't take no for an answer other times.

Rod: I agree with all those statements. I'm sorry for the way I treated you.

Kitty: Thanks.

Rod: There's a song by a band called Future Islands, *Seasons (Waiting on You)*. Maybe you've heard it. The lyrics are very good, very relatable. I remember listening to it while you were in eastern Tennessee and I was in Memphis. The lyric, "I tried hard just to soften you," stayed with me. Your mention of me taking away some of your shine reminded me of that lyric. It also reminded me that yes, I did try to grind away some of your rough exterior. I wanted you to lose some of your rebellious attitude because I deemed it unnecessary. I didn't want it *all* gone, I just wanted you to take the edge off. I wanted that because I thought you'd be a better person without it. I still feel that way. I had good intention. My execution, however, wasn't very good. I should've just let you be you. I'm sorry for my behaviour in this case.

Kitty: I think you need to deal with your shit before you start to try and change others. That's really egotistical of you to think that you know what's better for me.

Rod: I can see how dealing with my issues left you exhausted. In Memphis, I was shocked when you admitted you wanted to drive a car from Florida to Canada because you wanted/needed a break from me. I was almost clueless. You appeared fine most of the time, so I thought things were okay. Things were not okay. As time went on in Memphis, I noticed how exhausted you were. I'm sorry that I was the cause of this. An ex of mine used to call me a *vampire* because she felt I sucked her energy. I found her reference derogatory, but true nonetheless. It's hard for me to admit it was true.

"I didn't have anything left for myself." I'm sorry this happened to you. I'm sorry you had to take some time, once again, to top up your reserves, to do more work on yourself, to bring yourself up. You had to do the same after your relationship with Adam. I'm sorry to be a contributing factor to that unfortunate cycle in your life.

I remember when you had those pains. You were in a lot of distress. I didn't show very much empathy. I'm sorry.

I definitely felt entitled to have sex with you. That's hard for me to admit. There was a possessive mindset at work. Sex should've been much more consensual. I'm sorry for taking advantage of you for my own pleasure.

Kitty: Thank you.

And somehow, I have to leave it at that. I don't think Kitty wants to have anything to do with me anymore. Communication has been sparse, usually initiated by me. It all takes place on Facebook Messenger. No face-to-face. No phone conversations. It ended as it began, with me pining for a woman who chooses to remain distant. Somehow, I have to accept that. Somehow, I have to move on, wounded heart and all. I am not proud of my ugly actions, but I stand by my beautiful ones—actions of love where it was *less Rod, more Kitty*. Storm clouds may have plagued us from time to time, but we still had quite an adventure.

My relationship with Kitty Pawlak was never common knowledge among my friends. A few friends met her, but many didn't. She was never comfortable introducing me as her boyfriend or partner. In rare instances when she *did* introduce me (oftentimes she did not), she would say, "This is my friend, Rod." She presented no evidence that I was anything more than a friend. I found her choice of words hugely disrespectful and tremendously embarrassing. Many times, the people I was introduced to appeared confused, not knowing whether to ask if we were more than just friends, or to simply take it at face value. The majority of them never sought the deeper truth.

Kitty steadfastly refused to be labelled as my *girlfriend*. To her, the term was derogatory. "Why can't I just be called Kitty?" she'd ask, seemingly unaware that I considered the term endearing. To me, the term signified a significant bond, an expression of commitment and love. To introduce someone as my *girlfriend* does not, to me, seem negative, abnormal, or derogatory. I don't believe the term degrades a woman's status. I believe it recognizes her as something more than a friend. It communicates, in a very common language, that two people are in a relationship. People use the phrase millions of times every day without incident. It seems like a very common occurrence. Kitty, however, has made a habit of rejecting anything that may be considered *common*. It is her duty to be different. It is her duty to challenge societal norms, and damn anyone who dares to challenge her beliefs. Kitty is never wrong. Fault lies in the laps of others, not in hers. This inner deception, I believe, will inevitably contribute to her downfall. I admire her rebelliousness—it's part of what attracted me to her in the first place, and it reminds me of my own disdain for society—but even *my* elevated patience level was topped by her incredibly feisty rejection for most things conventional. I'm glad her endless critique of the commonplace is gone from my life.

Kitty was never fully comfortable with sharing our relationship on social media, something I definitely wanted to do, but did not. I admit to being scared that going public with the relationship might contribute to its demise. Oftentimes, relationships shared on Facebook suddenly become everyone's business. If things go sideways in the relationship and the fallout is displayed on Facebook, chances are everyone will know about it. That's not a situation I wanted to find myself in. I didn't want to get caught in the embarrassing trap of sharing my love for someone, and then, later, sharing the hate. I've never been a fan of putting my drama on full display, at least not online. The thing is, I've never been in a relationship where I ever felt comfortable enough to post about it on social media. To me, that's just fucking sad. I liked those women very much. I wanted the world to know how much they meant to me and how happy I was at the time. For various reasons (all quite valid), those women didn't want me to publicize our relationships. Of course, out of respect for them, I kept details out of the public eye, even though my work as an author, speaker, and adventurer is very much *in* the public eye. In that sense, I felt like I was living two lives. My private life was stuffed with depression, isolation, suicidal ideation, emotional pain, and the occasional relationship drama. Those things never appeared on Facebook. Facebook friends got the selfies with captions like, "Still smiling!" Truth be told, some of those smiles were fake. My life in the Age of Facebook has not been all smiles, adventure, and book writing. Those are just the aspects I chose to share with the world via social media. Perhaps Facebook should be sarcastically dubbed *Façadebook*, because real life and social media are rarely combined. The News

Feeds we view on Facebook are simply thin veneers concealing the unfortunate, unspoken desperateness of our private lives. Perhaps if I had shared my relationship with Kitty on Facebook, it would've deepened my value of the relationship. Perhaps it would've helped alleviate the feeling of being trapped in the relationship. Perhaps by freeing myself from my own censorship, I may have had a greater sense of self-worth. The same can be said of my decision not to share my Australian paddling expedition online. Sharing may have altered the purpose of the trip in a positive sense. Instead of feeling trapped inside my head with a secret suicide plan, sharing the expedition online might've given me reason to live. Social media is useful in some ways, but it can be a scourge in others. I look forward to the day when I finally jettison it from my life.

I hate that I censored what the public saw of my relationship with Kitty Pawlak. I hated keeping things secret. I did it because I didn't want Kitty to be upset. I sacrificed my happiness so she could be happy. In our time together, I never saw her post an image of herself, or of us, on social media. I hated that she did this, but I never shared my displeasure with her. I have always thought that if a relationship has to be kept secret, it's not worth being in. I should've taken the cue early on and jettisoned Kitty from my life.

Throughout my relationship with Kitty Pawlak, I regularly visited a therapist. It was the only way I could cope with the confusion I felt during the ups and downs of the relationship. Therapy helped me revisit the drama. It helped me refocus and move forward with a plan. I continue to see that therapist as I continue to wade through the relationship residue.

I wish therapy wasn't necessary. I wish the drama never happened. I wish I never had a part in creating the drama. I wish Kitty would come forward and claim responsibility for her part in all this. A sincere apology would be nice to hear. Does she owe me an apology after everything I've put her through? Absolutely. She let her anger get the best of her many times.

You don't often hear men speaking out about their female partner physically and verbally abusing them. It happened to me in a previous relationship, and it happened with Kitty. I never thought I'd have to endure it again, especially with a woman I wanted to spend the rest of my life with. Those abusive episodes left me shaken, sad, and scared. My trust in Kitty waned. I did a lot of eggshell walking, nervously anticipating another outburst. I censored myself, curbing my behaviour in hopes it would keep the mood civil. My docile approach simply led to more drama. She criticized me for being withdrawn. I was damned if I did, and damned if I didn't. I felt this way throughout the whole relationship. Unfortunately, so did Kitty.

Kitty and I were two difficult and complicated people desperately trying to remain on our feet during a tumultuous relationship that measured 8.2 on the Richter scale of *can't-fucking-get-along*. When something happened that went against her moral code of conduct, the rest of the world heard about it. She rode around on a mobile soapbox, unafraid to call out anyone who violated one of her unwritten rules. Many times, I found myself embarrassingly caught in the crossfire, shirking away from the rain of ridicule she showered on others. Many times, I was the target. I was left questioning my own motives, wondering whether to feel guilt for having done nothing wrong.

I tried to reframe the way I viewed her rants. I tried to believe she spoke in a *love language*, that the root of her scorn lay buried in good intent, that it came from her warm heart and not from some cold, angry corner of her brain. Kitty cares for the world around her. She wants love to reign supreme. She wants equality and respect for everyone. But it's in the way she conveys her love that leaves us doubting her as well as doubting ourselves. I wish her communication was clearer and calmer, maybe even *silent*. Perhaps her concern for the world can be best conveyed through actions, not words. When she plants a garden and shares her yield, *that* is when she is most effective. When she meditates at a river's edge, *that* is when she is most effective. When her only communication with a stranger is a smile, *that* is when she is most effective. She can be the change she wants to see in the world, but she needs to curb the boundless broadcasting of her opinions. The world doesn't want to be preached to. It wants to be led silently to a fenceless garden by nameless heroes and handed a bag of seeds. It wants to reap its own reward, and thank the leaders later.

I remember well the night I met Kitty Pawlak. I remember how close she sat next to me at the restaurant where she worked. I remember her flowing scarf and woolly jacket. I remember her exquisite smile and saucer-like eyes. I remember the questions she asked me while seated cross-legged among her peers at the public library in Dunnville. I remember her shy reply when I offered to return to her workplace to help clean up. I remember the sadness I felt when she left the library without me. She seemed intrigued with me, yet very hesitant. The spontaneity I'd seen throughout that night was shuttered for a short second, just long enough for her to say, "Thanks for the offer, but Frances Jane and I will be fine."

Thirteen months later, she shared a secret.

"You probably don't know this," she said to me following a dinner date in Hamilton, "but I went back to the library that night. I thought a lot about you when I was cleaning up at The Minga. I tried to talk myself out of going back to talk to you, but I couldn't. I wanted to see you. I wanted to hang out with you. So, I plucked up the courage and drove over. When I arrived, the library door was locked. You were inside with Jody, packing up your books and stuff. I guess neither of you could hear me knocking. Sadly, I walked back to my car and drove home.

"So, I just wanted you to know. I went back because I liked you. I went back because I saw something good in you, something I wanted to know more about. You are special to me. You've been special to me since that night at the library. Thank you for being part of my life."

~ ~ ~

A return to Australia is on the horizon. The desire to see every inch of the Darling–Murray river system has definitely been fuelled by the writing of this book. I'll stick to the original summit to source to sea plan—hiking, biking, and paddling my roundabout way to the Southern Ocean. The expedition will likely take six months to complete. The suicide ending won't be included this time. From a business point of view, it'll be more beneficial to live to tell about it. A longer life means more books written and more potential book sales, hopefully. A longer life means another opportunity to experience love, hopefully. A longer life means another opportunity to give myself a second chance, to reframe the future into a place filled with wonder and possibility. If everything in life is cyclical, then it's comforting to know every drought will eventually pass and every river will eventually flow again. I intend to ride that flow as long as I can. Peace.

During the writing of this book, I came across a link to the following article in my Facebook News Feed. The link had been posted by an acquaintance of mine, a hospice liaison nurse based in Memphis, Tennessee. As sometimes happens with things of this nature, the article came into my life at a time when I needed it most.

The decision to go public with my mental health issues was not made easily. I worried about how people would perceive me once they discovered my "secrets." Would my "audience of readers" abandon me? Would they view me as weak? Cocooning in my comfort zone was, without a doubt, the safest approach. But being an artist means taking risks. In order to grow as an artist, and as a human, one must make oneself vulnerable, one must face the fears one has created.

After weighing the possible outcomes, I decided it was worth the risk to share my truths. I decided it was time to challenge the outdated social stigmas surrounding depression and suicidal ideation. I decided it was time to "come out of the closet," so to speak.

At a time when self-doubt and self-criticism plagued my days, this article and its positive content helped reframe my approach to the future. It helped me view myself as strong, not weak. I've included the article here in hopes that it may further the much-needed discussion about mental health issues. Those who struggle with depression and suicidal thoughts deserve our respect and support. Please offer them acceptance. Offer to listen. Offer to help.

If you're struggling with depression and suicidal thoughts, please reach out to someone. You do not have to suffer in silence. Use your voice. Share your story. You made it this far. You are strong. You are loved. Your life matters.

The article below is from elephantjournal.com. It was published on March 7, 2018 and was written by Alex Myles.

Those Who Live with Suicidal Thoughts
Are Strong, Not Weak

I know many people who live with daily thoughts of suicide, including someone who is close to me.

The one thing that strikes me with each one is their immense strength to continue to stay and live, despite their minds barraging them with harmful thoughts about why they should end it all and leave.

These incredible souls, who are in constant battle with a powerful and controlling darkness, are not weak—they are some of the toughest and most resilient people I have ever known.

Only those who are either going through, or have gone through, an existence where your main concern is trying to silence overbearing voices in your head persistently attempting to convince them that they, and everyone else, would be better off without them on this planet, knows the amount of mental strength it takes to carry on and try to heal.

It is courageous and brave to keep going despite depression, anxiety, stress, or chronic pain, along with a concoction of toxic chemicals and hormones infiltrating their lives to the extent that they consider suicide a viable option.

That is not weakness—it is sheer determination against unimaginable illness that may not be visible, but is valid and extremely real.

When we shame people by labelling suicidal thoughts as a sign of weakness when a person is doing their damn best to survive, we only add to the problem rather than showing compassion, empathy, and support to help them through their dark times.

When people lose hope and the will to live, yet their heart still beats to survive against the odds, it is a sign that they are clinging to the possibility that there may be a small chance for improvement.

Telling people to just "toughen up" or to "get over" whatever it is that is poisoning their mind, is futile, and, in my opinion, beyond cruel.

Holding their hand and letting them know they are loved, appreciated, supported, and significant in the world will achieve far more than judging and berating what we do not fully understand.

There is so much social stigma around expressing suicidal thoughts and feelings that many people don't reach out and talk freely about what they are experiencing, and tragically this can be one of the things that leads people to feel alone and as though how they feel is "wrong." This is why it is vital that we re-frame and change the perception about suicidal thoughts.

One reason people are unable to comprehend how it feels to be suicidal is that generally we fear what we don't understand, so we prejudge what is unknown as something to be afraid of; therefore, we become scared to even talk about it. Instead of this, we could open up and accept that we do not need to be experts in anything to be able to listen and be compassionate and supportive. The only thing we need to keep in check is our willingness to harshly judge or condemn things we have no personal experience with.

Persevering in life when your body, mind, and spirit are exhausted and want to give up and give in to treacherous thoughts is commendable. The fight to stay alive when life has become overwhelming, and support and treatment do not seem to be alleviating the difficulties, is one of the hardest things to endure.

There are a variety of reasons that cause people to feel suicidal. When someone is suffering with agonizing physical illness, we would never try to tell them they are weak for not being able to cope with excruciating, unimaginable pain. Yet, the opposite seems to be true when it comes to mental illness.

The people who experience suicidal thoughts are not weak and selfish. It is weak and selfish to dismiss those thoughts and think we know better about something we are fortunate enough to never have lived with.

To tell someone who feels suicidal to "stop being negative and think positive" is possibly one of the most harmful things we could say. Instead, we can offer them a safe space to talk about why they are contemplating suicide, and do as much research as we can so that we get a glimpse into how it feels to live each moment with chemical imbalances that cause chaotic and reckless thoughts.

From an outside perspective, it may appear that someone's life may be perfect, but what's on the exterior is worthless when the interior is intensely disturbed. When we hear that someone is feeling suicidal, let's not think about what we would do, how we think we'd cope, or what we believe to be right for the other person. Let's try to consider for a moment that we truly have no idea how it feels to live with someone else's body and mind. No one else can truly ever know or understand.

I'm not an expert on the subject, so I don't hold all the answers. I don't think anyone does. But, one thing I know for sure is when I look into the eyes of someone I love who has fought off suicide month after month, year after year, the one thing I see is strength—and desperation to not cause pain or suffering to those around them.

That is not selfishness, and it's most definitely not weakness.

Some people feel broken, and some eventually break. Unless anyone knows the internal storms that they have weathered, no one on this planet can possibly judge them.

These suicidal people, who are part of all of our societies, and who many of us have either in our families, set of friends, or work colleagues, are some of the strongest people you will ever have the pleasure to meet. So, let's cherish, love, appreciate, and support them as best we can. The acceptance that they are incredibly courageous souls, exactly as they are, might just be the healing elixir they need.

For support and assistance in Canada, call the Canada Suicide Prevention Service at 1-833-456-4566. In an emergency, call 911.

For support and assistance in the United States, call the National Suicide Prevention Lifeline at 1-800-273-8255. In an emergency, call 911.

For support and assistance in the United Kingdom, call 111 or contact a local accident and emergency center, and ask for details of the nearest CRT (Crisis Resolution Team). In an emergency, call 999.

For support and assistance in Australia, call 13 11 14.

Alecs Alecs commented:

Thank you, Ms. Myles. You have very accurately explained what life is like and what goes on inside the mind of a person who's daily dealing with suicidal thoughts. I can say that in all confidence because it describes my situation completely. I have tried suicide twice and, against all odds, survived both attempts. My family and friends have *all* asked me not to talk about my suicidal thoughts with *them* as *they* cannot cope with it. It makes *them* feel guilty and it makes *them* cry and upset to hear of it. It is my hope that your article will help people understand how important it is to just listen to someone when they are expressing their suicidal thoughts. Just the act of listening, offering a shoulder to cry on, and expressing love can make the difference between thoughts remaining thoughts and thoughts becoming action.

I have decided to speak openly about my own major reoccurring depression in the hope it will help lift the stigma attached to it and help others understand how to deal with the issue. It's like coming out of the closet, if you will—tough, but necessary. Once again, thank you for raising this subject so beautifully and compassionately. I hope it will inspire more people to talk about it from all perspectives.

ACKNOWLEDGEMENTS

Big thanks to those who helped throughout the evolution of this book:

My family for their love, patience, and understanding: my mother Darlene Wellington (rest in peace), my father Robert Wellington, my sister Carrie Formosa and her family, my sister Sharon McLean and her family.

Kitty Pawlak, Richard and Judy Day, Norm Miller, John Ruskey, Janet Moreland, Jerico Lefort, Churchill Clark, Peggy Manes, Joe Wilson, Tanner Aljets, Dean Klinkenberg, Robin and Connie Kalthoff, Steve Schnarr and Melanie Cheney, Patrick Dobson, Cheri Becker, Renée Appleman, Thomas Holman, Shane Perrin, Ellen Falterman, Dave Cornthwaite, Mark Kalch, Laura Kennington, Sarah Outen, Traci Lynn Martin, Tom Dunn, Peter and Gemma Dodds, Mike Bremers, Trevor Davis and family, Jeremy Bruneel, Tony Culotta, Angela Speller, Candice Cottingham, Tim Turnbull from Aquapac.

Cheryl Marshall and Mark Cundle (rest in peace, my friends).

REFERENCES

1. Murray River Summit to Source to Sea Blog (Australia). (n.d.). Retrieved March 1, 2018 from www.rodwellington.com/murray-river-summit-to-source-to-sea-blo.

2. Following My Inner Compass. (August 2, 2014). Retrieved March 1, 2018 from www.rodwellington.com/blog/14049298.

3. Lead with Your Heart – Part One. (May 30, 2015). Retrieved March 1, 2018 from www.rodwellington.com/blog/14148835.

4. Top 150km, Murray Source–Bringenbrong Bridge (12–18 Dec. 2017). (n.d.). Retrieved March 1, 2018 from www.sites.google.com/view/murrayrivercanoetrip/home/top-150-murray-source-bringenbrong-bridge/murray-source-tom-groggin-2013.

5. Millennials. (n.d.). Retrieved March 1, 2018 from www.en.wikipedia.org/wiki/Millennials.

6. Why Trump Supporters Love Calling People Snowflakes. (February 1, 2017). Retrieved March 1, 2018 from www.gq.com/story/why-trump-supporters-love-calling-people-snowflakes.

7. Caspian Challenge: Early Retirement. (June 27, 2015). Retrieved March 1, 2018 from www.medium.com/laura-kennington/caspian-challenge-early-retirement-850df2d42c27.

8. What Did I Learn from My Round the World Adventure? Never Let the Demons Win. (November 9,

2015). Retrieved March 1, 2018 from www.the-guardian.com/commentisfree/2015/nov/09/round-world-adventure-sarah-outen.

9. Day 143 – The Pick-Up. (October 10, 2015). Retrieved March 1, 2018 from www.sarahouten.com/phonecast-day-143-the-pick-up.

10. Lost and Cold in Fog and Ice, Kayaker Delays Great Lakes Record Attempt. (March 28, 2017). Retrieved March 1, 2018 from www.mlive.com/news/saginaw/index.ssf/2017/03/record-attempting_kayaker.

11. Traci Lynn Martin Seeks Record and to Set Record Straight. (April 22, 2017). Retrieved March 1, 2018 from www.piadvance.com/2017/04/traci-lynn-martin-seeks-record-and-to-set-record-straight.

12. Murray River Expeditioners Facebook page. (April 17, 2017). Retrieved March 1, 2018 from www.facebook.com/groups/313507932124918.

13. A Dying River. (July 7, 2017). Retrieved March 1, 2018 from www.whattomhasdunn.com/single-post/2017/07/07/A-dying-river.

14. Missouri River Paddlers Facebook page. (November 30, 2017). Retrieved March 1, 2018 from www.facebook.com/groups/MissouriRiverPaddlers.

15. Those Who Live with Suicidal Thoughts Are Strong, Not Weak. (March 7, 2018). Retrieved March 14, 2018 from www.elephantjournal.com/2018/03/those-who-live-with-suicidal-thoughts-are-strong-not-weak.

ABOUT THE AUTHOR

No stranger to adventure, Rod Wellington has toured more than 16,000 miles by bicycle, including continental crossings of North America and Australia. He has also logged over 8500 miles of river travel, including source to sea descents of the Missouri–Mississippi river system (3800 miles), the Mississippi River (2300 miles), and the Murray River, Australia's longest waterway (1580 miles).

Rod is an accomplished public speaker and author. *Wet Exit* is his third book.

Find out more at rodwellington.com.